Praise for INCOME INVESTII

"Rick Stooker is on the right track. We also intend to pursue a more income-oriented strategy in the years to come. Capital gains are subject to both the risk of a decline in economic fundamentals and a deterioration in market psychology. High-quality dividends and income are subject only to the former, and that makes a big difference in modeling your portfolio returns in retirement."

-- *Charles Lewis Sizemore CFA, Senior Analyst HS Dent Investment Management, LLC http://www.hsdent.com/*

"I am a Chartered Accountant in Canada and spent most of my career teaching in a community college.

"Over the years, I have used various "plans," with varying degrees of success, but had never given much thought to dividends, so I fell prey to the hype about capital gains. So what was I thinking? Should have been investing for dividends.

"I also learned about some new investment vehicles, and got a "heads up" on some investments that I was aware of, but put on the back burner.

"Wish I knew about all this stuff when I was in my 20's, or at least paid attention to the theories involved in my 40's."

 --- *Dennis Wilson*

"What an eye-opener!!!

"I had heard about REITs, MLPs, BDCs, but you really explained their advantages and disadvantages. Thank you, Rick. You have set me on the right path to generate a steady income stream."

-- *Kenny H*

While the financial markets are collapsing . . .

Finally, you too can discover the old-fashioned -- yet now revolutionary (and updated for the 21st century) -- "gold egg" income investing secrets for lazy investors

Despite following the conventional financial wisdom, many senior citizens are now asking what happened to that worry-free fun and relaxation they promised themselves after a long career of hard work.

Many people in their fifties and early sixties are wondering when -- or even if -- they'll be able to retire.

What's the alternative?

Investing for income.

Learn how to make money whether the stock market goes up, down or sideways.

Income Investing Secrets

How to Receive Ever-Growing Dividend and Interest Checks, Safeguard Your Portfolio and Retire Wealthy

by Richard Stooker

Published by Info Ring Press

ISBN: 1450516661

EAN-13: 9781450516662

DISCLAIMER

I am not a broker.

I am not a licensed securities dealer or representative of any kind.

I am no legal right to sell you securities and I'm not trying to do so.

Nothing in this book is to be construed as a solicitation or offer to sell you securities.

Nothing in this book is to be construed as personal financial advice.

I have no legal right to give you personal financial advice. Even if I was a registered financial advisor, I don't know you or your individual financial situation.

This book is the result of my research and is believed accurate. It consists of my opinions and suggestions.

I'm not making any representations as to how much money you will make if you invest according to the guidelines I set forth -- that will depend upon the payouts of dividends and interest of the precise securities you decide to invest in, and nobody can predict the future.

That is part of the problem with mainstream financial advice -- it assumes the future will repeat the past. It doesn't.

Past performance is not indicative of future results.

This book is for education and entertainment.

Nothing in this book is to be construed as professional advice. For that, you should consult your attorney, accountant or financial advisor.

I am not responsible for the results of your investment decisions.

I follow my own advice. The only financial investments I own, besides ordinary checking, savings and money market accounts, are ones I recommend in this book.

You must read, think over what I say, make your own investment decisions and take responsibility for your own life, including the results of your investment decisions.

Continuing to read this book implies your acceptance of these terms.

LEGAL NOTICE

Dedication

To Paul Jacoby ("Grandpa"), for constructing the income investment portfolio that fed and clothed my sister and I after our father's early death.

Table of Contents

My Promise to You

You're about to learn a revolutionary way of investing.

It's not magic, and it's not any more guaranteed than anything else in this world.

It's not a short-term quick fix. The short term buying and selling of financial securities is more properly known as "trading," and is most akin to gambling. Even if you're a good guesser, the "house" -- your broker who gets paid commissions on every transaction-- is the only guaranteed winner. And sooner or later, you'll guess wrong more often than not.

But for long-term investing, as you'll soon see, it's the way that makes the most sense. It's building a foundation so that your investments can support you for the rest of your life.

And just so we're clear -- this method of investing is for the long term, especially for retirement.

It's not about saving up for a vacation, a house downpayment, or a child's college tuition (although if the child is still young it could be adapted to that). If you want to save up for a short-term goal, you should keep your funds in a money market account. In the short term you can always lose money in the stock and bond markets -- as they've proven so dramatically since the summer of 2008.

The younger you are, the better it'll work for you -- but we're all younger than we think.

We All Wish We Could Turn Back the Calendar

I do understand that the people who could benefit most from it (young adults) are not likely to be reading this, because they tend to value what they can buy now more than saving money for the future.

Income Investing Secrets

Most of them will have to learn the hard way -- just as we did.

Those of us who are already old enough to understand that someday we'll want to stop working, or at least stop being dependent on employment income, need this advice the most.

But frankly the sooner you start this program, the better.

If you want to do any young adults you know or in your family, given them this book and make them follow the program.

But don't think you can't take advantage of these principles just because you're already 60 or 70 or 80. We're all living longer than before. Many of you who read this are going to live past 100. You may not think so now, but many of you will, thanks to advances in medical science.

And if you take advantage of advances in alternative medical science, you'll probably live even longer and enjoy it more . . . but that's not the subject of this book.

(I suggest reading THE FANTASTIC JOURNEY: Live Long Enough to Live Forever by Ray Kurzweil and Terry Grossman).

This Book is About Ordinary Investing and Investments -- Nothing that Requires Trading or a Lot of Work

Also, this book assumes you're investing in widely available, publicly traded financial vehicles. It's not about investing in real estate, tax lien certificates, penny stocks, art work, foreign exchange trading, stamps or coins, IPOs, commodities, diamonds, start-up companies or private placements. Nothing that requires special expertise, travel, inside contacts, extra time, or that you be an accredited investor.

If you're interested and you acquire the necessary information and put in the necessary sweat-labor and leg work, you might make money with any of those things. However, they are in effect businesses in their own right.

This book is about ordinary, passive investments which you can profit from for the remainder of your life -- with only a few mouse clicks.

Much of what I write is not news, and so some of my advice overlaps with "conventional wisdom." Some of what I advise incorporates the findings of Modern Portfolio Theory and academic studies, but adapts it toward the point of view that income is what's important.

You Must Accept Principle 1

To truly understand this system and make it work well for you, you must grasp the First Principle and understand its implications. It's a "consciousness-bending" change from the conventional wisdom, so I ask you to keep an open mind.

One of my inspirations was the book RICH DAD, POOR DAD by Robert Kiyosaki. He upset a lot of readers by telling that their homes aren't assets, because they don't produce any income (assuming you're not renting out a room in your house or running some type of business out of it.)

Yes, he points out, when the value of your home rises, you can make a profit when you sell it -- but then you must still spend some money to live somewhere. Putting some type of roof over our heads is a necessary expense of living.

His point was to encourage his readers to invest in income-generating properties and businesses.

I maintain the same logic applies to financial investments. If they're not generating cash, what good are they? Sooner or later, to realize that profit, you must sell them, and then you must either reinvest that money, or lose net worth by spending it.

The smart money of previous generations knew that selling off capital was a financial sin. They put their wealth into stocks and bonds that paid an income, because that's all they allowed themselves to live on. To need to sell those stocks and bonds was a signal they were going financially downhill.

Just as smart farmers would rather starve through a winter than eat the "seed corn" they will need to sow in their fields come spring, sophisticated investors hang on to the stocks and bonds that produce income for them.

This program updates this once-common sense investing wisdom for the financial investments available in the 21st century, and combines it with the relevant findings of financial academics to reduce risk.

Put your money into the most sophisticated forms of income investments, and rely on businesses that meet the fundamental needs of human beings.

I wish all of you a prosperous, secure and comfortable life now and when you retire.

Let's first answer the question -- why invest for income?

Chapter One

The Case for Investing for Income (Dividends and Interest)

"The power of the basic principle of investor return is magnified when the stock pays a dividend."

-- Dr. Jeremy Siegel in THE FUTURE FOR INVESTORS

Income from your investments are:

1. Cash in your pocket you can spend for things you need now, or reinvest for the future.

Newspaper listings of current stock prices AND checks in the mail are just writing on pieces of paper -- but only checks can be exchanged for the hard green (or whatever the color of your national currency) stuff that you can use to put food on your table . . . or buy a new table.

2. Dividends aren't guaranteed but, once shareholders are in the habit of receiving them, well-run companies hate to reduce or eliminate them, and do so only when absolutely necessary.

3. In absolute terms, dividends generally increase as time goes by.

(That is, yields as measured by current market stock prices have been going down for decades, but over time the amount of money paid per share usually goes up.)

4. Dividends from the best companies keep up with or even exceed the inflation rate.

Some companies have averaged 14% annual dividend increases.

5. Encourage you to hold on to your investments -- not buy when you have a profit or sell to prevent more losses.

A firm named Dalbar, Inc. has been studying investor behavior for over 20 years. They have found that most individual investors consistently buy when the market is high and sell when the market is low. Equity investors on average have earned only 2.57% per year even though the S&P 500 has gone up about 12% per year (on average). Bonds have gone up about 11% per year on average, but the average bond investor earned only 4.24% per year.

People investing for capital gains, whether in the stock or bond markets, woefully underperform the markets.

Investing for income encourages you to stop trying to time the market -- a futile and self-defeating effort, as documents by countless studies.

6. Allow you to enjoy cash from your investments without selling them.

7. Allow you to diversify by using you income you receive to buy a different kinds of securities.

8. Using bonds, you can obtain the highest possible market interest based on the amount of risk you're willing to assume.

9. Indicate a company has a positive net cash flow.

10. Dividends indicate a company appreciates its owners, by treating them as real partners.

11. Dividends indicate a company's cash flow is well-managed, without fraudulent bookkeeping to enhance "earnings" through accounting tricks.

"Earnings" consist only of numbers required by taxing governments, but dividend checks have to be backed up by cold hard cash in the bank.

12. Can be received by you and your descendants into the far future.

Dividend-paying companies keep paying them for as long as the companies prosper.

Income Investing Secrets

Interest-paying securities can be reinvested when your principal is returned to you at maturity.

13. You must pay taxes on this income, but the IRS never forces you to have to touch the income-producing investments themselves.

14. TIPS and other inflation-indexed investments will increase their interest payments along with the cost of living.

15. Give peace of mind to the elderly, because once they have enough income investments to live on, they know they'll never run out of money.

16. Encourage you to never sell your investments at a profit or loss, thus saving on commissions and taxes.

This is a much bigger deal than you might think. Few investors realize how much their portfolio has been reduced by paying unnecessary expenses.

17. Allow you to sleep well at night, not knowing or caring what happened in the stock market that day.

18. Most investment income is, to a large degree, predictable -- though never 100%.

19. Make it easier to evaluate different investments based on current hard numbers, not a stock tipster's subjective analysis or predictions of future market demand for a company's products.

Many companies, especially new ones, are sold by their "story." I love good stories. I've written some. If you like good stories too, I suggest you try out my novel VIRGIN BLOOD or one by any other author you enjoy reading.

But choose your investments based on numbers.

20. Allow you to compound your investments over time -- what Albert Einstein called the greatest miracle on Earth.

According to Roger G. Ibbotson in STOCKS, BONDS, BILLS AND INFLATION HISTORICAL RETURNS (1926-1987), if you invested $1 in the U.S. stock market in 1824 and did NOT reinvest dividends, by 2005 that $1 was worth $374.

If you DID reinvest dividends, by 2005 that $1 would have been worth $3,200,000.

Big difference.

21. You get paid bond interest so long as the issuer entity survives (or unless the government "bails them out," and stock dividends so long as the company is able to pay them. Capital gains depend 80-90% on the market's performance, and the remainder to the market believing the company is going to grow.

22. If you don't sell a bond, you get your principal back at maturity whether interest rates have risen or fallen (during the 20 year average lifetime of a bond, interest rates will probably do both).

23. If you start investing for income soon enough, you can retire early.

24. If you feel compelled to the market price of your securities . . .

During bear markets, stocks that pay dividends don't go down as much as stocks that don't, because investors know they will receive some benefit from their investment.

During the bear market of 2000-2002, the S&P 500's dividend-paying stocks actually went up 10.4% -- nonpayers went down 33.19%.

Studies by Standard & Poors and the University of Georgia have found that the total return of dividend-paying stocks exceeds nonpayers in both bear and bull markets.

BOTTOM LINE:

You can't have your cake and eat it too, but so long as the "cake" sends you checks to buy other cakes with, you don't want to eat that cake.

Chapter Two

The Case Against Capital Gains

"In contrast to skeptics who claim that high-dividend paying stocks lack 'growth opportunities,' the exact opposite is true."

-- Dr. Jeremy Siegel in THE FUTURE FOR INVESTORS

It just makes the most sense to increase your wealth by letting your "gold eggs" hatch into many more geese that lay more gold eggs that hatch into more geese that lay gold eggs . . .

Than to feed ONE goose until it's so fat you think it can't get any fatter, and then sell it.

Problems with capital gains. They are:

1. Transitory

One day the stock or bond markets are up, the next day they're down.

We like to think that the market price of the past few years is an established "floor," but in reality, we just don't know.

On October 9, 2007 the Dow closed at 14,164.

By October 9, 2008 it was 8579, down nearly 40% in one year, returning to its September 1998 level. The gains of almost 10 years -- up in smoke.

And it didn't stop. As of March 9, 2009 the Dow hit 6547, which it first hit in late 1996. The gains of almost 13 years, up in smoke.

It's rebounded since then, but far how long? Nobody knows.

Income Investing Secrets

Will it ever go down to 5,000 again?

We hope not, but who knows?

Nobody knows where the bottom of this current financial crisis is.

It would take a great disaster, but there are people in this world who are actively planning such a great disaster for the U.S. and all democratic countries.

Nor can we rule out natural disasters. People have forgotten that a severe earthquake could put half of California into the ocean, but that ignorance doesn't affect the San Andreas fault. Climate change, whether caused by humanity or natural events, will cost us.

Nor can we rule out economic cycles. We think the Great Depression could never happen again, but who knows?

Maybe baby boomer retirements will sink the market by 40-50% (as Dr. Jeremy Siegel says is possible), but nobody yet knows.

2. Fluctuate in irregular, unreliable, unpredictable and uncontrollable amounts and directions

Nobody knows when the markets will go up (or by how much), or when they will go down (or by how much).

Yes, historically the stock market returns an average of 10% (which includes inflation and dividends as well as capital gains), but these returns are quite volatile. They can go up -- or down -- by as much as 40% in one year.

3. Useless until you sell the security

You can spend dividend/interest checks, and yet continue to own the underlying stocks/bonds.

4. Borrowed against, they are no longer yours

Yes, you can use securities as collateral for loans of cash. However, when you do so, there's a lien on them. You've lost control until you repay the loan. Plus, you must pay interest on the loan, so it's costing you money which you must have some source of income with which to pay. Instead of being an asset that provides you money, you've turned that security into an expense that's costing you money. You can default on the loan and keep the cash, but then you'll lose the security. You may as well have just sold it on the market.

5. Based on hope

You buy the latest "hot" stock based on its story of how it's going to take over a particular market. Maybe it succeeds, but many don't. Most glamorous companies stories have unhappy endings, especially for investors.

6. Exist only on paper until you sell the security

I'm tired of hearing how owners of Berkshire Hathaway are millionaires. They don't get a dime in dividends.

Warren Buffett is a great investor, and so he buys up cash-rich businesses such as newspapers and insurance companies. Berkshire Hathaway has prospered because Buffett himself does not practice what he forces Berkshire Hathaway investors to practice . . . he buys businesses such as Coca-Cola -- which pays dividends.

7. Cannot be reinvested by compounding

If I could go back in time to the 1970s, even knowing the tremendous gains Berkshire Hathaway was destined to make, I'd still put my money in stocks such as Philip Morris (now Altria) and Coca-Cola. If I reinvested the dividends from those companies I'd probably have a bigger portfolio -- as well as a much bigger dividend income -- than buyers of Berkshire Hathaway (whose dividend income is zero).

8. Are shared with the government when you do sell the security

True, income investors must pay taxes on the dividends/interest they receive, and this does reduce the number of "gold eggs" we can buy from reinvesting our income.

But the "geese" -- the securities we've bought -- are still ours. Tomorrow, and next week, and next year, those geese will lay new gold eggs for us to spend or reinvest.

When you sell the fatted goose of a stock/bond with capital gains, the government takes a big cut of your profit, reducing the cash you have left to produce new investing profits in the future.

9. Require research to discover a hot new growth stock after being realized through a sale

You have a stock you bought for $10 and now it's selling for $110, so you sell it for a $100 profit. After sharing your profit with the government, you have $85 to reinvest. (Less, if the government raises taxes on capital gains or if you owned the security for less than a year.)

Assuming you are smart enough to want to keep those funds growing for your retirement and not blow it, you must now find a NEW hot growth stock you think will be a "ten-bagger."

10. May indicate fraudulent or questionable accounting by a company

All the infamous corporate frauds (Enron, Global Crossing, and so on) of the early 2000s paid no dividends (except one that once paid a one-time penny per share dividend). They used bookkeeping tricks to make their profits look higher than they were. This artificially boosted market demand for their stocks.

I can't say that all dividend-paying companies are 100% honest . . . but every quarter they must come up with enough real cash to pay their shareholders the promised dividends.

No smoke and mirrors accounting sleight of hand can cover up bounced dividend checks!

11. May hide poor management decisions on the use of cash

The conventional wisdom is that because dividends are paid out of a company's retained earnings (its net income after paying taxes), they reduce the company's ability to reinvest its profits and therefore to grow in the future.

In some businesses, this makes sense. In some industries, companies must spend all their cash on the latest, most modern and efficient equipment and factories, just to keep up with the competition.

I salute those businesses, but don't want to invest in them, and advise you not to also.

In many companies, management uses the cash available to buy up other businesses which it doesn't know how to properly run, makes other inefficient purchases, or simply wastes it.

Robert Arnott, editor of FINANCIAL ANALYSTS JOURNAL, and Clifford Nasness, president of AQR Capital Management, did a study that found that a company that began paying higher dividends actually had higher than average earnings in following years.

12. May reflect other factors affecting the market price, rather than efficient reinvestment of retained earnings by management

The conventional wisdom says that when management efficiently and effectively uses retained earnings to grow the company, its stock market price rises proportionately, reflecting that growth.

This assumes that there's a rational, clear-cut, cause-effect relationship between a company's financial standing and its stock price. So that when a company's financial standing improves, its stock price will rise proportionately.

Unfortunately, modern finance has found that a stock's market price is only about 10-20% determined by the company's financial standing.

The other 80-90% is determined by the overall market or by the industry sector.

Let's say a nondividend-paying company's management avoids the flaws mentioned in reasons #10 and 11 above. They efficiently and effectively reinvest all retained earnings into growing the company's profits by 10% in a year.

Does that mean that the company's stock price will rise by 10% in that year?

Of course not. It may drop because the president of another company in the same industry is indicted for fraud. It may rise because the Federal Reserve announces a cut in the federal funds interest rate. It may drop because the United States' trade deficit goes up. It may go up because Congress cuts taxes.

In short, although you are foregoing current income with the expectation it will make you more money through capital gains in the future, that may or may not happen, based on many factors totally out of not only your control, but the company's.

13. Encourage you to sell too soon

If you invest for capital gains and your stock goes up a lot, there's always the temptation to sell it. No matter how many financial pundits tell you not to sell too soon, there's also that little voice inside you that says, "You can't go broke by making a profit."

You may also a less rational little voice inside you that says, "You could buy a new car and take a trip to Hawaii and meet a hot babe/dude."

It's human nature to desire instant gratification. And in some ways that's rational -- we really don't know whether the good we see now will still be there in the future, if we pass it up now.

Capital gains are transitory. Investors sitting on capital gains know that, and know that if they don't sell now, their profits may disappear next month.

Therefore, capital gains encourage you to fear losing money (and fear of loss is the most powerful human motivator), and therefore encourage you to want immediate pleasure from your profit.

Thus, many people sell profitable stocks, then watch as their market prices continue to rise.

You know how people say, "Gee, I wish I'd bought Wal-Mart in 1980 . . . " or Intel or Microsoft or Dell Computer or Berkshire Hathaway, and so on?

Chances are, if you had, you'd have sold the stock decades ago, and you'd now be moaning about, "If only I hadn't sold that Wal-Mart/Microsoft/Dell/Berkshire Hathaway stock to buy that new motorcycle. I'd be rich by now."

Investing for income works with the human need for immediate gratification. Regular checks are fun to receive, so they encourage you not to sell the security that's sending you those checks.

Capital gains encourage the fear/greed emotional seesaw that makes most investors buy too late and sell too soon.

14. Create an illusion of investing success

Years ago, in looking over the balances of my retirement funds on my job, I had a simple revelation.

I enjoyed seeing the balance of the account go up, but I figured out that so long as I was working and buying shares in that account, I'd be better off if the market stayed LOW throughout my entire working career.

If I could manipulate the market price, I'd make it as low as possible while I was still buying shares out of my paycheck.

Then, right before my retirement, I'd shoot the market up 10 ten times!

Yet, so far as I know, only Warren Buffet and Dr. Jeremy Siegel have pointed out that continuing to buy shares for a low price is more important to your long-run investing success than a high market price for the shares you've already bought.

It's human to look at a brokerage account balance and want it to go up every month . . . but it's the number of shares you will own when you retire that will count -- not the current market value of what you've already bought. And you can buy more shares with the same number of dollars only if the share price is low.

15. May encourage you to lose money by buying high and selling low.

Most ordinary investors in common stocks lose money. They're scared of the market when stocks are low, and don't jump in until stocks have risen a lot. Then they hold on, thinking stocks will go even higher and they're greedy for even more profits -- and then the stock crashes. Discouraged and afraid of losing even more money, ordinary investors then sell at a loss.

What happened to investors from 1995 to March-April 2000 is a good example.

But when an investor wants yield, they're happy to buy dividend-paying stocks at a low price. When those stocks go up with the market, they're not tempted to sell, because they want to continue to receive those quarterly checks.

When the stock market crashes, they don't sell, because they want to continue to receive those quarterly checks.

15

Income Investing Secrets

Income investing encourages you to buy low and buy high -- and never sell.

16. Worry elderly people who rely on them to finance their retirement. They are afraid that a bear stock market will cause them to run out of money before they die.

This is a legitimate fear. What if you had retired in 1929, 1973 or 1999? Some people did, and they suffered for it.

If you want to retire now and you've been depending on stock market gains . . . you're going to keep working for many years to come. If you retired in the past year or two, you're either an income investor already, rationing your Social Security check or looking for a job.

17. Cause you to waste too much time paying attention to every little up and down in the stock market.

I enjoy reading about investing, but consider the daily financial news a waste of good radio time. It's noise. I'd rather listen to a good song. I don't understand why people not employed in the industry pay any attention to daily DJIA, S&P 500 or NASDAQ fluctuations.

18. Can encourage you to plan to retire early, then be forced to cancel your plans once the stock market crashes.

Many people had to delay their retirements because of the 2000-2002 bear market. I suspect that, also, many people left retirement during that period because they had to return to work.

The same is happening now. Please, don't retire now unless you're wealthy enough to get through this crisis.

19. Contribute a lot less to the stock market's long term performance than you've been led to think.

Historically, the stock market has averaged a total return of 11%.

Here's what the big media financial writers fail to tell you:

According to Peter Arnott and Peter Bernstein in the Financial Analysts Journal, that includes over 3% from inflation and about 5% from dividends.

Only 3% of the market's long term historical, "real" total return has come from capital gains.

Dr. Jeremy Siegel, who came up with the famous graph comparing stock returns to gold, bonds, cash and the cost of living over nearly 200 years, which he published in his book STOCKS FOR THE LONG RUN, explained in his recent book THE FUTURE FOR INVESTORS that 97% of the stock market's rise -- which trounced every alternative by a long shot -- came from REINVESTING DIVIDENDS.

"From 1871 to 2003 97 percent of the total after-inflation accumulation from stocks comes from reinvesting dividends. Only 3 percent comes from capital gains."

20. Don't always exist.

That's the very worst thing about capital gains -- sometimes they add insult to injury by not even being there at all!

Sometimes you only have capital losses.

If you happen to retire just before a drastic market downturn such as we saw from 2000-2002 and November 2007 to March 2009 . . . you could easily wind up selling far more of your stock than you'd expected, just to meet your expenses, and be faced with running out of stock to sell in your much later years.

Even though the Dow is now (early January 2010) up dramatically since its March 2009 low, it's at a place it first reached in early 1999.

If you have bought stock in the past ten years, you have not made money unless you're also receiving dividend checks.

The Dow Jones Industrial Average didn't break its September 3, 1929 pre-Black Tuesday record high until November 24, 1954. How would you like to have been a retiree relying on stock market capital gains during that period (before Social Security checks, remember!)?

The Dow Jones reached 1000 for the first time in 1966 -- and didn't break that mark again until 1981 . . . after 15 years of the most extreme economic and political turbulence in American history since the Civil War. During those years we lived through several gas shortages, The Vietnam War, Watergate, skyrocketing meat, sugar and other food prices, and 20% interest rates.

Investors in certificates of deposit got double-digit returns. If you'd been relying on capital gains from either stocks or bonds, you'd have fallen FAR BEHIND the cost of living.

Can't happen again?

Do you have a signed guarantee from God to that effect?

I don't pretend to have a 100% accurate crystal ball, but when I think about 82 million baby boomers selling off stock -- or even just failing to continue to buy as much stock as they are now -- to retire over the next 10 to 20 years . . .

. . . the rising costs of energy -- including where most of the world's accessible oil fields are located and how vulnerable they are to terrorists . . .

. . . and how many fanatical terrorist jihadist Muslims want to destroy the U.S., all democracies, and all countries not ruled by sharia . . .

. . . how China's current leaders seem bent on achieving the ancient dream of China -- ruling the world (China's emperors have traditionally always believed they ruled the world in spirit. But in ancient times they couldn't do much in practical terms, besides sometimes invading Tibet, Vietnam and Mongolia.) . . .

I could go on, but I don't want to turn this book into a political rant. Let's just say that too many Americans -- and Europeans, Canadians, Australians and Japanese too -- take their freedom and prosperity too much for granted.

Having your wealth in the form of capital gains means it's tied up in the shares of stock you own. You may as well as well keep cash in a safe. Capital gains can't be stolen as cash can, but they can -- and often do -- simply vanish, when the market (or just the stocks you own) turns south.

You can lock and hide a safe, but no burglary alarm in the world can protect your capital gains from a bear market!

Just ask millions of people around the world who've been in the markets for the past two years.

BOTTOM LINE:

You can't continue to have capital gains and still enjoy, or reinvest, them.

You can't have your cake and it too.

Next: Objections to investing for income.

Chapter Three

Objections to Investing for Income

Here are the arguments against investing for income:

1. Stock dividends are double taxed.

This is absolutely true, and it's disgraceful that class warfare political rhetoric in the U.S. is so powerful that it's going to remain true for the foreseeable future.

Here's how it works. You own 100 shares of the XYZ Corporation. Let's say that's 1% of the total shares of the corporation. The XYZ Corporation figures out that their 2007 net income is $1 million. Logically and technically, 1% of that -- $10,000 -- belongs to you.

However, the XYZ Corporation has to pay income taxes on that $1 million. For the purposes of illustrating this point, let's just say they have to pay 40%, which is $400,000. They write that check to the IRS and send it in with their tax return.

Therefore, they have $600,000 left.

Remember -- your 100 shares of XYZ stock makes you a 1% owner of the corporation. So you as 1% owner just paid $4,000 in taxes to the IRS. You as 1% owner now have a remaining $6000 in XYZ Inc.

XYZ Corporation's Board of Directors votes a 50% payout dividend. Soon after, you get a check for $3000. That's one-half of the remaining $6000.

If the corporation didn't have to pay income taxes, you'd be getting $5000 (One half of $1 million times 1%).

But now that you've gotten your $3000 dividend check -- guess what?

The IRS wants some of that money too!

In effect, as a 1% owner of the XYZ Corporation, you have already paid $4000 in taxes.

Yet now that you've gotten a $3000 check with your name on it, the IRS wants a cut of that too.

So it's true that dividend investors get whacked twice by the IRS.

Yet just go to the floor of Congress and try to lobby for the end of this unfair situation. Mention "double taxation of dividends" and you'll immediately have a bunch of closet-socialist politicians spouting a lot of hot air about how fair it is that "the rich" should pay more taxes. And they get away with it.

It's unfortunate that most Americans don't understand this, but no matter what your politics, as an income investor you should understand it.

2. Interest is taxed at the recipient's normal tax rate. In most places and times, so is dividend income. The tax on capital gains is usually lower, so it's better to receive capital gains.

In the United States, the tax rate for dividends was reduced to 15% for most taxpayers for 2003-2010. (For low income taxpayers it was reduced to 5% through 2007 and 0 for 2008-2010.) However, unless this reduction is extended or made permanent -- which does not appear likely -- dividend interest received by U.S. taxpayers will again be taxed at nominal rates beginning in 2011.

Therefore, it's better for companies with excess cash to buy back their own stock. By reducing the number of shares of stock outstanding, they increase the value of each of those outstanding shares.

Stock repurchases began in 1983, due to a change in regulations. The total amount of repurchases was about $30 billion annually in the 1980s. But by 1998, for the first time, the total money spent on stock buybacks exceeded the amount of dividends paid out by companies.

The September 10, 2007 BARRON'S reported on a study by Douglas J. Skinner, a professor of Accounting at the University of Chicago Graduate School of Business. The title: "The Evolving Relationship Between Earnings, Dividends and Stock Repurchases."

Income Investing Secrets

He concludes that eventually companies will eliminate dividends.

His basic case is that stock repurchases are more flexible for companies. If they pay out dividends this year, shareholders will want at least the same amount next year, if not more.

Unfortunately, the company's business next year may not be as profitable. If they repurchase stock this year but not next year, nobody complains.

Skinner says that the number of companies doing repurchases but not paying dividends is increasing.

Eventually, he concludes, dividends may be eliminated.

I don't know whether the study examines the tendency of companies to buy back shares on the open market, but not to cancel them. These shares then remain in the company's treasury until needed to be given to employees who're exercising their stock options.

Therefore, there's not always a net reduction in shares outstanding, so the apparent benefit to shareholders in capital gains is temporary and illusory.

A report published by the management consulting firm McKinsey & Co indicates that some share repurchases may simply be for management's benefit, since their compensation packages are tied to the company's earnings per share.

If management is unable to increase the earnings, they'll decrease the numbers of shares outstanding.

Simple arithmetic, but bad business.

So stock buybacks can be a signal to shareholders that management doesn't have any better ways to invest the company's capital.

There is a counter trend. In 2004 high-tech Microsoft began to pay dividends.

My own contention: I want money to reinvest or spend. I don't want to have to sell shares of stock to benefit from my investment in a company.

If all corporations stop paying dividends, I'll stop investing in the stock market.

3. Companies that pay dividends are cutting their own growth rates, because they won't have the capital necessary to fund their growth. That will reduce their future potential income.

This is a nice academic argument, which seems to make sense.

If a company needs to build a new factory to expand its widget business, how dare its shareholders demand it pay them dividends instead?

So it's better for a company to build new factories than to pay dividends to stock holders.

Frankly, for some companies, it even makes sense in real life. Many industries are both capital-intensive and competitive. The leading companies in them need to constantly spend their profits by reinvesting in new factories or more modern equipment.

Or they fall behind, can't compete and therefore go out of business.

So they just can't afford to pay dividends to stock holders.

Avoid Companies Too Desperate for Your Money

My advice is -- don't invest in such companies.

Your responsibility is to provide for you and your family, not to fund a hyper-competitive industry.

Besides, many companies are able to both pay dividends and still keep growing their businesses.

Coca-Cola is one.

Would Coca-Cola grow any faster if it didn't pay dividends?

Coca-Cola Has Been Paying Dividends -- AND Growing -- for Over 90 Years

I don't know. Would Coca-Cola sell twice as much soda if it took out twice as many TV and magazine ads?

Could it sell more soda in more countries? I don't know, but I strongly suspect that Coca-Cola is now in every country in the world that will allow its products to be sold there.

It could be that many companies have just plain reached a point of diminishing returns. That means, they so dominate their markets that they just can't sell any more, no matter how much money they spent.

How much more gum could Wrigley sell, if it spent all its retained earnings on advertising?

I don't know. I do know that I'm not going to start chewing gum even if I see 300 Wrigley gum commercials every day for a year.

I'm not in their market, so they'd be wasting their time trying to make me buy their gum.

So it's better for them to send the rest of their money to their shareholders.

Next: is the market really too "efficient" to beat?

Chapter Four

The Efficient Market Hypothesis and What It Means for Income Investors

"Anybody who tells you that they know the direction of the economy, interest rates or the stock market is either a) inexperienced or b) selling you something you don't want."

-- Dylan Jovine THE TYCOON REPORT

I'm not so sure that markets are efficient -- at least as in all the connotations I associate with the word "efficient."

However, I am sure that the markets -- however inefficient -- are the markets.

That is, you can't argue with them. You'll lose, because they're a lot bigger than you.

I've spent years of my life studying how to trade. I've read all about commodities, options, Japanese candlestick charts, and so on and on.

In the many chapters of Jack Schwager's MARKET WIZARDS books, each successful trader emphasized over and over that their success came from following the market's direction, not arguing with it.

It's Easy to Know the Market's Direction -- When You Read the Charts in Books

Only trouble is, although you can look at a trend line and see in what direction the market's been going, you can't tell where it's going to go in the next five minutes, let alone tomorrow or the next day or the next month.

Sometimes what you think is a market peak is just the beginning of an upward trend.

Sometimes what you think is a slight pullback is the beginning of a downward trend.

You just don't know. I recall watching a video of options author David Caplan giving a lecture. He told about how during the 1980s he used to see a guy on TV always telling investors to put on option spreads that profited so long as the stock market stayed within particular (and highly reasonable) limits.

Which they almost always did.

ALMOST always.

Caplan reported that after the 22% drop in the Dow during October 1987, he didn't see that guy on TV anymore.

Caplan taught a great system of making money from options by putting on a spread that profited so long as U.S. Treasury bonds stayed within certain wide, and historically reasonable, boundaries.

I went to a free seminar and got very excited as I watched the lecturer explain the system.

Putting My Money Into a 90% Successful Trade . . . A No-Brainer, Right?

Treasury bonds, I kept thinking. How boring boring boring -- how wonderfully boring. They didn't crash like the stock market could. They didn't shoot up like orange juice futures prices hit by a unseasonable Florida overnight freeze. They changed only due to interest rates and demand.

Controlled by the Federal Reserve, interest rates change slowly.

And demand -- how much could demand for U.S. Treasury bonds fluctuate?

These option spreads were over 90% successful.

I dug up some money I couldn't afford to lose, and put on one of those trades -- an option spread that would remain in profit as long as U.S. Treasury bonds stayed within some wide limits for just 30 days.

How much could demand for U.S. Treasury bonds change in only 30 days?

In the chapter on hedge funds, I describe how, after Russia's stock market melted down, every wealthy person in Russia, Asia, Africa and South America sold everything they could put their hands on and sent it to the safest, most economically and politically stable country and currency in the world.

Like the infamous Long Term Capital Management LLC hedge fund, in the summer of 1998 I had a government-bond related trade going.

As the value of U.S. Treasuries shot off the charts, my 90% sure-thing position quickly turned into a negative $2000. I closed it out, thankful that I'd followed Caplan's advice to hedge my trade, so my loss was limited. Otherwise, I'd have lost a LOT more money.

You just don't know what's going to happen -- even with such boring investments as U.S. Treasury bonds, let alone highly volatile stocks.

Buying Stocks for Capital Gains are a Crap Shoot Where You Pay Your Broker Instead of the Casino

Another time, following some system I've forgotten, I bought a cheap stock, and the very next day, its price shot up 60%.

Why? I didn't know then and I don't know now. I don't know what could happen to make one company worth 60% more in just one day.

I don't believe that financial markets are "random" in the same sense that a casino slot machine is random. People buy and sell stocks for reasons.

The markets are the sum totality of all those reasons, and I just don't believe anybody can predict them.

In his 1900 dissertation, "The Theory of Finance," Louis Bachelier intensely analyzed the French capital markets. He concluded, "The mathematical expectation of the speculator is zero."

In 1931, having noticed that few to none stock forecasters predicted the 1929 Crash, Alfred Cowles began analyzing the long term records of stock forecasters. He asked the question: "Can stock market forecasters forecast?"

After years of recording and analyzing stock market predictions, he concluded, "It is doubtful."

He founded the Cowles Commission and spent many years recording the forecasts of the forecasters (analysts and newsletter editors of many different types), and then comparing their forecasts to the actual performance of the individual stock or the stock market.

He never discovered anyone who in the long term could forecast the future of any individual stock or the market as a whole any better than randomly selected cards.

Some Stock-Pickers ARE Superior to Others

Now, it's important to understand that the efficient market theory doesn't say that it's impossible for anyone to get better than market results for a long period -- just extremely difficult.

I don't think the "if enough people flip coins somebody will flip many more heads than average" argument explains Warren Buffett's success.

To me, it's even more of a coincidence that the champion "coin flipper" (that is, stock picker) of the 20th century just happens to have taught himself how to do complex math in his head while still a child, just happens to have been a success raising money in his own businesses while still a child, has deeply studied accounting, finance and stock picking, and received the only "A" Benjamin Graham ever awarded to a college student in his stock picking class -- and that was just his early preparation.

In retrospect, it's easy to see that Warren Buffett is an unusually gifted, stock picking genius.

Yet, because he's also honest, he'll also be the first to tell you he's not always accurate. In 2009 Berkshire Hathaway suffered its worst year since 1999 -- badly lagging the broad markets. The S&P 500 was up 23% -- Berkshire Hathaway was up a mere 2.7%.

Now -- find the "next" Warren Buffett. Are they managing YOUR mutual fund?

Maybe -- you'll find out in 20 to 30 years. Until then, you're just a'wishing and a'hoping.

And they can still underperform the market.

If You're Investing for Capital Gains, Make Sure You Follow Wade Cook's Advice -- Don't Buy Stocks That Won't Go Up in Price

A lot of people like to quote Will Rogers: "It's easy to make money in the stock market. Just buy a stock and sell it when it goes up. If it doesn't go up, don't buy it."

Years ago I bought a tape set from Wade Cook before he became infamous (I never went to his $7000 seminar, though!) I was astounded to hear him say something similar but, unlike Will Rogers, he wasn't joking.

He was describing one of his option strategies, the success of which depended on the underlying stock's price going up. It went like this: "Sometimes people tell me they lost money because the stock's price didn't go up. I ask them, 'What're you doing buying stocks that don't go up in price?'"

Advice like that may be why his stock market seminar business in now bankrupt.

So, my conclusion is that although a few unusually talented and hard-working people can beat the market in the long run, you can't know who they are in advance, only in retrospect -- and then it's too late.

You can't predict the performance of a stock (or any security) picker any more than you can predict the markets.

Yes, I know that many of them boast of their records. Of course they can make successful picks. You can do that too, just by throwing darts at the stock listings.

Their copywriters play up their successes and play down -- or totally ignore -- their losers.

To obtain a newsletter's real success rate, you should check with Mark Hulbert of The Hulbert Financial Digest. He tracks the real performance of over 180 stock and mutual fund advisory newsletters.

You Can't Rely on Finding "Inefficiencies" in the Market

In his book A RANDOM WALK DOWN WALL STREET Burton Malkiel tells the story of a student walking along with his finance professor. The student spots a $20 bill on the sidewalk and bends down to pick it up.

"Don't bother," says the professor. "If it were really a twenty dollar bill, it wouldn't be there."

Now, I actually once found a $20 bill on the sidewalk. And if it wasn't real, it was still accepted as currency by the store where I spent it.

So, opportunities do exist -- but not for long. For the $20 bill to stop being in the sidewalk, somebody has to pick it up. But after that, it's gone.

It's fine to take advantage of good luck when it happens, but you can't depend on it to finance your retirement.

I don't spend my days walking along all the sidewalks I can, looking for $20 bills.

The Markets Don't Seem Efficient At All -- But Don't Let That Fool You Into Thinking They're Predictable

To my way of thinking, if the market were "efficient," that means rational, and stock prices would go up only as a company's earnings and other financial information improved. Stock market prices would closely track the performance of the overall economy. They would not zoom up as they did from 1995-2000, nor crash as they did in the summer of 2008.

Why Do Stock Prices Keep Changing?

We like to think that a stock's price keep changing because of its business prospects. We learn that its main product is selling better than expected, so its price goes up. We learn that a major lawsuit has been filed against it, so its price goes down. Analysts expect it to earn $10 per share this quarter.

And so on. In this model, investors and analysts are tempted to think that, based on what they know of the business, it's "true" price is really above or below its market price.

However, according to modern financial theory, these rational ways of analyzing a stock account for only 10 to 20% of its stock price. And this does not account for the daily fluctuations in stock prices.

I mean, it just doesn't make sense that on a given day ABC's stock can go from $30.10 to $29.50 to $31.80 and wind up at $30.20, based strictly on the company's business numbers. Except for exceptional events, a company's business does not change much on any given day. Its employees go to work. Sales people make sales. It pays some bills. It incurs some expenses. It manufactures product. Everybody goes home.

Yes, on some days unusually big changes can happen: layoffs, new product rollouts, ad campaign failures, buyouts, and so on. Those are major events that are new information that justify a re-evaluation on the part of stock analysts. But most days are just one more day on the calendar. If stock prices were rational, they wouldn't change much from day to day. But we know that they change constantly.

The only way you can know something important that other investors don't is if you have inside information. If you are high enough up in a company to have access to inside information, you know it's illegal to buy or sell stock based on it. Yes, I'm sure it happens. And I'm sure that some people do it and get away with it. Maybe you won't get caught.

But it's not something a system for the rest of us.

Besides, even if you know today's inside information, you don't know tomorrow's. It's only good for a quick profit.

For example, let's say that an executive at Coca-Cola years ago knew that its rollout of New Coke was a marketing disaster before the company released the sales information to the public.

They could have made some money by selling KO -- in the short term.

But they couldn't know that the company would handle the problem, and that its stock would continue to go up.

And there's another hiccup.

You as an investor cannot know more about the business than everyone else in the market. That's a delusion.

Let's say you perform the fundamental analysis that many books advise you to perform. You decide that Company A's stock is "really" worth $50 per share. It's selling for $45, so you buy it.

You're putting your analysis against that of thousands of fund managers who have billions of dollars to spend on the latest in computer hardware, databases, proprietary software, specially designed mathematical models and Ph.ds in finance. They are constantly analyzing markets around the world to find undervalued stocks. You're not going to discover anything they don't.

If other investors thought the stock was really worth $50 instead of $45, they'd be putting in buy orders until the stock price rose to $50.

The truth is, the stock price's may well rise to $50 -- but not until it's fallen to $41. And you don't have any true idea what it will be next year. Maybe $30, maybe $80. You don't know whether its next product release will succeed or fail.

In fact, nobody does. Not even the teams of quants working for hedge funds. They don't know the future any more than you do, no matter how much more they can massage the data.

Yet Stock Pricing is Not Even That Rational

However, let's face it, even that doesn't account for why stock prices continually change.

Some characterize the markets as a constant struggle between the bulls and the bears.

That is, people who believe Company B's stock is going to rise are buying. People who believe Company B's stock is going to fall are selling.

Frankly, I don't think it's even that rational. People and institutions buy and sell for many reasons.

Much of them are emotional. Many writers point out that Wall Street is dominated by greed and fear -- one at a time.

In periods of "irrational" exuberance such as the 1995-2000, greed controlled the markets.

Now it's fear.

According to the disciples of Ben Graham, when Mr. Market is in the depression phase of his manic-depression disease, it's a good time to buy good value. That seems to make sense.

In the long run, the market will reward true value.

When Do We Ever Reach the "Long Run?"

Many analysts acknowledge that they don't know what a stock's market price will be next week, but can determine from its fundamentals whether it's undervalued now. They claim that they'll be proven right in the "long run." Value will always win in the "long run."

Trouble is, when the long run ever happen? Never.

Coca-Cola had its IPO in 1919, over ninety years ago. It has proven to be a winning company, nobody can deny that.

But does that mean its current market price is "right?" Does that mean that its true value has surfaced, finally? Then why has its 52-week price ranged from $37 to $59? Was its business so bad in the past year that a drop to $37 was justified as its true value? Did one out of three Coke product buyers suddenly switch to Pepsi? And since its price is now about $56, does that mean that almost all of them switched back?

No, none of those things happened. The U.S. stock market as a whole took a big hit, bottomed out in March 2009 and has been rising since then.

If KO hasn't reached the mythical "long term" yet after ninety years of selling soft drinks, we better stop waiting. We don't have time for "true value" to be discovered by the market.

The truth is, stock investors are trying to use current information to anticipate the future, but nobody knows the future.

There is NO "real" price for any security. There's the current market price. If you want it, pay the current market price. If you don't want to pay it, you don't want that security.

Maybe its price will go up, maybe it will go down. You don't know and neither does anybody else.

It will move as demand fluctuates, mostly because of random reasons, and as new information about the company comes to light, and as overall stock market sentiment shifts in response to the overall economy.

I don't claim all this is rational, which is why I object to the term "efficient" -- but it is unpredictable.

The Drunkard's Walk Down Wall Street

Burton Malkiel invented the comparison of the stock market with a drunk walking. He's had too much to drink to know where he's going, so he might go up or down, and will frequently switch back and forth. Maybe he'll find his way home and maybe he won't, but it's unpredictable.

Thinking that you, or any other analyst, broker, fund manager, pundit, newsletter editor, expert or talking head on TV knows where the drunkard is heading next is an illusion.

Furthermore, this isn't just speculation. It's backed up by numerous studies of those same analysts, brokers, fund managers, pundits, newsletter editors, experts and talking heads on TV.

Their predictions come true -- but no better than random chance. Their choices are about as good as picking stocks by throwing darts at the market listings in THE WALL STREET JOURNAL. In fact, WSJ editors have done exactly that.

If you went to a roulette wheel in a casino, bet on Red and won -- would you feel justified in proclaiming yourself a financial guru?

So How Can We Beat an Unpredictable Market?

We can't beat it, so we join it.

Burton Malkiel's solution was to advise investors to buy broad index funds such as the S&P 500. That way you're not predicting any particular company or timing the market. You're just there to take advantage of the economic growth of all those companies.

To me, that is optimizing a dysfunctional strategy, because you're still investing for capital gains. You're just doing it the most intelligent way possible.

In his book THE SECRET CODE OF THE SUPERIOR INVESTOR, James Glassman divided investors into two classes: "outsmarters" and "partakers."

Outsmarters think they can come up with some system or follow some guru with a system that will let them beat the market. Partakers simply partner up with good businesses and share in the rewards.

My only problem is with Glassman's application of this setup. Although he devotes a chapter to the importance of dividends, he also gives a lot of credence to capital gains.

By now you can figure out that if I'm going to "partake" with a good business, I want to PARTAKE! I want to share in the profits . . . now! not in the vague never-never future when I terminate or reduce the partnership by selling the stock.

It seems obvious to me that a good partaker should remain a partner in the business -- hopefully, forever. But they must be suitably rewarded for their participation -- which means paying them dividends.

To me it's now painfully obvious that it's a contradiction to say that people can't benefit from their partnership with your business -- unless they end the partnership (or some fractional share of it) by selling some or all of the stock.

Next: "Risk" as defined by finance academics and the "real world" risk that can actually hurt your finances.

Chapter Five

Income Investors Need Worry Only about "Real World" Risk -- There's More Than Enough of That

The vast majority of financial books and articles you read implicitly or explicitly define "risk" as the volatility of the market price of your investment. In technical terms, even the tendency of your investment's market price to RISE is termed "risk."

However, when the market price of a security goes down, that's not cash out of your pocket. (Just as, when its market price goes up, that's not cash in your pocket. It won't buy you even a cup of old school coffee, let alone a glass of Starbucks cappuccino.) The market price of one of your securities going down is a problem only if you are planning to sell the security.

And you shouldn't be selling.

While You're Buying, You Should Want the Price to Remain Low

And for ongoing accumulation of assets, as when you're having money taken out of your paycheck to fund your 401(k) account, the market price going down is a good thing -- it allows you to buy even more units of the security when you reinvest your income or add more money from your next paycheck.

Since it's inevitable that, over time, market prices will go up and down, the vast majority of financial books and articles you read equate risk with volatility.

Volatility is normally measured by "beta." Beta is the degree to which a security goes up and down in price.

"Standard" beta is the number 1, and that is defined as the volatility of the market as a whole. Therefore, if a stock's beta is 1, its price goes up and down identically with the market as a whole, and just as much as the market as a whole.

If a stock's beta is below 1, it's less volatile than the market. If the market drops 5%, that stock may drop only 4%. But when the market goes up 5%, its price will go up only 4%.

If a stock's beta is above 1, it's considered more risky than the market as a whole.

According to Academics, Enron was a Safe Stock

Is this beta/volatility the same as "risk?" I read recently that Enron's beta was 0.85 -- comfortably below the market's beta of 1.

If you owned Enron stock, I'm sure you're relieved to know that Enron was 15% less risky than the market as a whole.

Isn't it just a funny thing that the stock market as a whole still exists -- but Enron doesn't?

That should tell you what you need to know about equating volatility with "risk."

In my book (and this is my book), REAL "risk" means just what it does everywhere else -- DANGER!

NOT price volatility. But . . .

1. Loss of income -- the security reduces or doesn't pay you the dividend/interest due you.

2. Loss of principal -- the security issuer goes out of business, and so your stocks/bonds are now worthless.

3. Loss of purchasing power -- inflation and loss of currency purchasing power.

Certainly there are times to worry, and times to sell your investments to cut your losses:

When your dividend/interest checks bounce, or don't arrive at all.

When you see the CEO and CFO of the company on TV being led away in handcuffs.

When the company's product or service is obsolete. (Airlines go in and out of bankruptcy all the time, but remain flying because there's a demand for that. But when DVDs come out, get rid of companies that manufacture VHS tapes.)

BOTTOM LINE:

All investments have some risk. Not because their prices fluctuate, but because security issuers can fail to make payments and go out of business.

Nobody can guarantee you absolute safety with your investments (or anywhere else, for that matter). We live in an imperfect world. Bad things happen.

Your best protection against Risks 1 and 2 (loss of income and/or principal) are:

a. Investing in businesses that meet basic human needs and desires (Principle Number 4)

b. Diversification (Principle Number 5)

Your best protection against Risk 3 (inflation) is:

a. Reinvesting and compounding your returns (Principle Number 2)

b. Investing in income growth investments (Principle Number 6)

Chapter Six

The 7 Foundation Principles of Income Investing Secrets

You're not going to stick with any investing program unless you understand why it works.

I could keep this book a lot shorter by just including the final chapters (and some readers will cheat themselves by skipping to the final chapters), but then you'd soon forget about this book and would be reading the next thing that catches your eye.

This is a complete program for long term investment, especially retirement. I want you to understand why this program can work for you and your family, so you stick with it through the many years to come. It'll will work for you, if you work it.

I've read a lot of books on investing, personal finance and so on. This is the result of wide and deep research. There's more to this program than just me telling you, "Hey, invest for income."

In the chapters to follow I'll measure your income investment options against the 7 Foundation Principles of Income Investing Secrets -- pointing out where they're weak and where they're strong.

(No investment is perfect, unfortunately. In the markets, as in life, there are always trade-offs. However, you can and should construct your portfolio to take advantage of the advantageous investments while minimizing their weaknesses.)

Conventional advice is to diversify using asset allocation and rebalancing. I believe rebalancing is a form of market timing. I believe in income allocation.

I'll discuss each one of these in its own separate chapter, so you understand its importance to your financial future.

But here's the list:

1. An investment's true value is in the income it generates.

Geese that lay gold eggs are valuable for the gold eggs they lay -- not for the market price of their meat, which goes up and down anyway. Tons of academic studies have proven that in the long run, financial markets are not predictable enough to overcome transaction costs.

2. Increase your income by reinvesting that income. The longer you compound your income, the higher it grows.

Unless you need all of your income to meet necessary expenses, trade some or all of your gold eggs for more geese that will also lay gold eggs, and trade those gold eggs for yet more geese that lay yet more gold eggs . . .

It's better to have 20 skinny geese that lay gold eggs than one fat goose worth only the market price of its meat.

3. The lower the market price at which you reinvest your income, the more income-generating securities you can buy, which will increase your future income.

The lower the market price for geese that lay gold eggs, the more new geese that lay gold eggs you can buy when you reinvest the gold eggs.

4. Invest in businesses that meet basic human needs and desires.

If you feed your geese that lay gold eggs with common grain, they'll always have enough nutrition to lay gold eggs. If they eat an exotic, imported delicacy and it's no longer available, they'll starve to death and you will lose your gold eggs.

5. Use diversification to reduce risk.

The more types of geese that lay gold eggs you have, the less vulnerable your entire flock is to foxes, bird flu and other hazards.

6. Grow your income to keep up with or beat inflation.

Make sure the size of the gold eggs keeps increasing at least as much as the price of geese feed.

7. Guard your income generation power by reducing expenses: taxes, brokerage fees, commissions, management fees and so on. Your personal time is also an expense to keep to a minimum.

The less of your gold eggs you spend on food, veterinarian bills and other geese-related expenses, the more gold you have leftover with which to buy more geese that lay gold eggs. The less time you spend reading annual reports on geese or gold-egg laying geese periodicals (such as THE WALL STREET JOURNAL), the more time you have to either earn more gold (to buy more geese that also lay gold eggs) -- or simply to enjoy life.

Chapter Seven

Principle 1

An investment's true value is in the income it generates.

This is the most important concept to get into your head. And it's hard, I know, because you as well as everybody else in the investment/financial community from professors to stock brokers to your neighbors make the assumption that because (most) investments are liquid (which means that they easily and quickly be bought and sold on the open market), they are equal to money.

They're not.

An investment is an interest in an ongoing business or other income-generating organization.

A share of stock is a direct ownership interest in a business. A bond is a loan to a business (or other organization). Partnership units are direct ownership in a limited partnership. Trust units are direct ownership interest in a trust.

Ownership interests and loans are not money.

Yes, investments are worth money. Yes, they have current market values. Yes, to obtain stocks and bonds you must pay money for them. Yes, you can sell them for money. Yes, their market prices fluctuate so that you may sell them for a profit or a loss. Yes, most people -- from Nobel prize-winning economists to the slimiest of bucket shop penny stock pushers -- think the purpose of "investing" is to sell investments for a profit. Yes, I'm asking you to ignore what you read in other investment books, what your broker advises you and what you hear the talking heads on TV say.

Get Your Head Around This

Yes, I'm asking you to change the way you think about investments and to look at them in a way your family and friends will not understand (unless you refer them to this book). Yes, I'm asking you to think about investments like you never have before, and it'll take some practice and getting used to.

The good news is . . . once you free your thinking from the tyranny of capital gains, you feel so relieved. No more stress over every up and down in the market. You can listen to music on the radio instead of "The Wall Street Report." You can play a game with your kids instead of checking on stock prices. No more worrying about whether the Federal Reserve is going to raise or lower interest rates at their next meeting. You can watch a movie on TV instead of listening to so-called market experts jabber on about why stocks rose or fell.

You spend less time with your broker or financial advisor and more time with your family. You don't agonize over your monthly brokerage statements -- as long as they show you got paid.

The smart reason to buy investments is not to sell them in the future. It's to receive a perpetual, lifetime stream of income from those investments.

I want you to think of investments not as money, but as money-makers. Money machines. Money generators.

I Accept Only the Practical Aspects of This Theory of Investment Value

In 1938 John Burr Williams wrote, and Harvard University Press published, "The Theory of Investment Value," which described the theory of Discounted Cash Flow. Williams held that an investment's true value is the present value of the sum total of the future cash flows it's expected to bring to its owner.

According to Williams, the sum total of future cash flows includes all dividends plus the appreciation realized when selling it for a profit.

But what if you never sell the investment? Then there's no capital gains profit.

If that investment doesn't pay dividends or other income, then it's effectively and mathematically worthless. Worse than worthless, actually, since you could spend the money on something of value. So you lost the price of the commission you paid, plus suffered the opportunity cost of not investing it in a security that gives you a cash return.

The present value of zero is zero.

Would You Rather Have an Investment Worth $0 -- or Infinity?

If a stock or other investments pays out income, theoretically into infinity (assuming the company never goes out of business), then the present value of that stream of money is actually infinite.

OK, in real life you're not concerned with what a security will pay throughout eternity. What's important to you is the money you'll get in your lifetime.

Most of us don't think about more than ten or twenty years into the future, but we're living longer than ever before. If you're 65 now, chances are good you'll live another 20 or 30, or even more years. Of those of us who're younger than 65, many more of us will reach 100 than we ever thought before.

Every year that you stay alive is another year that medical science in general advances, and another year that you demonstrate you own personal survivability.

And if you're still alive by 2020-2030, chances are good you'll live MUCH longer.

Therefore, unless you are now over 70 years old or you have a terminal disease, you should plan on making your investments last at least another 30 years.

Looking at them from a long-range perspective is the best way to do that. That means -- buying them for income rather than to sell them later at a profit.

And if you have children, you can also think about leaving them these income-generating investments.

Some stocks have been paying steadily increasing dividends for over a hundred years. Don't you wish your great-grandparents had bought some shares of those companies, reinvested those dividends and held on to them?

Yes, by putting your money into income investments, you could not only assure yourself of a prosperous retirement, but found a family fortune.

Don't Rely on Greater Fools

Some say that a share of stock is worth whatever someone will pay for it. This is certainly true, but if you don't think further, you'll buy stock at any price because you think it will go up, and that a greater fool will buy it from you.

You run the risk of winding up the "greatest" fool. That is, you could be the last one left standing up in a game of Wall Street Musical Chairs.

You could be the one holding 1000 shares of DotComDotBomb when everybody else has already sold it, and its website is shut down.

The "Real Value" Theory of Stock Valuation -- Who Defines What a Stock is "Really" Worth?

Others say that a share of stock can "really" be worth something different than the current market price.

"Value" investors look for companies that, they believe, are undervalued by the marketplace.

You must understand that anybody who tells you that a given stock or the overall market is "over" valued or "under" valued -- for whatever reasons -- is playing God.

Unless you believe they really are God, ignore them.

The Theory of Discounted Cash Flow is very logical. Only it's not very practical to determine. What discount rate should you use? Current interest rates? Future interest rates? How do you know what those will be?

A bond's interest payments are fixed, but a stock's dividends are not. You can make a rational estimate of how much they'll grow, but you won't be precisely accurate unless you're psychic.

You can't know how much profit you'll make. Usually you don't know when or if you will sell it. A bond's principal will be returned to you at its maturity date, but if interest rates go down before then, you could sell it for a capital gains profit. You could be forced to sell the bond because the company exercises its right to call the bond from you You might sell it at a loss because of a financial emergency.

The Dividend Paying Stocks of the Dow Might Reach 36,000

In their much unjustly maligned book DOW 36,000, James Glassman and Kevin A. Hassett point out that common stocks pay dividends for a potentially infinite period, and the present value of any infinite value is infinity, so stocks are really underpriced. However, most of us place a lot more value on next year's income from our Coca-Cola stock than the dividends our great-grandchildren will receive from it.

This is good in theory but in practice you need a financial calculator that doubles as a crystal ball.

As an investor looking for "partners" to invest your hard earned money with, you are in effect treating these partnerships as your own business. IRS rules don't allow you to treat investing that way for tax purposes, but in practice, that's what you're doing . . . running your own investment business.

What if You Wanted to Go Into Another Type of Business?

Would you buy a money-losing McDonald's franchise you thought was priced too high, with the plan of selling it in 3 months to a "greater fool?"

If so, you're a 1990s style dot com investor.

Would you buy a McDonald's franchise because you thought it was undervalued, and so the price would go up in the long run, and then you'll sell it?

If so, you're a value investor.

Would you buy a McDonald's franchise if you couldn't receive any income from it? That is, if McDonald's told you that you MUST reinvest all your profits into the restaurant, to build its value, so that you wouldn't get any benefit from your business until you sold it (assuming it would be worth a lot more money, because of all the profits you'd reinvested?)

If so, you're investing for capital gains.

Would you add up all the profits you expected to receive from the business in the future, discount them by the U.S prime rate and then compare this present value to the price given by McDonald's, and buy only if your calculation of present value was higher than the price McDonald's was charging you?

If so, you're investing based on the present value technique.

Do you believe that ANYBODY buys a McDonald's franchise for ANY of these reasons?

I thought not.

When we consider buying a McDonald's franchise -- or a lemonade stand -- we want a business that will give us a good profit for years to come, at a price that is fair in relation to the risk, the profits and the prices of other, similar businesses you could buy.

As our own investment business, the securities we buy are worth the money we receive from them. Some pay less income, some pay more. The goal of a rational income investor is to maximize income -- yield -- from securities while minimizing risk.

I emphasize the income that businesses receive for yet another reason.

Sure You Want to Buy That $1.50 for $1?

Classical "value" investing as advocated by Benjamin Graham emphasized finding and buying stocks that were cheap based on the value of the assets the business owned. In one of his books, he gave as an example finding a company that owned a rock quarry that nobody else in the stock market was paying any attention to. Therefore, he was able to buy shares in a company that had a higher "real" value per share than what he paid. Occasionally you hear about companies that are in some kind of trouble, yet their stock is bought by value investors because, despite their business problems, they still had large amounts of cash in their bank accounts.

On paper, this sounds terrific. Buy $1.50 worth of assets for $1? That's the "no-brainer" all good value investors "get." At that price, give me all you've got, right?

Well . . . maybe.

Remember, unless we're talking about a very small business where you can exert control (and that's not what this book is about), you as one small fry investor have no say-so over what the company does with its assets.

Sure, the value of buying $1.50 for $1 is obvious -- except the company is not going to send you that 50 cents as a reward for buying their stock (especially if it's in the form of a rock quarry!)

How can you benefit (that is, receive spendable cash in your pocket) from finding such traditional undervalued situations?

Assets are nice but unless a company is using them to generate more profit, they may as well be gathering dust in somebody's attic. If you're not going to enjoy Grandma's antique lamp, why not sell it on eBay? As an ordinary investor, you don't control what a company does with its money.

In his early career, Benjamin Graham's star pupil Warren Buffett found a small company that was sitting on an underused asset -- a classical "value investing" situation. He bought enough of the company's stock to gain a seat on the Board of Directors (not an option for most of us).

Yet the rest of the Board of Directors resented an outsider coming in, telling them how to run their business. Buffett could not convince them to use that asset, and so he finally sold his shares.

Sure, it's nice to buy $1.50 for $1, but not when that $1.50 remains in somebody else's pocket, out of your reach.

BOTTOM LINE:

Every income-generating investment is a goose that lays gold eggs.

And geese that lay gold eggs should be kept for more gold eggs, not sold for the price of their meat, no matter how fat they are.

Next: all long range investors should know that the true value lies in using their investing income to produce yet more investing income.

Chapter Eight

Principle 2

Increase your income by reinvesting that income. The longer you compound your income, the higher it grows.

If you could live long enough, you'd become the richest person on Earth just by putting $100 into an ordinary savings account and reinvesting your interest income until it compounded into a fortune.

Granted, nobody lives that long (yet!), and you don't need to become the wealthiest person on the planet to have a comfortable retirement.

The concept of reinvesting and compounding your investing income so that you earn interest on interest works -- that's the point.

Sure, you want to speed it up as much as possible by putting as much money as possible into your investments and by getting the highest return possible.

Yet over the long run, you'll make the most money from the reinvestment of your earnings.

Reinvestment and Compounding Allows You to Profit from What Albert Einstein Allegedly Called the 8th Wonder of the World

When I was a kid, I remember reading a "brain teaser" about a little boy who outfoxed his father. He told his father, "Dad, I'll never ask you for money again as long as I live, if you'll do just one thing for me."

"What's that, son?"

"Tomorrow's the first of the month. Give me a penny. The next day, give me twice as much -- that's only two pennies. Every day of next month, give me twice as much as the day before. Do that until the end of the month, and I'll never ask you for money again."

The indulgent father agrees, thinking that it'll no problem to give the boy a few pennies a day.

Check a calculator. 1 cent X 2 to the 30th power is . . .

$5,368,708.80

And that's just what the father had to fork over on the final day, not the total for the month.

That's the power of compounding.

OK, you're not going to double your money every year.

What if you start with just $100 and earn just a reasonable 5% per year?

In 20 years you'll have $252.69.

In 30 years you'll have $411.60.

In 40 years you'll have $670.46.

In 50 years you'll have $1092.11.

Why do I go out to 50 years? You say you're not going to live that long? Maybe.

The More Time You Have, the More You Can Take Advantage of This Principle -- and Most of Us Have a Lot More Time Than We Think

First of all, although I expect most readers of this book are getting close to retirement age, I hope there'll be some who are young enough to use this information to get filthy rich -- just by saving money now, while they're still very young, investing for income and reinvesting their earnings.

Secondly, although you may be in your 50s or 60s now, that doesn't mean you're going to die soon. Odds are, you'll live at least another 20 years. And many more of us baby boomers than realize it now are going to live past 100.

And once we're that far along, who knows what advances in medical science will keep us alive even longer?

So even if you watched the The Beatles debut on the Ed Sullivan Show, that doesn't mean it's too late for you to start saving, reinvesting and compounding your savings.

You can still get rich.

One Woman Started With $5000 at Age 51

Anne Schieber is a good role model to mention here. At age 51, in 1944, she retired from the IRS with $5000 in savings. She put that money into stocks (having observed during her career with the IRS that wealthy people owned a lot of stocks), and reinvested the earnings for the rest of her life.

In 1995, at age 101, she died. Her estate was worth $22 million.

When she retired in 1944 she probably didn't think she was going to live another 50 years, but she did -- and you're going to have the advantage over her of the vast increase in medical knowledge and technology. Heck, when she retired penicillin was the first Wonder Drug.

If you are currently retired and seeking to maximize your income from investing to meet your current expenses, you can't reinvest all your interest and dividends. However, I strongly suggest reinvesting at least 10%. That will grow your total income through the future.

If you're under 80 years old, you have a reasonable chance of living another 10 to 20 years -- at least.

You can and should at least partially harness the power of compounding your income.

Here's a Real-World Example

If you bought 200 shares of Philip Morris (now Altria) in November 1986 (cost: $14,700), and reinvested all dividends, twenty years later in 2006 you received $20,430 in dividend income.

That is -- the per year return on your original investment is now over 150% . . . and you still own the shares (gold eggs), so you'll keep getting more and more in dividends from Altria every year.

Oh, and by the way, the market value of your shares of Altria would have increased to $483,021.

That's 3.66 times what you would have made by investing that same money in the S&P 500 in November 2006.

Oh, yes -- in case you care about "risk"/ volatility, Philip Morris's beta was 22% less than the market's.

Here's another one. The Dow Jones Industrial Average is the most well-known stock market bench market. But it measures only rises in capital gains -- that is, in market price.

It began in 1886 and broke 10,000 for the first time in 1999.

What if the Dow Jones measured the results of reinvesting the dividends paid by those 30 companies?

In 1999, the Dow would have been 905,259!

This principle is mathematically sound, but psychologically difficult, because we tend to emotionally discount the future. That is, the future benefit of receiving large amounts of money from our investments seems less important to us than the current pleasure of spending money RIGHT NOW.

Think of It This Way . . .

No matter how old you are now, don't you wish you'd started saving, investing and reinvesting when you were much younger? I started earning money from a paper route when I was 14 years old. If I'd put half of that money into a savings account, let it build up, reinvested the interest, added to it as I kept working, let it build up and reinvested the earnings, kept adding to it as I grew older and made a higher income from working better jobs and kept on letting it build up, reinvesting the earnings . . .

I'd be rich now!

I'd live in some tropical paradise and would do ONLY what I wanted, when I WANTED.

Unfortunately, when I was young I wasn't that smart -- and odds are, neither were you.

During my extreme youth, the immediate pleasures offered by sex, drugs and rock n roll seemed more important.

Don't you wish you'd saved money back then?

Well . . . now you DO understand the importance of saving!

You know that time IS going to pass. You ARE going to grow older, have more responsibilities, get tired of working for other people, want to relax and enjoy life while feeling financially secure.

You know that having lots of money is the key to enjoying the rest of your life.

So start doing now what you now wish you'd done when you were younger.

Invest for income -- reinvest and compound your earnings.

Principle 3 points out that while you're reinvesting and compounding, it can make a big difference to your final result how much you pay for additional shares.

Chapter Nine

Principle 3

The lower the market prices at which you reinvest your income, the more income-generating securities you can buy, which in turn will give you more income to reinvest, so you receive even more income in the future.

"From 1871 to 2003 97 percent of the total after-inflation accumulation from stocks comes from reinvesting dividends. Only 3 percent comes from capital gains."

-- *Dr. Jeremy Siegel in THE FUTURE FOR INVESTORS*

Years ago I looked at a statement of my retirement account at work and had a revelation . . .

I realized that if I could control the stock market, I'd be best off if I kept the S&P 500 very low while I was working and buying up the index mutual funds shares -- and allowed it to go up in price only just before I retired.

I'm not the first one to have this kind of insight. Warren Buffett has written about the same thing.

Yet, it felt weird to think about that, because I recognized that I'd never read anything in a financial book or article that explained how investors are better off with low stock (or bond) prices -- while we're still buying/accumulating stocks and bonds.

It's somehow human nature to prefer to see prices go up after we've bought some stocks and bonds, and be happy at the rise in price of our investments, without thinking about how that same price rise would reduce the number of the shares we buy in the future.

Care More About the Price You'll Pay the Next Time You Invest in That Security, Rather Than What Its Paper Value is Now

And just as this applies to making continuous investments out of your paycheck, it also applies to the reinvestment of your earned dividends and income. I'm indebted to Dr. Jeremy Siegel and his book THE FUTURE FOR INVESTORS for pointing out this key fact.

In his book he describes the results of two studies he made. One compares the results of investing in a boring "old school" stock -- Standard Oil -- and an exciting "high tech" growth stock -- IBM -- from 1957 to 2003. The other study compares the results of investing in two "developing" countries -- one (Brazil) a highly volatile, politically unstable, economically hazardous country prone to currency crises and the other (China) the much hyped glamorous growth story.

He assumed reinvestment of all dividends -- that's an important point.

He found that investors who bought Standard Oil in 1957 and held it through 2003 beat investors who bought and held IBM through that same period.

He also found that investors who bought shares of companies in Brazil in 1992, by 2003 had beat those who invested in that darling of international investors, China.

Yet, during those periods, the market price of IBM did grow more than Standard Oil, and the market price of China's companies grew more than that of Brazilian companies.

So how come investments in IBM and China didn't outgrow Standard Oil and Brazil?

Simple math.

Because IBM and Chinese companies were expected to grow a lot, the prices of their stocks were priced much higher in relation to their earnings than Standard Oil and Brazilian companies.

Investors in high-growth IBM and China paid more than investors in boring Standard Oil and troubled Brazil.

Here's Another Example of Why You Should Buy When Securities are Cheap

It's widely known that stocks crashed in 1929, and the Dow Jones didn't again reach its September 3, 1929 peak until November 24, 1954 -- over twenty-five years after the crash.

Twenty-five years of the Great Depression, World War 2, the Korea "police action" and the Cold War with Communism. A bad time to own stocks?

On average, stocks during that time paid out 6% in dividends. If you'd bought $1000 in dividend paying stocks at the 1929 Dow Jones peak, then reinvested those dividends, by 1954 your stock portfolio was worth $4440!

The Dow Jones average remained negative for 25 years -- but your portfolio went up by 444%!

How can that be?

Because you reinvested the dividends, thus buying more and more shares of stock.

But if on September 3, 1929 you'd bought $1000 worth of non-dividend paying "growth" stocks, the market value of your portfolio would have remained below $1000 until November 24, 1954.

Depend on capital gains --

Income Investing Secrets

Receive no return on your investment for over 25 years.

Reinvest dividends --

Grow your portfolio -- and your dividend income as well -- by 444%!

The Great Depression was a great time to BUY stocks, because they were so cheap.

I remember my grandfather commenting once that he could have become rich during the Depression by investing in stocks (he had a good job so he had the money to invest), but my grandmother stopped him. Her fear -- shared by almost all Americans -- kept my grandfather from accumulating the wealth that would have made him and his descendants (including me) wealthy.

Don't make the same mistake!

I promise you -- in years to come your children and grandchildren will wish you'd bought all the dividend-paying stocks you can afford.

Principle 4 helps to bear-proof your portfolio. Invest in businesses that are too basic to not succeed.

Chapter Ten

Principle 4

Invest in businesses that meet basic human needs and desires.

"Business" is a word widely used in everyday language, and we all have a good idea what we mean by it -- but few people keep in mind the most basic fact of what a business is.

You can go to a bookstore or Amazon and buy a hundred business and investing books, and learn about accounting and management and international negotiation skills and options and much more -- without ever learning what the foundation of a business really is.

A business is an organization for meeting the needs and desires of human beings.

A profitable business meets the needs and desires of human beings at a cost that is lower than the price those human beings are willing to pay.

That is, revenue must exceed expenses.

Whether the business is a lemonade stand in your front yard or Microsoft.

Many businesses start off losing money due to their startup costs, but they must take in at least more money than their ongoing expenses.

Many People Have Lost a Lot of Money by Forgetting This Basic Point

Now, I know this sounds painfully obvious, but remember back to the high tech, dot com boom of the late 1990s. Many companies did meet human needs and desires, although at a very abstract level, but couldn't do so at a price low enough to attract enough customers. Their ad and other costs exceeded their sales (some didn't even have any sales), so their cash reserves were used up -- at the time, it was called the "burn rate."

Some of those companies had only the promise of meeting human needs and desires in the future. Some had only the HOPE of meeting human needs and desires. They didn't know whether anybody wanted the "solutions" (a way overused high tech "buzz word") they were developing.

Yet stock investors and private venture firms threw money at these companies like crazy. Scratch that -- it wasn't "like" crazy. It WAS crazy.

Those companies couldn't pay dividends to their investors. They could barely meet their payrolls, and eventually couldn't do that.

To be fair, when you see or read a pitch for a new penny stock or over the counter stock these days, the company's story is spun from the angle of how popular their product or service is or will be. I see a lot of these in my mailbox . . . they're used to sell newsletter subscriptions. Every one of these new companies is in the forefront of a fantastic new trend, and each one has a product that will soon dominate its industry. Each one is the next Wal-Mart. If you believe their hype!

A good business must have a pool of potential customers who do need or want the product or service, and who have the money to pay a price that more than exceeds the cost of producing the product or service.

Basic Human Needs Have Not Changed Since We Discovered Fire

The word "basic" is important. I want my personal income from investing to be dependable. Many businesses meet human desires that fluctuate in intensity or with income.

For example -- water is a basic human need.

Having that water put into a plastic bottle and given a fancy name and sold in a retail store -- in developed countries with large supplies of clean and cheap tap water, that's not a basic human need.

(In countries without safe drinking water, it does meet the basic human need of protecting yourself against water-borne diseases, but only if you're a tourist or comparatively well-off. The local poor people must drink unsafe water).

In developed countries, if someone has enough extra income and they desire to drink bottled water for whatever reason, they will. However, if their income goes down, they can simply drink tap water.

Therefore, a water utility meets a basic human need but Evian doesn't.

We all need to eat, but in bad economic times people are more likely to stop dining at expensive French restaurants and go to McDonald's.

Modern Financial Markets Allow Us to Share in the Success of Businesses

The financial markets are a miracle of capitalism, because they give everybody who'll come up with a relatively small amount of money the chance to share in the profits of a big company.

You probably can't come up with the secret formula of a widely popular soft drink, but you can buy stock in Coca-Cola.

You probably couldn't obtain enough money to start up a car factory, but you can buy bonds directly from Ford.

You probably don't know how to revolutionize the computer industry, but you can buy stock in Microsoft, Apple and Dell.

Because stocks, bonds and other securities are pieces of paper with money values associated with them, it's only natural human behavior to "game" the system and thus to dream up ways to make money from manipulating those numbers and pieces of paper.

Too Many People Forget the Reality Behind the Numbers

People have devoted millions of hours of thought and work to coming up with systems to make money from trading the stock market, the commodity markets and the foreign exchange markets. People have spent millions upon millions of dollars buying books on trading and newsletters from financial gurus -- and lost even more millions of dollars by taking their advice.

There's scant evidence for anybody coming up with "systems" that work without fail, forever.

We do know, however, that the markets as a whole work. Well-run businesses that meet basic human needs and desires make a profit.

So we partner with them. It's a lot easier, simpler, cheaper -- and effective.

(Technically, only buying stocks gives you ownership in a company. Buying bonds is loaning those businesses money. However, once they owe you that money, you have a stake in their success. You get paid your semi-annual interest checks, and your money back upon maturity, only if that company continues to exist.)

Remember -- a share of stock is a piece of a business.

However, all investing entails risk. Investing in businesses that meet basic human needs and desires is one way to reduce risk. The next principle covers the most fundamental way to reduce investing risk to a minimum.

Chapter Eleven

Principle 5

Use diversification to reduce risk.

If there's any aspect of Modern Portfolio Theory (MPT) and asset allocation that makes perfect sense, although not for the reasons the academics think, it has to be diversification.

Harry Markowitz won the Nobel Prize for his work linking diversification and lowering portfolio risk.

Diversification is essential for reducing the risk of any kind of investing.

It only stands to reason that if all of your investment money is in one particular security, all of your investment money is at great risk. Every security has some type of risk. When all your funds are in that particular type of investment, they're all at the same risk. You can be wiped out by one event.

If you own one airline stock, your money is at risk if that company happens to lose out to all its competition, it goes bankrupt, and so on.

If you own stock in every airline company, you're protected from the risk of one airline going out of business, but you're at risk of something happening to the entire airline industry.

If you own stocks in a wide variety of industries, you're protected from the risk of any one industry going the way of the buggy whip sector.

I know that some people advise, "Put all your eggs in one basket -- and then watch that basket very carefully."

That's a catchy saying. But it works only when you can control what happens to the basket.

Do you control the market price of stocks and bonds? Or the behavior of Chief Executive Officers and Chief Financial Officers?

No. If you'd applied that catchy theory to owning Enron in the late 1990s, you'd have had no more idea than anyone else outside the upper echelons of Enron that they were committing fraud.

If you own only one investment, you can check its price every hour if you wish (though who would want to do that?) -- but if the CEO is arrested or if the company headquarters is exposed to anthrax powder or if their main plant in South America is taken over by communist revolutionaries . . . the best you can do is cut your losses ASAP.

But you'll be selling behind the Wall Street insiders.

The Theory

In MPT risk is defined and expressed as the volatility or up and down movements in the market price of the security. Therefore, reduction of portfolio risk involves reducing the overall volatility of your portfolio.

Diversification across asset classes accomplishes this through the mathematical term variance. Variance is the degree to which the market value of assets can be different.

For example, your local real estate market can go into a deep depression while the country's stock market is in a roaring bull boom. Therefore, there's a wide variance between investing in local real estate and the stock market.

During such a time, a local real estate-only investor will find their net worth shot to hell. The stock-only investor will be happy.

But their roles could easily be reversed when, in a few years, your local real estate market is again booming, but stocks are in a deep bear market.

The real winner is someone who's invested in both. Overall, the average value of their portfolio of both real estate and stocks does not go as far down -- or as far up -- as that of investors who own only one or the other.

Some asset classes are good because they have a negative correlation. For example, historically, gold moves in the opposite direction from the stock market.

Real Life Application

Since I don't regard up and down price volatility in securities as something to be afraid of (we should plan on holding our investments for the rest of our lives), I don't look at diversification as a mathematical construct of variances with the purpose of reducing volatility.

Again, we don't need to care about volatility.

However, let's face it -- real life does contain real risk for real businesses and other sources of income from investing. A company can pay dividends this year and go into bankruptcy next year.

It's just common sense to protect yourself, your portfolio, and your income by making sure you receive checks from various sources.

Therefore, I do advocate as wide a diversification as you can afford. Maybe you can start out buying only one stock or bond. OK -- you have to start somewhere.

But you should aim for diversification across:

1. Asset type -- stocks, bonds, real estate and so on

2. Geography -- various parts of the United States and countries around the world

3. Political as well as geographical -- other countries, both developed and developing, on every continent

4. Security sub-type -- Treasury bonds, municipal bonds, corporate bonds, and so on

5. Industry -- utilities, consumer goods, energy production, and so on.

6. Currency -- US dollars, Canadian dollars, Japanese yen, euros, and so on

The Opposing Viewpoint

Many people, including famed economist John Kenneth Galbreith, have understood that, taken to its logical extreme, diversification means that your overall portfolio results will reflect the average return of that type of security. And perfect diversification means that your overall portfolio reflects "only" the economic growth of the entire world.

Some writers are clever enough to refer to this pursuit of average returns as "di-worse-ification."

If you want to "beat the market," they point out, you must find just a few superior securities and put all your money into them.

That's all fine, well and dandy -- if you have a 100% accurate crystal ball.

Throughout this book, I'll refer to studies showing that the people paid millions of dollars to spend all their work time looking for those few superior securities -- pension fund managers, brokers and mutual fund managers -- fail to do as well as the overall market.

A vast amount of evidence shows that crystal balls are in short supply among the world's financial experts.

We must also guard against the biggest single threat to long-term investors. It's a war we have been fighting since the Bretton Woods agreement made near the end of World War 2.

Chapter Twelve

Principle 6

Grow your income to keep up with or beat inflation.

Most of us know that inflation has been a routine economic fact of life since the end of World War 2.

(Most people don't know that inflation was NOT a routine economic fact of life prior to World War 2. Yes, it sometimes happened -- Germany in 1923 is the best known example of hyperinflation. The purchasing power of the U.S. dollar did fluctuate between the founding of our currency and Pearl Harbor -- but overall during that period it was much more stable. Sometimes its purchasing power went up. Sometimes it went down. But it didn't go steadily downhill, as it has since 1945.)

Whatever the cause, inflation is now a routine fact of economic life in the world, and it's a great enemy of investors -- up there with death and taxes.

Inflation was a particular problem from the late 1960s to about 1982. Those of us who lived through that period can remember constant price increases in things we bought.

Even "Slow" Inflation Erodes Your Money's Purchasing Power

Inflation has gone down dramatically since that period . . . to a "mere" 2-3% on average. Thanks to the poor housing market, it was 1.8% in 2009.

Isn't that now too small to worry about?

If the government can keep inflation at a "mere" 2% a year (unlikely, given the fast-rising cost of oil and other energy, the plummeting of the U.S. dollar, plus the huge increases in government spending), then your purchasing power will be cut in half after 36 years.

If you retire at age 65 with just enough income to live on, your lifestyle will be cut in half by age 101.

Maybe you think you won't live to be 101 (although many baby boomers will live this long, thanks to the popularity of nutrition and exercise, and advances in medicine).

We Seem to Be Entering a 1970s-Type Era of High Energy and Commodity Prices

But it's more likely that inflation will not stay so low for that long. Remember, oil is getting scarcer, and many of the world's oilfields are under the control of politically threatened (Saudi Arabia and Iraq) or threatening (Iran, Russia and Venezuela) countries. Canada has a lot of oil in its tar sands, but that will be expensive to extract.

As I write, rising energy costs are already increasing the cost of groceries and other goods.

Also as I write, the United States government is spending much more money than it did just last year. And it's not alone. So are many European governments and Japan.

I don't have a crystal ball, but I wouldn't be surprised to see a return to 4-5% or even more inflation in the coming years -- at least until we solve our energy supply problems .

Also, U.S. consumers know that the falling U.S. dollar is making European and Japanese goods more expensive. The United Kingdom pound is falling even farther than the U.S. dollar.

And if you live in Europe, don't feel too smug -- when European baby boomers retire en mass and start demanding the benefits promised to them all their working lives, the EU is going to have to start running your printing presses on overtime, flooding the world with euros, devaluing that currency against the yen and dollar.

And Japan's government is spending a lot of money, making the yen's long-term outlook grim.

You Don't Want to Sit in a Rocking Chair Watching TV All Day

What this means is -- if you wish to maintain your purchasing power throughout your retirement, your investment income must keep up with inflation.

As with most things in life, this can get complicated in reality.

For instance, you'll probably want to do a lot more -- which means spending a lot more money -- when you're 65 than when you're 115.

Or maybe the age at which you feel really REALLY old -- too old to go on cruises, race sports cars and buy all the latest electronic toys -- will be 150.

Whatever -- the point is, at some point you're probably not going to be in physical or mental condition to have a lot of expensive fun. Yet, it's also true that may mean you need a lot more expensive medical care and therapy.

It's a cruel fact of life also, that this principle is most important to the people who can least afford to follow it (and who are least likely to be reading this book) -- those on low incomes.

After all, if you retire with a $500,000 a year income and your purchasing power is cut in half by age 100 -- that's still the equivalent of $250,000. Maybe you won't take as many trips to ski in the Alps, but you'll still live in plenty of comfort.

If you retire with a $25,000 annual income, you can't afford to see your purchasing power cut in half.

Don't Let the Risk of Inflation Trick You Into Not Saving Money Now

During periods of high inflation you'll hear a lot of advise to "spend your money now before it goes down in value."

This is logical but still misguided.

I think that it's most important that people save money for their retirement and invest it SOME way. Even if it loses some purchasing power, it'll be more useful during your retirement years than spent during your working years on extra luxuries.

Let's put it this way: you and your spouse save up some money, and now you can either go on a round-the-world cruise or invest it for your retirement.

You don't have any retirement money invested yet, and you just went on a round-the-world cruise two years ago. So you decide to invest it by buying some certificates of deposit which, on an after-tax basis, don't keep up with inflation.

When you and your spouse retire, the income from those certificates of deposit is just enough to pay for your monthly grocery bill.

Food for a month in your 70s may not sound as exciting as a round-the-world cruise now, but without it, you and your spouse will get very hungry.

BOTTOM LINE:

Your investment income must retain purchasing power over many years.

The long-term investor's next greatest enemy is expenses -- including taxes.

Chapter Thirteen

Principle 7

Guard your income generation power by reducing expenses: taxes, brokerage fees, commissions, management fees and so on. Your personal time is also an expense to keep to a minimum.

Few investors realize how critical keeping expenses to a minimum is to their financial future.

There's an old Wall Street story you may have heard before, but it's worth repeating.

A man goes to New York City to decide whether or not he should invest his savings in the stock market, so he visits a stock broker. The broker takes him on a tour and explains everything to him. Then, to impress the out of towner with how much money can be made in the stock market, looks out a large picture window facing New York City Harbor and points to the yachts there.

"See that large brown yacht?" the broker says, "That one belongs to Richard Smithson III, a successful stock broker. And that white one? That belongs to Robert Hampton, another stock broker. And that one in the middle, the biggest one - that belongs to Burton Langford IV, the most successful broker in the country."

Finally, the visitor asks, "Where are the customers' yachts?"

Nothing in life is free, and you should pay something for investing services. You can't expect brokers to buy stocks for you for free.

However, too many investors don't take the time to minimize expenses. They don't think about how they're buying yachts for their brokers.

Too many investors will drive 20 minutes to Wal-Mart to save $5 one time for a pair of bluejeans, but don't question the mutual fund expenses that will compound AGAINST their investment returns for the rest of their life, costing them thousands of dollars over the years.

The Money You Lose on Unnecessary Expenses is Compounded Over the Years Also -- It Subtracts From Your Final Total

This principle is, in a sense, the flip side of Principle 2 which advocates the compounding of earnings.

The money you lose from paying excess expenses is also compounded for the rest of your life -- in a negative sense, by its absence.

The money you could have made from compounding those dollars is . . . gone.

Investing expenses include direct expenses such as:

Commissions

Management fees

Taxes

Financial advisor fees

Online services fees

Record keeping and accounting fees

Large spread between bid/ask prices -- (This means that when you buy a security, you pay too much more than what the seller sold it for. There's always a middle ground, but it should not be too wide, or you're losing money by paying too much, and you don't even know it.)

It also includes the cost of your investor education:

Books, videos, CDs, courses, software, newspapers and magazines.

Active Management of Your Portfolio is Also a Luxury You Can't Afford

In 1986 Gary P. Brinson, L. Rudolph Hood and Gilbert L. Beebower published a paper in the July-August edition of FINANCIAL ANALYSTS JOURNAL: "Determinants of Portfolio Performance."

They studied the performance of 91 pension fund managers from 1974-1983. If these pension fund managers had simply invested in a stock index fund, bonds and money market funds, they would have earned 10.1% on average per year. However, on average they earned 9% -- the active management of portfolios cost the pension funds over 1% per year.

(1% compounded per year for 20 years means your final balance is 17% less!)

They did an attribution study to determine what contributed most to the pension fund manager's performance, and decided that 90% is due to the asset allocation. Only 10% is attributable to security selection and timing.

This study made the brokerage industry adopt asset allocation.

However, a staff writer for THE WALL STREET JOURNAL followed public recommendations of major brokerage houses from 1986 to 1997. He found that their performance was only about half the optimal results of dividing assets into stocks, bonds and cash.

Brokers still try to time the markets, only now call they call it rebalancing.

Therefore, I can't forget to point out that one of the costs of investing which you should minimize is the cost you'll pay for listening to brokers or any other financial advisors who claim they know how to get better than market returns.

Should You Even Subscribe to THE WALL STREET JOURNAL?

The story of Anne Schieber is worth mentioning here also -- that's the woman I mentioned in Principle 2 who compounded $5000 into $22 million.

She did her investing research. We know that she read THE WALL STREET JOURNAL every day -- but she didn't pay for it. She went to the library of a nearby woman's college and read THEIR copy!

(She did pay them back. She willed her entire $22 million estate to that woman's college, so in a sense, they got a great return on the money they paid for their subscription to the WSJ.)

Again, some expenses are necessary. But those that can be avoided, should be. Reduce your expenses as much as possible.

Your time spent on investing is also an expense you should minimize, and so that's the subject of the next section. No other financial writer will tell you what I'm going to. On this subject, even the best financial writers tick me off.

Chapter Fourteen

Use Your Time Well

I'm fed up with investing books that keep telling me to spend every single moment of my nonworking hours studying investment strategies.

Stay up with financial magazines, newspapers, websites and newsletters, the gurus tell us.

Read THE WALL STREET JOURNAL every day.

Hang out in online investing sites.

Read annual reports.

James Glassman says it in THE SECRET CODE OF THE SUPERIOR INVESTOR. The Motley Fool say it. Even Burton Malkiel in the 9th edition of A RANDOM WALK DOWN WALL STREET says it.

Yuck!

Once you have an investing system that will work for you long term -- spend your time during something useful!

That's my advice.

And I enjoy reading. I enjoy reading books about investing, or I couldn't have written this one. I have a B.S. degree in Accounting and, although I've never really worked as an accountant, still know how to read a balance sheet and an income statement. I've begun studying to take and pass the Series 65 test for financial advisors.

But give me a break --

Peter Lynch used to stay up until midnight reading annual reports -- but he got paid buku bux to do so. Warren Buffett knows the financial statements of every company on the New York Stock Exchange better than everybody else except the company's own CFO.

But those guys get paid to work full time at this. You and I don't.

If we want to have money to invest, we've got to work long, hard hours at our jobs and businesses.

Here I Step Outside the Normal "Investing Book" Box

In my years of reading about money and finance, I've noticed there are four categories of such books:

1. Personal finance: debt, retirement planning, how to save on insurance premiums etc.

2. Business opportunity: Make money in real estate, mail order, on eBay etc.

3. Investments (includes trading): stocks, bonds, commodities, options etc.

4. Business career development: How to give good speeches, how to network, how a famous corporation succeeded etc.

Within the covers of these books, there's no overlap. A book on Six Sigma quality doesn't tell you why you should buy term life insurance over whole life insurance. A book on eBay doesn't tell you how to choose mutual funds.

I'm Writing this Book for People Who Have to Live in the Real World

But in real life, people need to know just about everything. Assuming you have a responsible day job or business, you need the career development. You need to know how to budget your money. You need to know about investments. And if you have some spare time, then you can learn how to start a home business, to make even more money, so you have even more money to invest . . .

So it's silly to think that you have nothing to do all day but read investment books and annual reports.

Personally, I also think it's not realistic of you to think that even if you learned how to read a balance sheet, that you could properly evaluate a company's financial statements.

How many trained accountants knew Enron was cooking its books? Only its auditors, and they didn't tell anybody else (as they were supposed to).

And even if you could be certain that a company's public financial statements are accurate, that doesn't tell you about its future business prospects.

Maybe they have a terrific story. Maybe their product cures cancer, makes people thin, 20 years younger and irresistibly sexy. Maybe it grows hair on men. Maybe it does all these things at once.

Maybe they have a terrific buzz going on. Every talking head on TV predicts their success is guaranteed. The financial press says they're the next Microsoft, Wal-Mart and Starbucks rolled into one.

And maybe all those things are true.

You still don't know whether or not it's a good investment.

Some financial researchers look for crooked accounting by using company financial statements to track their cash flow -- they look for problems and discrepancies.

Thousands of mutual funds, pensions fund, insurance companies and hedge funds have computers running full-time to process all available information on public companies. They're running custom-designed software programs to analyze stocks, bonds and other investments using the most sophisticated mathematical investment models available.

And in the long run, they still can't beat the market!

So what makes you think you can beat them?

Just how arrogant are you, anyway?

The Efficient Market Hypothesis Makes All that Research a Violation of the Efficient Use of Time

Funny how many of the same gurus who tell us to spend so much looking for good investments, on the next page will explain how the Efficient Market Hypothesis makes all that effort pointless, because nobody can predict the market or the fate of individual stocks anyway.

You could analyze every security out there to the Nth degree -- bonds have their own language and financial analysis. Same with mutual funds, Exchange Traded Funds, and so on.

You could devote your life to studying all this, and in the end still not wind up with as much money as somebody who simply goes to work at their job every day and consistently invests as much as they can.

With what you learn in this book, you should spend some time setting up your investment plan. Once that's done, you should put it on "auto pilot."

You'll Make More Money From Investing If You Make More Money to Invest

Instead of reading endless investment books (you are allowed to read this one twice!) and annual reports and financial newsletters and hanging out in online investing forums, here're my suggestions for making more money from investing:

1. Get a part time job and invest all of those paychecks.

2. Clean up your house and sell all unused items on eBay. After that, help your friends and neighbors sell their unused items on eBay, for a 10% cut of the sale price. Invest all those profits.

3. Take college courses at a local or online school, so you get a higher degree and qualify for a higher salary at your job, or a new, better-paid job. Invest more from your now-higher income.

4. Run some type of home-based business. Invest your profits.

5. Take courses to obtain advanced certifications in your career. Demand a

raise or get a new job paying you more money. Invest more money with your now-higher income.

6. If you already own a business, research ways to market it better, or run it more profitably, or expand it. Invest your increased profits.

Did you spot the trend there?

Once you have a good investment plan in place to buy the securities we're about to learn are worthwhile . . .

You don't need to spend more time studying the prospects of one company's stock over another's.

You don't need to spend time on some online stock forum.

You don't need to read any annual reports.

You need to keep investing. The more money you can afford to invest, the more in the long term your portfolio will be worth.

So the best use of your nonwork time is to increase your value in the marketplace. Whether you choose to work a second job, to enhance your current career, qualify yourself for a more lucrative career, start a part-time business, or expand your current full-time business . . .

That's obviously up to you.

Oh, and by the way -- you're also allowed to use the time the gurus want you to spend reading annual reports on having more fun with your friends and family!

Near the end of this book, I have another chapter on how to increase the time available to you to make more money, both from these kinds of activities, and from compounding your investments. It's not what you may think. In it I break another "subject matter boundary taboo" so you're free to take its advice for what you think it's worth, or ignore if you choose.

Next we start to examine the forms of income investing securities we can buy. Some are better than others.

Chapter Fifteen

Forms of Securities

The next few chapters will examine the various ways you can invest in securities, and analyze them with the 7 Principles of Income Investing.

We'll look at the following:

1. Individual securities

2. Actively traded, open-ended mutual funds

3. Index mutual funds

4. Closed-end funds

5. Exchange Traded funds

6. Hedge funds

They're not all equal. None are perfect, though one type comes close.

Chapter Sixteen

Individual Securities

This doesn't need any explanation. One individual security can be a share of IBM common stock, a Treasury bond or shares in the Fidelity Magellan mutual fund.

If you are lucky and buy a security just before it zooms up in price, you can make a lot of money.

But if you're not so lucky, you can lose a lot.

Strengths:

You can start investing with a small amount of money ($25) through company Dividend ReInvestment Programs (DRIPs). Most major companies that pay dividends have them.

You open your account directly with the company, so you don't have to pay a commission to a broker. The quarterly dividends are then reinvested at no charge.

Weaknesses:

Obviously -- diversification. They're not. You can diversify by buying a number of different types of securities, but this requires a lot of money. And it's easier just to buy securities that are already diversified (covered in later chapters).

Bottom Line:

If you want to invest for income but have only a little bit of money to start with, DRIPs are the way to go.

Income Investing Secrets

If you have larger amounts of money, individual securities are too risky.

Next: the darlings of the mainstream financial media -- open-ended, actively-traded mutual funds.

Chapter Seventeen

Actively Traded, Open-Ended Mutual Funds

"The historical record is that on a cumulative basis, over three-quarters of professionally managed mutual funds underperformed the S&P 500 Stock Averages."

-- Charles Ellis in WINNING THE LOSER'S GAME

These are what most people refer to simply as "mutual funds." But closed-end mutual funds are also a kind of mutual fund (though different), and we'll look at them in a later chapter.

Open-ended mutual funds have no doubt been the most over-hyped form of investing in the past 40 years. They're the darlings of the mainstream financial media. Some successful managers (Fidelity's Peter Lynch) are celebrities.

The first recorded one was started on March 21, 1924 when three Boston businessmen pooled $50,000 to form the Massachusetts Investor's Trust, to invest in the stock market boom.

Open-Ended Mutual Funds are Enormously Popular

One source says that in 2006, 8606 mutual funds held $9 trillion.

Another source says that as of the beginning of 2007 about 13,000 mutual funds held $16 trillion.

Either way, there's a lot of funds holding a lot of money for a lot of Americans -- over 50 million.

My personal theory is that most average investors know that they should diversify, but don't trust their own judgment about which individual stocks to buy, so they're glad to hand the responsibility off to a mutual fund manager.

A famous mutual fund "family" (such as Fidelity, T. Rowe Price, and Putnam) starts up a fund for a specific purpose. It could be investing in corporate bonds or Canadian junior mining stocks or whatever.

Investors send in their money. The fund company creates shares in the fund as it receives the funds, and uses the money to buy the particular investment which is the purpose of the fund.

As more investors send in more money, the fund manager buys more investments. These may or may not fit the fund description in the prospectus. Some managers have a lot of leeway to buy securities they think are going to go up in value, whether they're in line with the stated purpose of the fund or not.

You'll never know when a fund deviates from its stated type of investments -- mutual funds don't keep you informed of every security they buy. They do report periodically, but those reports don't represent everything they've bought and sold, just what's left at the time of the quarterly report, which is designed to keep customers happy.

As money continues to be invested with the fund, the manager buys more investments.

By the way, they must pay commissions for everything they buy. They get lower commissions than you and I pay, but they can't buy and sell stocks for free.

When they feel it's necessary or when mutual fund shareholders redeem their shares, the fund manager sells investments. This costs more in commissions.

At the end of the day, the fund tallies up its total value, divides by the number of outstanding shares, and reports on the net asset value (NAV) of each share. If you're buying or redeeming shares, this is the price they give you.

(This point doesn't seem too critical -- but it was to many investors during market panics such as October 1987. On such days, mutual fund holders call the company and want out NOW, before the bleeding continues. They don't know that their shares will be redeemed using the end of trading day value, even if they called at 9:01 AM. If stocks drop 22% that day, their shares get redeemed at a value 22% less than the previous day's. Again -- even if the customer called at 9:01 in the morning.)

If a lot of shareholders redeem their shares, they can force a mutual fund manager to sell securities at a loss, just to raise the cash to meet the redemptions.

An open-ended mutual fund's "inventory" of securities goes up and down depending on how many people buy new shares and redeem shares.

If ordinary companies were run like this, Ford Motor Co could not buy a new forklift truck until someone wishing to buy shares of stock sent the company enough money. If more investors redeemed their shares, the company might have to sell off part of an assembly line to raise the cash.

Sounds silly, but that's how open-ended mutual funds are run.

Strengths:

1. Diversification.

Actively traded mutual funds are not as diverse as index funds, covered later, but they're more diverse than you buying a few individual securities.

2. Reinvestment.

They allow you to easily reinvest your money to buy more shares.

Weaknesses:

1. Expenses.

Here is where actively traded, open-ended mutual funds really stink.

According to the Greenwich Association, the average actively traded mutual fund spends $16 million per year on trading expenses.

Taxes Cost Mutual Fund Investors a Lot More Than They Realize

Robert Arnott and Jaffney reported in the June 1999 issue of TRUSTS AND ESTATES that according to their study, the typical mutual fund lost 3% per year to taxes.

Income Investing Secrets

According to Arthur Levitt, former chairman of the Securities and Exchange Commission, taxes can reduce mutual fund returns by 2.5% to 5.5%.

The SEC itself found that the average tax loss to mutual fund investors was 2.5%.

When the fund manager buys and sell securities at a loss or gain, they are incurring capital gains and losses. By law, these are passed on to mutual fund shareholders of record as of a particular date, usually in November or December.

When the fund incurs net capital gains from selling securities at a profit, it distributes the capital gains late in the year.

Shareholders of record as of that date receive capital gains distributions which represent capital gains for the fund for the entire year -- even if they did not invest in the fund until the day before the date of record.

Yet they must pay capital gains taxes on these distributions.

Many people don't realize that it's risky to open up a new mutual fund account late in the year.

(By the way, just because the fund incurred net capital gains from selling securities during the year, doesn't mean that you the shareholder are in profit. On December 31, due to a market downturn, your shares could be worth a lot less than they were on January 1 -- yet you still must pay taxes on the capital gains distributions for transactions made throughout the year!)

Many people don't realize that they can lose money in an open-ended mutual fund and still owe taxes on the capital gains distributions.

In fact, if the fund is losing so much money that a lot of investors redeem their shares prior to the record date, the capital gains are divided among a much smaller number of investors, increasing the taxes of those who did not redeem their shares.

Large capital gains distributions can make you lose money in many tax-related areas. They can affect your eligibility for tax exemptions, deductions (which are based on Adjusted Gross Income), and credits. They can make your Social Security benefits taxable -- the entire list is a long one.

Actively Traded Mutual Funds Costs You More Money Than You Realize

Various academics studies suggest that, on average, active management costs investors about 1% a year.

That's low, according to the results of a study by Mark M. Carhart, published in the March 1997 Journal of Finance. He analyzed the performance of 1892 equity mutual funds for the period 1962-1993. On a pretax basis, these funds underperformed the market on average by 1.8%.

And remember that this 1.8% is compounded over the years.

Mutual Funds Rack Up the Expenses

According to Morningstar, the average actively managed mutual fund has an expense ratio of 1.33%. That's average -- some (especially at Vanguard) are lower, but many are higher. According to the Investment Company Institute, from 1990 to 2002 the average mutual fund expense ratio went from 1.47% to 1.64%.

Plus, according to a study by Wake Forest University, the University of Florida and the Zero Alpha Group, 44% of mutual fund fees are NOT disclosed in the prospectus!

To find them, you must examine the fund's Statement of Additional Information -- which is even weightier and more sleep-inducing than a prospectus. Plus, the companies are not required to send it to you.

According to this study, these additional fees (which include the transaction costs of buying and selling securities) amount to an average of 1.25% per year.

That's a total of 2.58% average fund expenses

Add the 2.5% you lose to pay taxes on capital gains distributions.

Add the 1% you lose because the fund's manager underperforms the market.

The average actively managed mutual fund costs you 6.08% per year.

According to Charles Ellis in WINNING THE LOSER'S GAME, from 1984 to 1995, investors gained only 6% on average a year, half of what the funds actually earned, because they bought and sold too quickly.

According to the industry monitor Morningstar, over half of its 5 star - rated funds underperformed the market the year following their 5 star rating.

They must keep track of all accounts. This includes mailing out monthly statements, paying a staff of customer service representatives to answer questions, and so on.

Traditionally, open end mutual funds have charged a large commission to open an account for you. These are called "front loads" and have been as high as 8 percent, especially if you're foolish enough to buy mutual funds through a broker.

Many mutual funds have also charged people a fee to redeem their shares -- a back end load.

Plus, some funds charge a 12-b fee, which is you paying for their advertising costs.

One good thing the mainstream financial media has done is to publicize what a rip off load funds are.

If you're not already aware of this, you need to know it -- despite what your broker (who wants a commission) and the load mutual fund families tell you -- there's no evidence that expensive load mutual funds perform any better than no-load mutual funds.

Plus, you must pay their management expenses.

Plus, there's the costs of taxes and trading expenses.

BOTTOM LINE:

Actively traded, open end mutual funds are not the ideal investment they're hyped up to be. They do allow you to easily diversify (though not to an ideal extent), but do so by incurring a lot of expenses, including significant negative tax consequences.

Chapter Eighteen

Open-Ended Index Mutual Funds

"Most individual investors would be better off in an index mutual fund."

-- Peter Lynch, famous former manager of Fidelity's Magellan Fund

"Most of my investments are in equity index funds."

-- William F. Sharpe, Nobel Laureate in Economics 1990, creator of the Sharpe Index for measuring reward versus risk

Open-ended index mutual funds operate basically the same way as actively traded open end mutual funds, so I won't repeat all that.

The important difference is that index funds simply try to replicate a particular index. The fund manager doesn't have much to do except buy and sell securities if and when the index changes, which should be infrequently.

The first and still the most famous is Vanguard's S&P 500 Index fund, which simply holds all the stocks in the S&P 500 in their correct proportion.

This saves on expenses, since the manager is not buying and selling new securities.

This saves on capital gains distributions, because these are not realized unless a change in the index forces it.

This also saves us from suffering from the mistakes of active management.

This makes the process more open. You know what you own, because the makeup of indexes is public information.

Strengths:

1. Diversification.

You get the benefit of owning piece of a broad market, so one company's stock failing does not hurt you much.

2. Low expenses.

Index funds still have to service customers, but they avoid the loads, the commissions, the market underperformance and capital gains distributions of actively traded mutual funds.

3. Reinvestment.

They also allow you to easily use any earnings to buy new fund shares.

Weaknesses:

The normal broad market indexes include many stocks that don't pay dividends.

BOTTOM LINE:

Open-ended index mutual funds are an inexpensive, attractive -- though not ideal -- way to partner up with a market and profit from its economic activity.

However, they pay only as much income as the broad index does, which these days is very small. You're buying a lot of stocks that don't pay dividends.

If you insist on investing for capital gains, buy index funds is the way to go. It's how to optimize your dysfunctional goal.

Next: Closed-end mutual funds -- the kind of mutual fund the mainstream financial press doesn't want to tell you about.

Chapter Nineteen

Closed-End Mutual Funds

Closed end mutual funds are formed by a company that issues a number of shares -- say 100 million -- as an Initial Public Offering or IPO. They use the money they raised to buy up a large amount of stocks or bonds or other securities, depending on the type of fund they're creating.

So each share of a closed-end mutual fund represents an ownership interest in the basket of securities that the closed-end fund bought with the IPO money.

The shares of the closed-end fund are then bought and sold on the secondary market, by brokers, just like shares of Microsoft or Ford. That is, investors buy and sell these shares from and to each other, not from and to the closed-end mutual fund company. You need to use a broker and pay commissions just as when you buy stocks.

The closed-end fund does NOT issue any more shares. It will always have 100 million shares outstanding.

If you want to own some of those shares, you must buy them from somebody who wants to sell them.

The Closed-End Fund Company Doesn't Have as Many Expenses as Open-Ended Mutual Funds

The mutual fund company simply manages the fund, buying and selling securities as the fund manager sees fit. Since the mutual fund company does not have the expenses of dealing with customers, tracking accounts, sending out account statements, selling securities when customers demand refunds, buying more securities when deposits come in -- as open-ended mutual funds do -- their management fees are a lot less than those charged by open-ended mutual funds.

The actual value of the shares themselves, based on the market value of the securities held by the mutual fund company, is called the fund's net asset value, or NAV.

Remember -- the NAV is calculated using the current market value of the basket of securities owned by the mutual fund. Naturally, this goes up and down on a day to day basis as the securities themselves go up and down in market price.

The shares of the closed-end mutual fund are trading on a stock exchange just like other securities. And just like other securities, the closed-end mutual fund's market share price fluctuates from day to day based on the ups and down of market demand for that fund's shares.

Therefore, it's entirely possible -- indeed, common -- for a fund's NAV and its share price to be different.

Most Closed-End Funds Sell for Less Than Their NAV -- Some for More

Sometimes popular funds trade at a premium to their NAV. That means you'd have to pay more for the fund shares than justified by their underlying asset values. I recommend you never buy a closed-end fund at a premium.

In many cases, however, the fund's shares are trading for a price lower than the fund's NAV, sometimes by as much as a 30% discount. When the fund is introduced, participating brokerages push it to keep the price up. But after a few months they've unloaded their inventory, and demand sinks down, and the share price with it.

Many closed end funds issued by the same mutual fund company are virtually identical. That's because they make more profit the more money they have under management, and it's easy to write up a new prospectus, get approved by the SEC and issue shares of a new fund . . . which for all practical purposes is identical to an earlier fund.

This helps you find bargains, though. It could be one reason many closed-end mutual funds trade at discounts -- it's difficult for investors to get excited about one more cloned fund.

Buying $1.50 in NAV for $1 Sounds Good, But You May Never Get That Extra 50 Cents

However, you should keep in mind that while the discount the fund trades to its NAV will fluctuate randomly over time, very often it will NEVER trade at full NAV. Which means that although it's good to buy a basket of securities at less than their full market value, you can't count on selling them later for full market value. If you sell, you may lose money by selling at an even greater discount to NAV.

Also, when you own shares in a closed-end mutual, since the manager of the closed-end mutual fund is always buying and selling securities, you don't know from day to day exactly what you own.

And since the securities within the closed-end fund are being actively managed, over the long term its NAV will suffer from the same underperformance against the market that all actively managed funds do.

Weaknesses:

1. Diversification.

This can vary a lot with the fund, but many contain only one or two types of securities. Therefore, they're riskier than broader index investments.

2. Reinvestment.

You cannot easily reinvest in closed-end mutual funds.

Strengths:

1. Income.

Many closed-end mutual funds invest in securities that pay an income. If you buy them for below Net Asset Value, you're getting a higher yield than if you bought those individual securities yourself.

For example:

You buy shares in a closed-end bond mutual fund for a 10% discount to the fund's NAV. The securities held by the bonds owned by the closed fund pay an average of 5% interest. Therefore, your net effective yield is 5.55%.

2. Expenses.

Closed-end mutual funds have many fewer expenses than open-end mutual funds.

However, they are actively traded so you do lose money on management underperformance and on buying and selling transaction fees.

BOTTOM LINE:

Closed end mutual funds can be an effective way to buy certain types of income-paying assets, and possibly get a higher yield because the fund is trading at a discount to its NAV. The key is to select the funds holding the types income investments you want to own.

Chapter Twenty

Exchange Traded Funds

Exchange traded funds are a form of closed-end mutual fund, but with several important differences that make them more attractive.

Just as with all closed-end mutual funds, a company starts an exchange traded fund (or ETF) by raising money through an Initial Public Offering (IPO) and then using the funds to buy various securities, in line with its purpose.

After the IPO's over, the company doesn't sell any shares of the ETF. They are traded on exchanges just like ordinary shares of stock. If you want to buy one, you put the order in to your broker, and they buy it just like any stock, charging the same commission.

One share of an ETF is an ownership interest in the basket of securities the ETF owns, just as one share of General Motors common stock is an ownership interest in the business of General Motors.

But as mentioned, ETFs are different in two ways from ordinary closed-end mutual funds.

1. They replicate an index.

For instance, the very first ETF holds shares of stocks in the S&P 500 index, and replicates that index closely. (The ticker symbol for this ETF is SPDR, and it's nicknamed "Spiders." Spiders are one of the most actively traded securities in the world.)

Thus, the company that owns the SPDR ETF does not buy and sell any stock, unless and until Standard & Poor's decides to remove and add companies to its index.

Because the composition of indexes are public information, with an ETF you always know what you own.

Because you are in effect buying an index, you do not suffer from a fund manager's mistake when buying and selling. This also saves you the expense of paying their commissions and capital gains taxes.

2. Certain individuals, called authorized participants, can create or cash in shares of the ETF, usually in 50,000 lots.

What this does is allow these authorized participants (who are obviously already wealthy, savvy and well-connected), to seek opportunities to arbitrage the ETF if the market price gets out of line with its Net Asset Value (NAV).

If the NAV of an ETF is only $40.00 but the market price is $40.01, these authorized individuals can buy up the underlying index (which cost $40), then give them to the ETF company, which creates 50,000 new shares of the ETF. Then they sell these 50,000 new shares of the ETF on the open market for $40.01, for the $500 profit.

The increased supply of shares of the ETF then helps to drive the market price back to $40, in line with its NAV.

It's not important to understand all the mechanics of this (not being one of those authorized participants, I sure don't). But the upshot is, ETFs always trade for very close to their NAVs.

This is unlike closed-end mutual funds, which may trade at a discount or premium to their NAVs.

Weighting of Indexes

When somebody puts together a list of securities, a big issue is how to "weight" them. That is, how to decide which companies make up what percentage of the index value.

The Dow Jones Industrial Average is price-weighted, which means that the relative share of each of the 30 stocks is determined each day simply by the market price of their stock.

But almost all other indexes are cap weighted. That is, their percentage of the

97

index is determined by the capitalization of their stock. That is, by the market value of their stock TIMES the number of shares outstanding.

Think that each company in the S&P 500 makes up 1/500th of the S&P 500 index? Nowhere close. Each company comprises a percentage of the index based on its market capitalization. Most of the value of the S&P 500 index is made up of the ten largest stocks in it.

If the market price of the smallest S&P 500 company stock dropped to zero one day, the index would hardly budge.

Dr. Jeremy Siegel, a financial writer and researcher mentioned often in these pages, studied this issue and decided that it'd be better to weight indexes based on some fundamental criteria -- for this book, we prefer dividends.

He helped found a company called Wisdom Tree which has come up with some fundamentally-weighted dividend indexes and corresponding exchange traded funds. They are the first family of funds to focus on dividend-weighted indexes.

Only time will tell whether cap weighting or fundamental weighting will make a great difference in your returns. I suspect that for most investors, just investing for income and compounding their returns over the long run will be the most important thing.

Weaknesses:

1. Reinvestment.

You can of course always use your investment income to buy new shares of any ETF, but it's not as super-convenient as with DRIPs and open-ended mutual funds.

Strengths:

1. Diversification.

You are buying a broad market index of some kind.

Also, there are many kinds of ETFs, allowing you to focus on those that pay our dividends or income.

2. Few expenses.

It's much cheaper to run an ETF than an actively traded open-end mutual fund or even an index fund. You're also not penalized for the active management mistakes. The fund manager is simply someone whose job it is to handle the basic arrangements. Their expense ratios are much lower than mutual funds.

There are no capital gains distributions unless the index behind the ETF changes composition. And then, unlike with mutual funds, the capital gains distribution is likely to be long term, saving you on taxes.

You just pay your discount broker a commission for buying the shares.

BOTTOM LINE:

Exchange traded funds offer the safety of diversification and the low cost of investing in an index.

They are not perfect, but they're as close to it as you can find in real life.

Next: the least well-known form of mutual fund. Or: why your broker may want to sell you a package of securities and why you probably don't want to buy it.

Chapter Twenty-One

Unit Investment Trusts

Another variation of a "mutual fund" -- that is, where money from investors is pooled together to buy a number of securities -- is the unit investment trust.

These are much like closed-end funds. However, their portfolio of securities is fixed. Plus, they have a definite life, such as 20 or 50 years. After its term is over, the remaining money is paid out to the trust's unit holders

Plus, the securities inside of the UIT are not actively traded. The only changes made are forced by some uncontrollable event such as a company takeover or bankruptcy.

However, unlike exchange traded funds, the securities in a UIT can be anything fitting the prospectus description. They don't track any kind of public index.

The Worst Time to Buy an UIT is When Your Broker is Pushing It

If you buy into a UIT during its initial public offering, you have no way of knowing what securities it will eventually hold, because they haven't been bought yet. They won't be bought and placed into the trust until the IPO has raised the cash necessary to buy them with.

Most large brokerages sell unit investment trusts. Most units have a $1000 face value ($500 for IRA accounts).

The sponsor of the fund writes up a document called the Trust Indenture, and names the trustee and the evaluator. The sponsor selects and assembles the securities included in the fund. The trustee holds the securities in trust for the owners, who are the unit holders.

A UIT can contain equities or fixed income assets. They can be designed to accommodate almost any investment goal -- capital gains, interest or dividend income, and so on.

You Can Receive a Return of Principal at Any Time

If an UIT contains bonds, then over time these bonds can be called by their issuers, or they could simply mature before the UIT is terminated. In that case, the principal is paid back proportionately to UIT unit holders.

And of course, bonds that are no longer in the UIT no longer pay any interest.

Therefore, UIT interest income is not as fixed as investors may be led to believe when they're quoted an "estimated current return" figure. Plus, they may get an unusually high amount in a particular month and not realize that the extra money is a return of their principal which they should reinvest, not spend.

This is dangerous for those of us who want to preserve our capital, to keep it generating income. Getting it in small pieces spread over years makes it hard to reinvest, and no doubt fools many people into spending it.

Therefore, when the UIT's termination dates comes, there may be few assets left to distribute to the unit holders.

Unit investment trusts are created to have a fixed number of units, like closed-end funds. They're pushed by issuing brokers after they're first created, during the initial public offering, then pretty much ignored. However, brokerages are required by law to redeem trust units for their Net Asset Value (NAV) -- which could be less or more than you paid for the UIT. Then they'll sell them to other customers.

You Pay a Lot of Money Upfront

Most UITs do charge an upfront load and deferred sales charges.

There is a secondary market for UITs, so if you're determined to own some, you can buy them when you can know and evaluate the securities inside them, plus pay only a commission to deep discount broker instead of the full load and sales charges.

Many UITs employ leverage to boost returns. This can work, but can also backfire.

There is one advantage of UITs -- unrealized capital gains are sheltered within the trust. You don't have to pay taxes on them until you actually receive the capital gains. Your tax basis is the net amount you paid for your shares. You must, of course, pay taxes on the interest and/or dividends you receive in income from the fund.

Weaknesses:

1. Diversification.

UITs are comprised of a "basket" of stocks or bonds, so there is some diversification. But they don't match any publicly available index. They are put together by the sponsor. They could simply consist of the brokerage's inventory of bonds that it couldn't sell to institutions.

2. Underperformance expense.

Their management expenses are less than mutual funds, but they can sock it to you with their upfront loads and deferred sales charges.

Although their securities are not actively traded, they also don't replicate an index. This means that the asset allocation will be less than optimal.

Strengths:

1. Income.

Most UITs consist of high-yield investments.

2. Reinvestment.

Fixed-income UITs normally allow unit holders to automatically reinvest distributions of interest and principal, although it's usually into a separate mutual fund that holds similar securities. In some cases, the UIT may allow you to reinvest into another series of the UIT. Equity UITs usually allow reinvestment into additional units of the same trust.

However, UITs have a fixed term of life.

Plus, if you're living on the income, you must make sure that you do reinvest the returns of your principal. These can be erratic, as this bond is called and then that bond is called.

Therefore, much of your principal is returned to you over the life of the UIT, in relatively small amounts. If you spend it, you've lost that income-generating power.

BOTTOM LINE:

I'm including Unit Investment Trusts to make this book as complete and helpful as possible. I can't recommend them in general, though possibly you may find some that are worth the money.

Still, I don't see that UITs offer any advantage over exchange traded funds.

Next: The most "romantic" form of investment: hedge funds.

Chapter Twenty-Two

Hedge Funds

Hedge funds have a huge romantic mystique associated with them. Because of their inaccessibility to most investors, plus stories about the multi-gazillion dollar trades done by hedge fund managers such as George Soros, many investors think that if only they could afford to let a hedge fund manage their money, they'd be rich.

You have to be rich before you can invest in a hedge fund. In the U.S., only accredited investors are allowed to send their money to them. "Accredited" means that you've made at least $200,000 a year for the last 2 years -- and will again this year -- or your net worth is at least $1 million. If you meet these requirements, the government will allow you to reduce your net worth by sending your money to a hedge fund.

You Pays Your Money and You Takes Your Chances

Hedge funds are private investment firms exempt from regulation by the SEC and NASD. They are often domiciled in an offshore country. Thus, although the manager and the fund offices may be in the United States, the company may officially be based in another country, such as the Cayman Islands, British Virgin Islands or Bermuda.

In other words -- let the investor beware.

Since they are private and not regulated, their true performance is often secret. Many do have their performances audited, but not all.

This tendency to remain in the background also results from the U.S. law that prohibits hedge funds from advertising and marketing themselves.

The first hedge fund was started in 1949 by Alfred W Jones -- A.W. Jones & Co., and lasted until the early 1970s. Before starting the fund, Jones published his idea for it in an article in FORTUNE.

Jones wrote that it should be possible for fund managers to achieve superior returns by hedging their positions. That is, to take both long and short positions. Ordinary mutual funds are only allowed to "go long." That is, they buy stocks or bonds or whatever, and hope the price goes up. If a bear market strikes their specialty, all they can do is hang on and hope it goes away soon -- and that they're losing even less than their competitors.

Jones said -- buy and sell, and make money on the difference. This in theory gives the fund manager the ability to make money in both up and down markets, or at least to hedge losses, which is why hedge funds are called hedge funds, though many don't hedge their positions.

Plus, he also used a lot of leverage, which is using borrowed money to multiply the return on investment.

(A good example of leverage is the mortgage on your house. You put down a 10% downpayment, yet the bank allows you to live in 100% of the house. But it cuts both ways. If property values in your neighborhood go down by 10%, you lose 100% of your equity.)

You're a Limited Partner in a Partnership, and the General Partnership is Officially a Corporation, Which Means the Fund's Manager is Limiting Their Personal Liability

Hedge funds for U.S. investors are often structured as a limited partnership. Investors are considered limited partners. The manager (often organized as a corporation) is the general partner of the partnership.

They require minimum investments ranging from $50,000 to $100 million dollars. Plus, many have a lockup provision, where you must agree not to withdraw any of your funds for at least 1-3 years.

Then you pay the hedge fund 1.5-5% percent of your account as a management fee, plus from 20-50% percent of the fund's profits as a performance fee.

(Jones did not believe in charging management fees. He felt that a hedge fund manager should make money if and only if the clients made money. He did set his performance fees at 20%.)

The theory is, the hedge fund manager is such a great trader, as long as they're well-motivated by the millions of dollars they'll make off you and other account holders, they'll find a way to make you even wealthier -- even after you pay their high fees.

Personally, I think people who believe hedge funds can accomplish this in the long run also stay up late on Christmas Eve waiting for Santa Claus to come down the chimney.

Mutual Fund Managers, Brokers and Pension Fund Managers Can't Beat the Market - But Somehow Hedge Fund Managers Can?

However, many people fall into this category, even institutions which use the ability of hedge funds to go both long and short to reduce risk through diversification. (Institutions such as pension funds putting money into hedge funds is scary -- aren't pensions endangered enough as it is? But it's good in some ways, because institutions demand more transparency and accountability from the hedge funds.)

Hedge funds are attracting a lot of top talent on Wall Street, because they can make more money that way. Allegedly, the best fund managers want to work for hedge funds, not mutual funds.

There're probably over 8000 hedge funds holding at least $850 billion in assets. The largest is worth about $20 billion. Many of them do have staffs and offices -- some large -- but others are operated out of the manager's apartment.

However, many of them are short-lived. Many are successful at first, but eventually meet a market they can't beat, lose a lot of money and go out of business.

Many hedge fund companies start a number of funds using different approaches. Some succeed, others fail. The company promotes the records of the successes but quietly closes up the failures.

Gamblers Sometimes Win, but They're Still Gambling

These facts support the idea that hedge funds can have success for a time, just as casino gamblers can win for a time, but that they can't beat the markets in the long run.

The ability to go short as well as long seems like it would alleviate risk -- but going short successfully in the long term still requires that a manager have some degree of ability to predict market direction.

If you find a hedge fund manager with proven psychic abilities, by all means hand over all the money you can to their care.

Although hedge funds allegedly can make a lot of money in volatile markets, they lost huge amounts of money during the 2008 financial crisis.

I have read that, despite their image at "gunslingers," most hedge fund managers are honest and do their best to preserve and increase the wealth of their clients.

Not all hedge fund managers are honest, even before Bernie Madoff. There are known cases where they've lied to their clients. It's true that every profession has its bad apples. Yet it's also true that a profession such as hedge fund manager, where wealthy people and institutions hand their money over to you to do whatever you please with it, with limited disclosure, with no oversight by government regulation, with 1-3 year lock up provisions, is bound to attract the smartest and slickest con artists in the world.

And Bernie Madoff is a great example of why you should beware of people who promise you they can beat the market.

Personally, I believe he was -- in a perverse way -- more honest than most fund managers, at least to himself.

He made promises he couldn't keep, but at least he didn't try. Other managers of funds (hedge funds, mutual funds, pension funds, and others) seem to believe they can beat the market even though they can't. They don't steal the money under their control, they throw it away.

Hedge Fund Managers Have Threatened the World's Financial Systems

The most famous example of a hedge fund trading success is probably George Soros (as manager of the Quantum Fund) going short the British pound in 1992. Although actively fought by the Bank of England, he had enough cash in his fund to force England to devalue the pound sterling.

He netted $985 million on that trade alone. However, he had $10 billion at risk. If the Bank of England had refused to blink, he'd have been out of business and his investors out of luck -- and money.

Sound investing is generally defined as getting the most return possible considering the risk you take. Is risking $10 billion for less than $1 billion sound? Especially in a situation where you don't really know the statistical odds, because you're not playing inside the market -- your trade is so big that you're making or breaking the market?

In the summer of 1998, the most high-powered hedge fund was Long-Term Capital Management LLC. Started by long time Salomon Brothers trader John Meriwether (he's written about extensively in the book LIAR'S POKER by Michael Lewis), plus Robert Merton and Myron Scholes, both famous for winning the Nobel prize in Economics for helping to formulate the standard valuation model for options.

Plus, they had a staff of "quants" with more PhDs than you could shake a stick at.

These financial wizards didn't try to "face down" one of the world's largest banks. They were much smarter than that. They weren't gunslingers. They analyzed the historical valuation of the U.S. Treasury bond index, and placed trades based on this.

All backed by solid math and historical relationships.

Rather than "hedging" this trade (as you'd expect a "hedge" fund to do), they leveraged it. By 100 to 1.

They not only used all the available funds from their investors, they found a number of banks willing to front them even more money.

For every dollar they could put up from their investors, they borrowed about $100, based on accounts I read.

(Don't try this with your home mortgage. You or I would be thrown in jail. Only Nobel prize winners are allowed to get away with this.)

In the summer of 1998, something interesting happened in Russia.

Their stock market melted down, losing 90% of its value. This, happening so soon after the Asian currency crisis in the fall of 1997, shook up investors around the world, especially the wealthy in developing countries.

Just about everybody who's wealthy in the developing world hocked the family jewels. They took all their spare cash out of their native currency and sent everything they could to a country with a secure financial and political system -- and a secure currency. It was a massive "flight to quality."

They sent money to Europe, no doubt -- but much of it went to the United States, and bought U.S. government bonds.

The Treasury bond index therefore spiked up.

Demolishing the old historical relationships of this index to the market.

Which made Long Term Capital Asset's derivative trades losers.

Multiplied by 100.

They had so much money involved, that when their trades went sour, the New York Federal Reserve Bank had to call an unprecedented meeting of large investment banks, trading houses and brokerages. All of whom are basically competitors to Long Term Capital Asset, and who would have liked to put the hedge fund out of business because it took investment money out from under THEIR management.

The New York Federal Reserve Bank told this group of high-powered traders, "You WILL kick in X millions of dollars to get Long-Term Capital Management through this crisis."

And they did. What was their alternative? Let major world banks go bankrupt? Let the U.S. and European financial markets meltdown along with Russia's?

In 1998 we came close to a financial catastrophe, yet most people have no idea this happened.

Prior to this problem caused by Long-Term Capital Management LLC, many other hedge funds had announced losing lots of money through direct investment in Russia. This included George Soros and Stanley Druckenmiller's Quantum Fund.

Weaknesses:

1. Expenses.

1.5-5% percent annual management fees, plus from 20-50% percent performance fees.

Ouch. Hedge funds make mutual funds look like a financial Wal-Mart.

In case you needed more evidence (after Bernie Madoff) that many wealthy people know how to make money in their businesses but are ignorant of investing principles.

2. Diversification.

You are subject to the fund manager's trading style. You're shooting for big time winners, not to equal broad market indexes. Therefore, your hedge fund balance will tend to resemble Babe Ruth's batting record -- lots of home runs AND lots of strikeouts.

2. Income.

Hedge funds promise to grow your portfolio, not generate income from it. They know you don't need them to do that. And if any of their investments do generate income, it's locked up for three to five years.

Strengths:

1. Reinvestment.

Because your money is locked up for a set period, the hedge fund manager automatically keeps using your gains to make additional trades -- which may or may not be winners. But they are trying to compound your returns.

BOTTOM LINE:

Hedge funds should only be invested in by people who can afford to lose a lot of money.

Personally, if I were super-rich I'm sure I could find lots of ways to lose my money that are more fun than writing a 7 figure check to a super-salesperson masquerading as a super-trader.

That finishes the formats of investments -- now I'll look at particular kinds of investments of interest to income investors, and evaluate them against the 7 Principles.

Chapter Twenty-Three

Types of Securities

The following chapters evaluate the possible types of investments.

We'll cover:

1. Equities

2. Utility stocks

3. Real Estate Investment Trusts -- REITs

4. Canadian income trusts

5. Master Limited Partnerships

6. Business Development Trusts -- BDCs

7. Income Deposit Securities -- IDSes

8. Guaranteed Investment Contracts -- GICs

9. Bonds

10. Treasury bonds

11.Corporate bonds

12. Direct Access Notes (DANs) or InterNotes or CoreNotes

13. Municipal bonds

14. Mortgage-Backed Securities

15. Short-term, Intermediate-term and Long-term bonds

16. TIPS and I Bonds

17 Preferred stocks

18. Fixed and variable annuities

19. Swiss annuities

Chapter Twenty-Four

Equities

Here I'm referring to common stock, although preferred stock shares are technically "equity" in a company also.

Legally, every share of common stock in a company represents an ownership interest in the company. The more shares you own, the more of the company you own.

Owning stock in a company gives you the right to attend its annual meetings and to vote on certain issues. Of course, for most of us this is not of practical concern. There's no way we can own enough shares in a public company to have any influence on how it's run.

As owners, we also have the right to share in the growth of the company. This includes of course seeing the market value of the shares of stock we own rise in price.

Most importantly for us income investors, it also includes the right to share equally in the profits of the company, when the Board of Directors votes to share them with stockholders.

That is, common stock owners have the right to receive dividends.

Don't Invest With the Worst-Case Scenario in Mind

Technically, owning common stock has a disadvantage if the company goes out of business. As owners of the business, stockholders are last in line for any leftover assets.

First in line are the lawyers. Next are the people the company owes money to: major banks, parts suppliers and service providers, and then ordinary bond owners.

(If the government bails out a company, as it proved with General Motors, all legalities go out the window. GM bond owners got thrown under the wheels.)

So if you own stock in a company that goes out of business, don't hold your breath waiting for a check in the mail.

To me, however, it makes no sense to invest on the basis of what happens in the worst case. If you have any reason to believe a company could go out of business, don't buy its stock.

Of course, it's true that we don't know the future. Your best defense against a stock you own going belly-up is diversification.

The best dividend paying stocks tend to group themselves into several major areas. One of these is basic consumer goods.

The Best Dividend-Paying Companies Meet Basic Human Needs

What do people need? They need food. They may not need Coca-Cola and McDonalds, but they eat them in good times and bad. In bad times they'll cut out expensive dine-in restaurants, but not McDonalds. If they're smokers, they buy cigarettes.

Some younger people in the U.S. are buying more energy drinks and tea . . . but much of the rest of the world is just discovering the refreshing taste of Coca-Cola on a hot day.

Also, if people are sick, they need drugs.

Also, people always need money.

Also, people needs lights, heat in the winter and water to drink.

Therefore, basic consumer goods, financial institutions, utilities and pharmaceutical companies often have lots of cash money to pay out to their investors.

Weaknesses:

1. Income.

I hate to write this, but it's undeniable that dividend-paying stocks have been going down in yield for at least 50 years. The good news is, they pay a lot more than stocks that don't pay anything.

Strengths:

1. Beating inflation.

Some companies have a history of raising their dividends at the rate of up to 14%. Some companies have raised their dividends every year for over 100 years.

Although dividend yields are low when you first buy the stock (at current market prices), if you hang on to it, the stock will eventually pay you very high dividends.

This is the best way for income investors to more than keep up with inflation.

2. Low expenses.

Stocks trade on many public exchanges. Stock prices are easy to find from newspapers, TV, and the Internet. Bid/Ask spreads are small. You can use a deep discount brokerage to buy stocks for a minimal commission. There are no additional costs except taxes on your dividends.

3. Meeting basic human needs.

Of course this does depend on which companies you buy, but many are available in industries that can go down but never out.

BOTTOM LINE:

Equities fall short in producing immediate income, but in the long run they have the power to make you wildly rich. You must buy and hold them for years.

Unless you're reading this on printed paper by candlelight, you're using the product of the first group of income equities.

Chapter Twenty-Five

Stocks of Utility Companies

Utilities are 4% of the total stock market, but are the traditional "safe haven."

Utility companies supply basic needs to household and businesses -- water, electricity, communications and natural gas.

Those of us who live in developed countries tend to take for granted getting light just from flipping a switch and water just from turning a faucet.

We should appreciate these luxuries more than we do.

In the past few years, my local electric company has had great trouble maintaining power during summer electric storms and winter ice storms. So I've experienced first hand what it is to swelter without air conditioning during the heat of the night and to shiver in my sweat suit during the cold of the night.

And I've seen many other people, including myself and members of my family, going without heat and lights.

Electricity Should Be Appreciated

It's as eerie experience to drive down a familiar major street late at night and not see any lights in front, behind or to either side of you, because all the street lights and business lights that you normally don't pay any attention to -- aren't there.

Plus, I've been in foreign countries during times they could not supply electricity on a 24 hour basis. It's no fun to be in a tropical hotel room at night and suddenly have the lights -- and air conditioning -- go out.

It's estimated that in the future electricity will be a scarcer resource than oil. Building electric power plants of all types is a major priority for China.

Similarly, water companies supply a basic need that we in developed countries take for granted. Many people around the world still use wells or the nearest creek or river. If water is not properly treated, it can spread cholera.

Many political analysts believe that in the near future more wars are going to be fought over fresh water than over oil.

Which liquid is more important? The human race lived hundreds of thousands of years without oil. We can't survive more than a few days without water.

Still Good for Widows and Orphans -- and the Rest of Us Too

So my conclusion is -- utility companies are businesses that are not going away, because they supply basic human needs.

Utility companies have traditionally paid good dividends -- they're the archetypal "widows and orphans" stock because they're considered so safe.

This would not be possible if utility companies had to compete as most other companies do. Because they are dependent on spending large amount of money for power plants, wiring and so on, most of their earnings would normally be reinvested in maintaining and expanding their capital equipment.

However, utility companies are regulated monopolies. This means that they are assured of a customer base, which must buy from them. The government agencies that regulate them are supposed to allow them to charge those customers for all their legitimate expenses, plus make a reasonable profit.

Therefore, well-run and well-regulated utilities make enough money to finance their ongoing need for capital to build new power plants and whatever else they need, and in addition pay a generous dividend to their shareholders.

Utility Companies Do Face Challenges

That's not to say that all utilities are well-run. Nor that all utility regulators do a good job. And utility companies face significant challenges in the years ahead:

1. Blackouts in recent years show that the grids of the U.S. and probably the rest of the world need updating.

2. Climate change activists are pushing for reduced carbon emissions. This may be enforced by a "cap and tax" law that will greatly increase the cost of energy.

3. Other countries in the world are pushing nuclear power, and some new nukes may be built in the U.S. despite opposition. Fortunately, new technologies mean that a fabled "China Syndrome" meltdown is impossible.

4. As consumers are squeezed on all sides by energy price increases, there'll be political opposition to electricity and natural gas rate hikes.

5. The water industry must upgrade to control pollutants and disease.

6. The deregulation trend could continue, but politicians must make sure all residents have access to basic services.

However, despite all obstacles, demand for electricity and natural gas will continue to increase. People will continue to pay their utility bills. And so utilities will continue to reward investors with ongoing income.

Weaknesses:

1. Expenses.

Utility companies tend to have high capital expenditures. It's not cheap to build a power plant. Of course, that's why they are regulated. In theory, local governments guarantees that local utility companies have the funds they need to meet the demand for their product.

However, utility regulatory agencies are political, and so subject to demands to lower utility rates.

2. Diversification.

Although local conditions can and do differ, owning one electric company carries much the same risk as owning every other electric company.

Strengths:

1. Income.

Utilities almost always pay dividends, though immediate yields are usually not as high as bonds.

2. Meeting human needs.

We need clean water, electricity with which to power our computers and desk lamps, and telephones to talk on. Many of us need natural gas to cook with it. In northern regions, we need it or heating oil to keep us warm through the winter.

Barring the discovery of revolutionary, science fiction-like technologies that give us convenient energy on demand, we will continue to need utility companies for the foreseeable future.

3. Inflation protection.

Utilities are highly regulated by state agencies. Although there're always disputes about how much their profits should be, they are allowed to make a profit -- and expected to share it with stockholders.

When their costs go up, so do consumer rates for electricity, natural gas and water.

BOTTOM LINE:

Owning stock in a diversified portfolio of utility companies is now (as it has always been) a good investment for income.

Unless you're now flying in an airplane or sitting in a cruise ship, you're using the product of the next group of income equities.

Chapter Twenty-Six

Real Estate Investment Trusts

Real Estate Investment Trusts (REITs for short) are large real estate companies with stock that sells on a stock exchange like any other company's stock. However, special laws apply to them that help make them particularly attractive to income investors.

First of all, I need to point out that real estate itself is one of the best investments you can make. Many wealthy people have become rich simply through real estate. Many get-rich quick real estate gurus advise you to stay away from stocks and other "regular" types of investments, because real estate is the best way to get rich quick.

This book is not about "investing" in real estate as a landlord or by buying and re-selling property for a profit. That's because:

1. There're plenty of such books, seminars and courses on the markct, by people who know a lot more about it than I do.

2. To me (and I realize I'm contradicting IRS rules here), when you go out looking for properties to buy, put in bids to buy those properties, look for financing to buy properties, paint the walls, advertise for tenants, fix leaky toilets at two in the morning . . . and so on -- that's operating a business, not "investing.")

I want "investments" that are pieces of paper I can buy and collect money from without ongoing effort.

If you want to make extra money and eventually get rich by buying properties and either renting them out or re-selling ("flipping") them, bless you and good luck. Buy one of the many books or courses that teach you how to do that.

This book is about how you can invest your profits so that you can set up additional streams of income that pay you without the effort of landlording (or any other home business you may want to start).

REITs Are a Terrific Way to Profit From Real Estate Without Fixing Toilets

Unless you're reading this on an airplane in flight or on a cruise ship at sea, you're now occupying some real estate.

It may be your house, your office or factory (on break, I trust), a public library, in a mountain cabin or at the beach (yeah!).

But everybody except those in the air and on water, are occupying real estate. Sooner or later, even the space station astronauts will come back down to real estate.

REITs cover a wide span of real estate types: apartment buildings, houses, golf courses, nursing homes, storage facilities, factories, hotels, condominiums, shopping centers, and undeveloped land.

They tend to be concentrated by geography and type of properties, so management is familiar with local conditions, businesses, rates and prices.

Traditionally, real estate has been owned by individuals or small companies. In immigrant cities such as St Louis, families would buy a 2-family (called "railroad" in other areas) flat, live in one floor and rent the other one out. Many people own from 1-10 different rental properties. However, as noted above, that is basically operating a business, since it involves a great deal of time and effort.

Over time, successful real estate landlords and developers have expanded their businesses. Most of these are still privately owned, but some are taking advantage of special tax rules to organize themselves as Real Estate Investment Trusts. This allows them to sell shares of common stock on securities exchanges such as the New York Stock Exchange.

REITs Have a Huge Tax Advantage

Better yet, REITs don't have to pay any taxes as long as they distribute at least 90% of their annual net profits to their investors. Thus, they avoid the dreaded double taxation of dividends.

No company-level taxes and a 90% payout = a big income yield for us.

For as little as $100 or so, you can own both residential and commercial real estate, earning a net profit that's comparable or better to what many landlords make.

Without fixing toilets at two in the morning.

Or buying a $300 real estate course from a late night cable TV infomercial "no money down" guru.

(To be fair, I once talked to a man who told me that he bought several of those courses when he got out of the Navy in the early 1980s. His friends laughed at him for wasting his money, but 10 years later he claimed to be worth several million dollars.)

By law, real estate depreciates. That is, its value is assumed to go down over time, whether it actually does so or not. (But it is true that nothing lasts forever.)

Tax Benefits of Depreciation Are Passed On to You

Real estate owners are allowed by the IRS to write off part of the cost of the property on their taxes as depreciation. This is an expense of owning property because -- remember -- nothing lasts forever. But it doesn't require any actual cash flow. Unlike fixing a broken window, which requires paying for the new glass and the labor of installing it.

Since REITs don't pay taxes, the depreciation on the property they own is passed through to us, the shareholders.

This means that when we do our taxes, about 25-30% of the dividends we're paid by REITS are considered by the IRS to be a "return of capital" and are taxed at the rate for long term capital gains. That's good, because the long term capital gains tax rate is lower than the tax rate for ordinary income.

123

The remaining 65-70% of the dividends you receive from REITs are taxed as ordinary income.

By the way, don't confuse REITs with the real estate master partnerships sold in the 1980s as tax avoidance schemes. These were scams that are now shut down.

REITs Have a Longer History Than Most People Know Of

The Real Estate Investment Trust Act was passed in 1960, and the first REIT formed in 1963, but they didn't become well-known until the early 1990s.

With 11 REITs now in the S&P 500, and a hundred more for sale on public stock exchanges, REITs are legitimate investments, and a necessary part of any well-rounded income investor's portfolio.

REITs can develop, acquire, renovate, lease, manage, tear down, rebuild and sell off properties based on their judgment and experience and market conditions. Of course, REITs are subject to all the risks of real estate -- tenant problems, high vacancy rates, overbuilding, rising costs, poor local economic conditions, higher interest rates, and so on.

REITs Are Becoming More Popular and Well-Known

REITs currently own about 10 to 15% of the $4 trillion U.S. commercial real estate market.

Some REITs invest in mortgages and mortgage-securities, not property. They are highly affected by changes in interest rates, and are highly leveraged. They don't own property - they speculate in debt. My personal advice -- don't go there. As the recent scandal in U.S. subprime mortgages has demonstrated, you can easily get burned. Some of those "mortgage REITs" did burn down in 2008. I recommend only property-based, equity REITs.

Weaknesses:

1. Diversification.

By definition, REITs operate in only one sector of the economy -- real estate.

And they tend to focus only on particular types of real estate. Many own expensive apartment buildings, but only one or two handle Section 8 housing. Few have much to do with ordinary private homes. One or two do handle trailers.

Shopping center REITs are more democratic, including lots of supermarket-anchored strip malls as well as expensive shopping centers.

Hotel REITs tend to focus on upscale hotels and resorts, not cheap motels.

Some AREITs (Australian Real Estate Investment Trusts) operate vineyards and chains of taverns.

Some REITs are extremely dependent upon one or just a few locations.

Strengths:

1. Income.

To maintain their tax-free status, REITs must pay out at least 90% of their profits to investors. Their yields go up and down depending on the market, but are generally high, from 4 to 7%.

You do have to pay taxes at the ordinary tax rate on most of the dividends you receive. However, receiving a high dividend yield helps to make up for this. Plus, 25 to 30% of it is taxed as long term capital gains.

2. Not expensive.

REITs don't pay taxes.

3. Inflation protection.

Inflation has a complicated effect on real estate. It may force some property owners to raise their rents, generating more profit to keep up with inflation. Or it could reduce profits for certain kinds of properties. However, in the long run real estate profits do go up with inflation, so in the long run REITs dividends do go up with inflation.

4. Meet human needs.

We all need someplace to live.

That said, I acknowledge that for the most part REITs don't provide individual houses or budget apartments. Also, expensive malls are threatened by online shopping.

However, many REITs own and operate small neighborhood strips of stores that will always exist.

Many others provide commercial facilities -- some quite specialized -- that will have demand fluctuating with the economy.

BOTTOM LINE:

With their high yields, REITs are one essential source of income for investors.

Next: why, until 2011, Canada is an income investor's best friend.

Chapter Twenty-Seven

Canadian Income Trusts

With The Income Tax Act of 1985, Canada initiated a new type of limited partnership intended to encourage development of its natural resources.

This law authorized businesses to organize themselves as trusts. They would not have to pay taxes so long as they paid out nearly all of their net earnings to the trust holders (also called unit holders).

However, until the dot com crash (which shook Canada's financial world -- Bay Street -- just as hard as it did Wall Street), nobody paid much attention to this law. The vast majority of trusts were CanRoys - Real Estate Investment Trusts and royalty trusts.

A trust is the holding of property for someone else.

A business converts into a Canadian income trust by becoming the settler of the trust -- it transfers ownership of its assets to the trust. The trust fund is the trustee. That is, it manages the assets on behalf of the beneficiary. The beneficiaries are the investors who've purchased shares in the trust

An income trust is a business that holds its assets to produce income to the owners -- unit holders. Ownership interest in Canadian income funds trades on stock exchanges just like shares of stock, but they're called trust units. Dividends are paid to the unit holders on a monthly or quarterly basis.

Often these are businesses that generate a lot of cash for investors, which then must be paid out to unit holders per Canadian law. Of course, to do this, the business must have plenty of cash from profits to begin with.

Canadian Companies Went Crazy for Trusts, Including Some Companies Trying to Conceal Business Weakness

By 2003, eight out of every ten dollars raised by Canadian Initial Public Offerings went to income trusts. The larger and more well-known funds trade on U.S. as well as Canadian exchanges.

In 2006, Standard and Poor's decided to include trusts in the benchmark Toronto Stock Exchange Index (S and P/TSX Composite Index).

There're about 250 income trusts and REITs listed on the TSX Toronto Stock Exchange.

Although they're focused on energy and natural resources, there're various types of Canadian income trusts:

1. Business Trusts

Current business trusts include the Canadian Yellow Pages, manufacturers, fisheries, and entertainment.

2. Trademark Royalty Trusts

Some trusts are set up so that they don't operate the underlying business, they just own the rights to the company's trademark, and they license it back to the company. In return, they receive a fee for each product sold. This is the income with which the "CanRoy" pays dividends to its unit holders.

For example, in Canada, the A & W Root Beer company runs the hamburger and root beer stands, but pays a fee on all franchise profits to an income trust (A & W Revenue Royalties Income Fund), which then pays its unit holders.

3. Oil and Gas Royalty Trusts

This type of trust is the major category of income trusts in Canada, and was the original intent of the law -- to encourage the development of Canada's rich supply of natural resources. For the good of Canadian investors and the overall Canadian economy.

Oil and gas royalty trusts own the right to profit from the oil or gas in a proven well. As long as the world needs these commodities, the trust will generate income by selling what's in its well.

4. Funds of Income Funds

These are basically mutual funds that hold nothing but the best (in the manager's estimation) of the available Canadian funds. You can buy units in these companies, which are themselves set up as trusts.

There are risks to Canadian income trusts:

1. Business risk

They're businesses. Duh.

2. Depletion of the Income-Generating Asset risk

Many Canadian income funds are natural resource businesses, since Canada is rich in natural resources and commodities. Therefore, it's possible that some trusts will go out of business when their oil wells run dry or their mines are depleted. These are known as wasting assets

3. Asset Price Fluctuation risk

We all know that the price of oil is going up -- but even though, when we're filling our tanks it seems as though the price keeps going up, it does sometimes go down.

Payouts from energy trusts will rise and fall with the price of the natural resources of the business.

4. Political risk

In 2005 the Liberal Party-controlled Canadian government attempted --but failed -- to impose taxation on Canadian business trusts. This became a big issue during the next election. When the Conservative Party barely won on January 23, 2006, trust investors celebrated. The Conservative Party had campaigned on a no new taxes (including on CanRoys) platform.

Then came October 31, 2006 -- the Halloween Massacre -- when Canadian Finance Minister Jim Flaherty announced that almost no Canadian businesses would be allowed to convert to trust status. Plus, beginning in 2011, almost all existing trusts (except Real Estate Investment Trusts) would lose their tax exempt status. The minister filed a notice of intent to table a bill in Parliament.

The bill must actually be passed by Parliament and signed into law. About one million Canadian adults own income trusts, and therefore would find their spending power reduced if these trusts are taxed. And they make up about 5% of Canadian voters.

Therefore, it's possible that by 2011 this proposal will be forgotten and that trusts will remain tax-free.

However, at this writing in 2010, it appears this change is going to take place.

In United States, the IRS has ruled that (except a few passively managed funds and limited partnerships) Canadian income funds are qualifying foreign corporations, which means their dividends are taxed at the 15% rate.

But early in 2007 Democratic Congressman Richard Neal of Massachusetts proposed a bill that would revoke this tax treatment of foreign entities, including Canadian income trusts and REITs. (If you live in Rep. Neal's district, please consider this bill to cut your income when you go to vote in the next election.)

5. Over-Distribution of Dividends risk

Some Canadian income funds pay out to unit holders more than their net income. In the long run this is obviously not sustainable. Therefore, it's a good idea to analyze a fund's cash flow. Compare its annual net profit per unit to its total annual dividend distribution per unit. Dividend distributions per unit should be under 100%, certainly not over.

Weaknesses:

1. Diversification.

Although there are income trusts for A & W Root Beer and the Canadian Yellow Pages, most of the big and successful trusts are connected with energy and commodities.

Strengths:

1. Income.

To maintain their tax-free status, they must pay out 90% or more of their profits to unit holders. Their yields tend to be quite high.

2. Human needs.

Most of them are invested in energy and natural resources. Human beings have an ever-growing need for these.
\
3. Inflation protection.

Energy and commodity prices do keep up with inflation in the long run, but in the short run can fall behind (as they did in the 1980s and 1990s).

BOTTOM LINE:

Until October 31, 2006, Canadian trusts looked like the income investor's dream. Some will undoubtedly still have good payouts even when taxed, but those will simply be one more stock to buy if it's in a good index. I can't now recommend you spend much time on the, especially if you live outside Canada.

Next: how to profit from energy pipelines in the U.S.

Chapter Twenty-Eight

Master Limited Partnerships

The Tax Reform Act of 1986 authorized businesses to organize themselves as limited partnerships, and yet have their partnership units trade on the public securities exchanges just like common stocks.

(Limited partnerships are common and nothing new, but are normally privately owned and operated.)

These publicly available limited partnerships are now known as master limited partnerships, or MLPs for short.

In 1987, the tax code was modified to limit these businesses to those receiving 90% of their income from natural resources, real estate and commodities, now referred to as qualifying sources. Some MLPs already in other businesses were grandfathered.

Most MLPs are pipeline companies. They charge energy companies to transport natural gas or crude oil or refined oil products. These businesses are regulated, and they do well no matter how much the price of gas and oil goes up or down -- because they charge by volume.

(So they may make less profits when the economy slows, and therefore the demand for oil and gas products decreases.)

MLPs Used to Be an Insider Investment

For many years, only wealthy investors "in the know" bought partnership units in these companies. In the 1990s, only 6 MLPs were listed on the New York Stock Exchange, for a market cap of only $2 billion. Now, however, thanks to the new, post-dotcom crash emphasis on income investing, plus the spread of investing information on the Internet, more investors are becoming aware of the opportunity. Their market cap has doubled in the past several years to $140 billion.

These limited partnerships have a General Partner (GP) which actually manages the operation of the business. Historically, these have been large energy companies, but now these businesses are attracting interest from large financial institutions. The GP is limited to owning 2% of the value of the company. Also, they receive at least 2% of the distributions of net profits, but meeting performance incentives can increase this, in the form of additional ownership, up to 50% equity in the MLP. This encourages the GP to manage the business well -- to grow it and increase cash flow and distributions to unit holders Also, the GP has all liability of the partnership.

The rest of the MLP is owned by the limited partners -- that can be you and I. Shares of the MLP are called units, and these trade in lots of 100 on stock exchanges just like shares of common stock of corporations. You can buy them just by putting the order in to your broker.

About two-thirds of the 70 or so MLPs now in existence are listed on the New York Stock Exchange. So MLPs are regulated by the Securities Exchange Commission and must file paperwork just like any corporation. They must also comply with the record keeping and disclosure requirements of the Sarbanes-Oxley Act.

From 2000 to 2007, MLPs returned an average of 26.1% a year.

What Makes MLPs Such Great Long-Term Income Investments?

MLPs do not pay taxes so long as they pay 90% of their cash flow to their limited partners (you and me!). They make required quarterly distributions. These checks are called distributions instead of dividends and, thanks to this provision of the law, their yields are higher than stock dividends.

MLPs often pay out consistent distributions of from 7 to 9% on your initial investment, and they have strong growth over time. Over the last 10 years, the average MLP has increased distributions nearly 10% annually. The median yield for Wachovia Securities' MLP Composite, 30 energy MLPs, has been around 6.4%.

There are complications, however, which often intimidate ordinary investors.

As energy pipeline companies (primarily), MLPs own a lot of heavy-duty equipment. Cost accounting and business tax law recognizes that this equipment doesn't last forever, even if well-maintained. Machinery goes downhill and becomes out of date, which is why we eventually have to buy new cars.

The running down of equipment (and need of eventual replacement) is a business expense that is recognized on business books and on tax returns as "depreciation."

But MLPs don't file tax returns. So what happens to the depreciation on all that equipment that won't last forever?

It's allocated to the limited partners as part of their distributions. Up to 80% to 90% of the checks sent quarterly to limited partners are considered by the IRS as a "return of capital," because it's your share of the MLP's depreciation.

And that's good!

Because, under the law, you don't have to pay taxes on "return of capital" (it's a "return" of the MLP's capital, by the way, not a return on the money you paid for your MLP units). It is tax-deferred until you sell your units or until the total amount equals what you paid for your share.

Therefore, you not only get quarterly checks that are a high yield from your purchase of the MLP units, about 80%-90% of that money is tax-deferred until you sell those MLP units.

If You Never Sell -- Which of Course is What I Advise -- the IRS is Out of Luck!

Every January, when most investments send you an IRS 1099 form to let you know what they paid you in the previous calendar year, to help you complete your tax return, MLPs send you a K1 partnership distribution form. It is more complicated, because of the tax deferral of most of the money sent to you.

If and when you do sell, and once the amount of distributions you've received add up to the amount of money you paid for the MLP units (which could take from 5 to 15 years depending on how much the dividends are), the distributions you receive are taxed as ordinary income.

Of the 10-20% of the distributions you receive that are not "return of capital," some may qualify for the 15% dividend tax rate (while the politicians still allow that rate to exist), but most is termed "unrelated business taxable income" (UBTI) and taxed as ordinary income.

However, tax-sheltering 80-90% of your distributions makes paying ordinary taxes on the remaining 10-20% fairly painless.

If you hold more than $1000 of UBTI in an IRA or other tax-deferred account, your IRA will be taxed on it at the ordinary income rate. Therefore, you should not hold MLPs in a tax-deferred account. (And this would be stupid anyway, because 80-90% of your income from distributions is already tax-deferred).

For years, mutual funds were not allowed to invest in MLPs. However, the American Jobs Creation Act of 2004 added MLP income to the list of acceptable sources of income for mutual funds. They may not invest more than 25% of their assets in MLPs, unfortunately, so you can't invest in an open-ended mutual fund specializing in MLPs.

One reason for MLPs remaining obscure until recently is that investors confused them with scam partnerships sold in the 1980s supposedly as a way to reduce taxes. However, MLPs are not at all the same type of investment.

MLPs Bring Business Risk, but They're Also Well-Regulated, Like Utilities

MLPs are businesses, however. They are subject to normal business risks. Their market values are affected by interest rates. Their managements can range from poor to great, but are most likely in-between. The demand for their products and services can vary. Pipelines can break down and need repairs.

As with all income investments, their price goes down when interest rates and inflation go up. However, pipeline MLPs enjoy a special protection -- the regulators will allow them to charge higher prices for transporting oil and gas, so their incomes will also go up in line with inflation.

A handful of closed-end mutual funds hold MLPs. Unfortunately, closed end funds have to pay taxes on the MLP distributions they receive, so if you invest in

MLPs this way, you still get the tax deferral, but lose some yield. To boost returns, most of these closed end funds use leverage. Therefore, the only one I can recommend is Tortoise North American Energy (TYN) -- the only one that I know of that doesn't use leverage. (But things can change, so make sure before you invest.)

At the end of the year, closed-end funds will report your total distributions to you with an ordinary 1099 form, not the K1 partnership distribution form which is so confusing.

The Alerian MLP Index, a composite of the 50 most prominent energy MLPs, is calculated by Standard & Poor's. The index is on the New York Stock Exchange as AMZ.

In association with the National Association of Publicly Traded Partnerships (NAPTP -- an MLP industry trade group), the Alerian Capital Management LLP also determines the Alerian MLP Select Index, which is 37 of the most liquid MLPs. These are the ones that conform with the New York Stock Exchange's standards for inclusion in Exchange Traded Funds.

So it's no surprise that Bear Stearns has just issued the first Exchange Traded Note (ECN), the BearLinx Alerian MLP Select Index ECN on the New York Stock Exchange (ticker symbol: BSR).

Therefore, by buying shares of the BearLinx Alerian MLP Select Index ECN, you get collective ownership interest in 37 of the top MLPs.

The top five, by market weight, are: Enterprise Product Partners (NYSE:EPD); Kinder Morgan Energy Partners (NYSE:KMP); Plains All American Pipeline Partners (NYSE:PAA); Energy Transfer Partners (NYSE:ETP); and TEPPCO (NYSE:TPP).

Weaknesses:

1. Diversification.

The only businesses allowed to use the MLP structure are in natural resources and commodities, especially pipelines.

Strengths:

Income Investing Secrets

1. Income.

MLPs don't pay taxes and so have high yields.

2. Basic human needs.

We all need and use the oil and natural gas that flows through their pipelines.

3. Inflation protection.

For the foreseeable future, people are going to need refined oil products and natural gas. Perhaps someday these energy MLPs will carry methane and ethanol as well (I don't know), but the human race has an ever-increasing demand for basic energy.

When there's no need for these pipelines, we'll either be living in a solar-powered eco-paradise -- or we'll have regressed to a pre-civilized state of barbarity.

Energy pipelines companies are regulated much like utilities. To keep oil and natural gas distributed where needed, regulators will have to allow these MLPs to raise rates when needed to match inflation. Over the past 10 years, their distributions have gone up on average nearly 10%, much higher growth than the rate of inflation.

4. Expenses.

Although MLPs do have high capital equipment costs, they are allowed to pass them on to customers and to write them off as depreciation, giving you a tax advantage. They don't pay taxes.

Thanks to their unique tax structure, normally 80 to 90% of the distributions paid to you (up until these equal the price you paid for your units) are tax deferred until you sell.

This creates a tremendous incentive to NOT sell your units. Therefore, you're encouraged to own your units -- and collect distributions that are high to begin with, and historically grow at nearly 10% annually -- forever.

MLPs have displayed strong growth in market prices, but you'd be foolish to realize these capital gains when you'd have to pay so much in taxes.

The annual K1 partnership distribution forms are more complicated and difficult to understand than ordinary 1099s, so this may cause you headaches or slightly higher tax preparation fees just before April 15, but this is more than offset by the power of tax deferring up to 90% of your (already high) quarterly distributions. brokerage fees, commissions, management fees and so on. Your personal time is also an expense to keep to a minimum.

BOTTOM LINE:

Master Limited Partnerships are powerful income investments. Although considered somewhat risky because they're concentrated in one industry, it's a much needed one. They are not proven by time, however, since this is a relatively new type of business entity.

Next: ever wanted to invest like a venture capitalist?

Chapter Twenty-Nine

Business Development Companies (BDC)

You've probably heard that the people who make really big money in the stock market are venture capital companies and angel investors who finance new companies.

These firms provide capital to start-up companies, and usually guide them through their early development. They do everything they can to ensure the success of the company, to protect their own investment.

Of course, they do this in return for a large ownership piece of the start-up companies.

Frequently, this is the only way a new company can obtain the cash it needs to survive.

When the new company launches its Initial Public Offering (IPO) onto the stock market, the initial owners, including the venture capital source, can profit enormously.

So -- if everything goes well (and that's a big IF) -- venture capital firms do make a lot more money from the IPO than anybody who buys the IPO's stock.

Venture Capital of All Kinds Entails a Lot of Risk

Not all new businesses that receive venture capital make it to the IPO stage. Not all IPOs are successful.

Nevertheless, there's a glamorous mystique associated with helping new businesses.

But until recently, only venture capital firms and wealthy "angel investors" could take advantage of this. Buying stock in a private company is called a "private placement," and the SEC requires that only an accredited investor may do this. To be an accredited investor you must have a net worth of at least $1 million or have an income of at least $200,000 in the past two years and be on target for the same in the current year.

Sometimes venture capital firms come in with financing and advice after the company is started, but before it reaches its IPO stage. This is known as "mezzanine" financing.

How You Can Get In On the Profits -- and the Risk

What if you, as a unaccredited investor, want a piece of this action?

Most venture capital firms will have nothing to do with you. They are private firms closed to new investors.

But now there is a way.

In the 1970s, venture capital firms convinced Congress to pass the Small Business Investment Incentive Act of 1980. This amended the "small private investment company" exemption contained in Section 3(c)(1) of the Investment Company Act of 1940 and the Investment Advisers Act of 1940 to add a new category of closed-end investment company known as a business development company (BDC).

BDCs are publicly traded, closed-end funds that invest in private or thinly-traded public companies. The 1980 Amendments were designed to encourage the establishment of public vehicles that invest in private equity.

For tax purposes, they are structured as a regulated investment company (RIC). That means they must pay out 90%+ of their profits to their shareholders as dividends. Also, they can't put more than 5% of their assets into any single company.

Successful BDCs Do Pay A High Yield To Shareholders

The potential of successful BDCs to pay a high yield to shareholders is why I'm including a chapter on them in this book.

However, BDCs didn't become very popular until this century. Now you can buy shares in BDCs on all the U.S. stock exchanges. There are now about 30+ BDCs worth over $9.5 billion.

Some BDCs focus on helping very new companies. Some aim for companies that are established. Some provide financing and management consulting to fairly well established companies.

Obviously, the newer the company the BDC supplies money, the greater the risk -- and the reward, if the new companies are successful.

Weaknesses:

1. Diversification.

You are investing only in new businesses. BDCs are not allowed to put more than 5% of their available funds in any one company. However, the other 95% is still in new and therefore risky companies.

Strengths:

1. Income.

Because of their status as a RIC, BDCs must pay out at least 90% profits to investors. However, that assumes they have profits to pay out. The business is speculative and so BDCs may have their ups and downs.

BOTTOM LINE:

Because of their speculative nature, I advise caution. BDCs deserve a place here, since they pay out a lot of income. However, this book is for long-term investing, and these are speculative investments.

Don't invest in BDCs unless you qualify for accredited investor status.

Next: How to obtain a high yield by investing in a company and loaning money to it -- through the same security.

Chapter Thirty

Income Deposit Securities (IDS)

These are single hybrid securities. They pay out a lot of money to their shareholders -- and it's partly a dividend for owning stock, partly interest from owning a bond.

Yes, that's confusing, and I can't explain the accounting mechanics. But when you invest in a IDS, you're partly an owner and partly a loaner of money to the company, as though you bought one of their bonds.

They can make higher payments than corporations, because the interest on the money they owe to you is a tax-deductible expense.

On average, IDS yields are large, up to 10%. Only mature, stable, small but cash-rich companies are allowed to convert to this type business entity, because they need a large cash flow.

Plus, IDS units trade on the American Stock Exchange. The IDS structure was in fact developed with AMEX.

IDSes must produce a lot of cash. There aren't many now. Examples I read about include a rural telephone company, a national laundromat company, a food company, and the company that sells food at most major U.S. sports stadiums.

Sometimes IDSes are called Enhanced Income Securities (EIS) or Enhanced Yield Securities (EYS).

The money you receive which is a dividend qualifies for the 15% tax rate on dividends. The interest portion is fully taxable as ordinary income. So this separation can be confusing to some people.

The debt portion of IDS units have widely varying maturities, though 10 years is typical.

An IDS Unit is a Common Stock -- and a Bond, All in One

So buying a unit in an IDS structured company is equivalent to buying both an intermediate bond from that company and shares of stock in it.

So it can easily be confusing, but the purpose is to maximize income to unit holders, which is good for us income investors.

The payments can be monthly but quarterly is more likely.

Many of the same bond/common stock rules apply. A company must pay bond holders their interest, or be in default, which adversely affects their credit rating. Dividends are subject to approval by the Board of Directors, and are subject to discretion depending on the profitability of the company.

So it's also possible to receive just the interest you're owed, but no dividends, if cash flow is currently a problem.

Yields are now running around 10%+, so you can easily see their appeal to income investors.

Weaknesses:

1. Diversification.

There are not many companies that qualify for or choose to switch to this type of structure.

Strengths:

1. Income.

They can yield up around 10%.

BOTTOM LINE:

Right now, there aren't many IDS companies. The future of this hybrid form of investment isn't certain.

Next: How to obtain a higher yield than a certificate of deposit -- by taking it out from a life insurance company instead of a bank.

Chapter Thirty-One

Guaranteed Investment Contracts (GIC)

Have you ever had the bright idea that -- like banks -- insurance companies have a lot of money . . . so wouldn't you get a little higher interest rate if you handed your money over to an insurance company instead of a bank, as the life insurance equivalent to a certificate of deposit?

Maybe you've never had that idea -- but the life insurance companies sure have.

Essentially, guaranteed investment contracts (GIC) are life insurance company versions of certificates of deposits. Only, of course, they are not insured by the Federal Deposit Insurance Corporation (FDIC). Therefore, they must pay you a little higher rate of interest, to compensate you for taking the additional risk of handing your money over to them instead of a bank.

Most life insurance companies offering GICs are rated AAA or AA, but your money's safety is guaranteed only by the successful existence of that life insurance company, so you should always check a company's credit rating:

1. AM Best -- http://www.ambest.com/ratings/guide.asp

2. Weiss -- http://www.weissratings.com/products_lh.asp

You Can Obtain Slightly Higher Yields with a GIC Than a CD

The insurance company contract with you guarantees you that they'll pay a fixed or floating rate of interest, plus will repay your principal after a set length of time -- generally from one to five years. Just like a CD. There is no secondary market for trading them.

Most customers for GICs are institutions looking to earn every last possible basis point of interest, but life insurance companies will take your money too if you choose to buy a GIC.

They're also known as fixed-income funds, stable value funds, capital-preservation funds and guaranteed funds.

You'll get a higher interest rate than you would from a savings account, bank certificate of deposit or money market account.

Though not as high as from bonds.

GICs are insured group annuity contracts issued by around 100 U.S. and Canadian life insurance companies.

Value of outstanding GIC contracts is now over $200 billion.

Weaknesses:

1. Diversification.

The insurance company will invest your money in various fixed income vehicles similar to what a bank does with your money in a Certificate of Deposit.

However, if you insurance company goes out of business, which is possible, you may get nothing. If you bank fails, in the United States the FDIC will give you back your money up to $100,000.

2. Expenses.

The life insurance companies allegedly charge high fees. Basically, you're paying them to use the leverage of the many assets under their control to make fixed income investments for you.

Strengths:

1. Income.

GIC yields are a little higher than bank CDs, to compensate you for the risk of company failure.

BOTTOM LINE:

I'm including a chapter on GICs in this book simply because you will probably come across them, yet they're not as well known as savings accounts, money market funds and certificates of deposits.

All these things are too safe and therefore small in yield to be worth mentioning further in this book.

Next: how to get rich by lending money.

Chapter Thirty-Two

Bonds

Bonds are the "traditional" means that people use to invest for income.

I put traditional in quotes because prior to about 1958, stocks on the average actually paid more money in dividends than bonds paid in interest.

Before 1958, stock holders required a higher yield than bondholders, to compensate them for the perceived risk of owning stocks. After that year, shareowners have been more interested in receiving the (potential) capital gains of stocks.

Bonds now pay a higher yield in interest than stocks do in dividends. That's the best reason to buy bonds -- for a high current income.

Bonds are a form of debt. They're fancy IOUs.

Owing Money Versus Being Owed Money

In one of the Rich Dad, Poor Dad books, Robert Kiyosaki writes that a banker once told him that a person is poor to the extent that they owe money. They're rich to the extent that money is owed to them.

Bonds are your opportunity to get rich by having big organizations owe money to you.

There're a huge variety of bonds. They're issued by the federal government, government-related agencies, local governments and by corporations. They can be for periods ranging from under a year, to 100 years.

Normally, they're issued for a face value (called par value) of $1000. They pay a set rate of interest, usually semi-annually (every 6 months).

Some bonds are secured -- that is, they're backed up by a specific asset. For example, a city might secure a bond with the revenue generated by a toll bridge. Most bonds are backed up by the "full faith" of the issuer.

All bonds have one thing in common: their value is affected by prevailing interest rates.

Changes in Prevailing Interest Rates Affect Market Prices of Bonds

That's because bonds pay a certain interest rate. If prevailing interest rates are now higher, the bond is worth less. If prevailing interest rates are now lower, the bond is worth more.

An example makes this easy to understand.

Let's say that in the year 2000, the General Computer Soft Corporation put out a bond that paid 5% interest for 20 years. Investors buying that bond in 2000 paid the par value of $1000 and are now receiving $50 a year.

In the year 2005, you're interested in buying a bond, but the prevailing interest rates are 4%. Since you'd rather get $50 a year from your bond investment than $40, you think you'd rather buy the 2000 General Computer Soft bond that pays 5%.

Good thinking, but things aren't that simple or easy. Since the prevailing interest rates have gone down to 4%, to buy a $1000 par value bond paying 5% you'll have to pay MORE than $1000. That means it's trading at a premium.

What if the opposite occurred? It's 2005 and prevailing interest rates are now 6%. You want to buy a bond. Since currently issued bonds (par value $1000) pay 6%, will you fork over $1000 for the same 2000 General Computer Soft Corp 5% bond?

Of course not. Nobody will pay the same price for $50 a year that they will for $60 a year. Therefore, the price of the old $50 a year bond when new bonds pay $60 will be reduced to a discount of about $833, so that the yield is 6%.

Bond Price Changes Are As Inconsequential as Stock Price Changes -- if You Simply Don't Sell

Therefore, although bond prices are not as volatile as stocks (because interest rates change slowly), you can have a capital loss if you sell after prevailing interest rates have risen. Over the course of a bond's life, it very likely will sometimes be worth more, and sometimes worth less, than its face value -- depending on the fluctuations of interest rates over its life.

The only way to avoid this is to hold a bond until its maturity date. At the end of the bond's life, the issuer returns to you the full face value, no matter what you originally paid for it. If you paid less than par, this guarantees you will receive a capital gain. If you paid more than par, this guarantees you will suffer a capital loss.

Another big factor affecting bond prices is the number of years left to maturity. Interest rates are going to fluctuate a lot more over the course of 20 years than in the next 6 months. This means that long term bonds are riskier than short term bonds. In general, the longer before a bond matures, the higher its yield must be to compensate the buyer for the increased risk.

Call Provisions Can Limit the Life of Bonds

Many bonds have what're known as call provisions. This means that the bond issuer has the right to "call" the bond from you. That is, give you your money back, even if you want to continue to own the bond. Actually, ESPECIALLY if you would rather own the bond!.

Why would they want to do that?

Let's say you own a bond paying 7% interest, but prevailing interest rates for similar bonds are now 5%.

Just as you'd rather pay your credit card company 5% on your outstanding balance than 7%, the bond issuer would rather pay you 5% than 7%.

So in such situations, it will call in the 7% bonds and issue new bonds at 5%.

Of course, this means you then have to reinvest your money at 5% instead of

7%.

So calls are generally a bad thing for bond investors.

Provisions for calls differ by bond.

Weaknesses:

1. Inflation protection.

This is the area in which bonds really and truly stink. A bond's interest is set for the life of the bond. Therefore, its purchasing power declines with inflation. When the bond reaches its maturity date, you get the entire principal back, but its value has also been lessened by inflation.

Strengths:

1. Income.

They pay higher current yields than stocks do.

BOTTOM LINE:

Bonds pay a higher rate of income in the near term, but are weaker in the long term.

The most important type of bonds are those issued by the government -- in the United States -- Treasuries.

Chapter Thirty-Three

Treasury and Government-Related Bonds

The Treasury Department raises money for the United States federal government by selling bonds with maturities of up to 30 years. These are considered risk-free because they're backed by the full faith and credit (and taxing power) of the U.S. government.

At $8 trillion, U.S. Treasury issues are the largest bond market in the world.

Treasury Bills

Treasury bills mature in three months, six months or one year. They don't make any interest payments. They are sold at a discount, and you get the entire face value upon maturity.

Treasury Notes

Treasury notes mature in two, three, five or ten years -- in denominations of from $1,000 to $1 million.

Treasury Bonds

Treasury bonds mature in ten to 30 years.

If the U.S. Government Defaults, Head for the Hills

If the U.S. government fails to meet its interest payment obligations, there's a world crisis going on so severe that you'll be worried about a lot more than your investment performance.

Treasuries don't have call provisions, so the government can't force you to sell it back to them if, in years to come, interest rates go down.

You must pay federal taxes on interest from Treasuries, but they're not taxable by state and local governments. This can be a large benefit if you live in a high-tax state.

Other governments around the world also sell bonds. All developed country government bonds are basically risk-free. Government bonds from countries with political instability obviously have the risk that a new government will take over and repudiate the obligations of the prior government/dictator.

Many government-related agencies in the U.S. also raise money by selling bonds. The U.S. government does not officially back these bonds as it does with its direct obligations. However, investors in the past have assumed that Congress will not allow them to miss any payments. In the fall of 2008. with the subprime mortgage crisis and Fannie Mae and Freddie Mac, we learned this faith was justified. These agencies were taken back by the U.S. government.

Most U.S. Treasury bonds are issued in $1000 denominations. The interest is paid every six months. You can buy them easily at:

http://www.treasurydirect.gov

You can also call 1-800-772-2678.

You can buy and sell a variety of Treasury securities with no dealer markup and without paying any commissions. You can have your interest payments sent directly to your bank account.

Outside the U.S. -- The governments of most, if not all, countries around the world want more money. If you live in a developed country, you should first of all invest in sovereign bonds issued by your own government. They'll probably be easier (cheaper) to invest in than U.S. Treasury bonds. Also, you may get some tax breaks -- check with a local broker or financial advisor.

If you live in a developing country, I strongly advise putting some money into bonds issued by politically stable governments: U.S., Canada, Australia, Japan, Great Britain, and the EU. However, you must check out the mechanics and expenses of doing this. Also, I advise diversifying. Interest rates will probably be fairly uniform, so you'll want to protect your funds by putting it into many different types of currencies.

You can set up a U.S. Treasury Direct account online or by calling 1-304-480-

Income Investing Secrets

7955.

I don't see anything on the website that restricts who can open up an account. So I assume that so long as your money can be converted into U.S. dollars -- and you can get it transferred into this account -- you can open up the account and profit from helping to finance the U.S. government's deficit spending (as a U.S taxpayer, I thank you -- we need all the help we can get!).

Government bonds have the same strengths and weaknesses of all bonds, but have one additional weakness:

1. Low income.

The government doesn't sell bonds because it loves you. It sells them to raise money and influence the economy. During hard economic times such as we're going through now, it keeps interest extremely low. Whether this will work or not is open to debate. The government of Japan has been selling its bonds with extremely low interest rates for nearly two decades, and Japan still has not recovered from its 1989 bust.

However, Treasuries also have an additional strength:

1. Low expenses.

U.S. treasuries are terrific in this area. You can open up your own account with the Treasury Department by going to http://www.treasurydirect.gov . You send your money and buy what you like, and they keep it there in your name, sending you the interest checks when due. There's no charge for this service if your account balance is under $100,000. Then they charge $25. And actually, you can save that charge simply by opening up additional accounts as needed. You won't pay a higher than market price. If you're buying a new bond, you'll pay the par value.

No commissions, no management fees, no inflated prices, no account fees for under $100,000 -- a simple, easy and cheap way to invest your money in a risk-free security that pays you regular income. Plus, in the US, you don't pay state or local taxes on the income.

If you're outside the U.S., you'll have to check with your own government to see if they have anything comparable.

BOTTOM LINE:

Treasuries are the lowest yielding bonds, but have the lowest risk and the lowest expenses to buy and own.

Corporations must pay higher interest than governments, since they're not risk-free.

Chapter Thirty-Four

Corporate Bonds

Companies need to raise money to finance their operations or to expand their businesses. They often do so by selling bonds.

The market for corporate bonds is dominated by institutions with millions of dollars to spend -- mutual funds, insurance companies, pension funds, and charities and other endowment funds.

So if you don't have at least $100,000 to invest -- bond brokers don't want you.

The Corporate Bond Market is the Opposite of the Stock Market

There are no organized market exchanges as there are with stocks, so the market is relatively opaque. In essence, that means you can't know when you're being ripped off by your broker. Which means that unless you're a Grade A customer, your broker will rip you off.

The price of corporate bonds is greatly affected by the credit rating of the issuing company.

Investment grade bonds pay lower interest rates than junk bonds, because they're safer. With corporate bonds, "risk" is not just a synonym for volatility. There's always the real danger that over the lifetime of a bond its issuing company will not have enough money, and will therefore default on the interest payments, or go totally out of business altogether.

Of course, some companies are riskier than others. A year-old biotech company is obviously more likely to default than Microsoft.

Income Investing Secrets

Less than investment grade bonds must have a higher yield to compensate investors for taking that additional risk.

Some companies rate bonds, to help guide investment decisions. The three most important are Moody's, Standard & Poor's, and Fitch. Here are their rating systems.

The more letters, the better.

INVESTMENT GRADE

	Moody's	Standard & Poor's + Fitch
Highest Quality	Aaa	AAA
High Quality	Aa	AA
Upper Medium Grade	A	A
Medium Grade	Baa	BBB

SPECULATIVE GRADE

	Moody's	Standard & Poors + Fitch
Lower Medium Grade	Ba	BB
Low Grade	B	B
Poor Quality	Caa	CCC
Most Speculative	Ca	CC

IN DEFAULT

	Moody's	Standard & Poors + Fitch
In default	C	D

Also, S&P can add a plus sign "+" or minus "-" sign, which indicates that the rating is trending up or down.

Moody's adds a number: 1, 2 or 3. The lower the number, the higher the quality. Thus, an A1 bond has a slightly higher quality than an A2.

These same ratings apply to all kinds of bonds (except Treasuries, which are assumed to be in effect Aaa/AAA), such as municipal bonds, convertible bonds, preferred bonds and so on.

Historical studies over the past 20 years have found that investment grade bonds have a less than 1% default rate.

The higher the credit rating of the bond issue, the lower the coupon rate, because the risk of default is lower.

In the 1980s "junk" bonds were used to finance leveraged buyouts of one corporation by another, and got a deservedly bad name. Today, less than investment grade does mean that you're taking the chance that the company will fail, but the abuses of 20 years ago are pretty much over.

Below investment grade bonds have default frequencies running from 1.5 to 12.5%, depending how just how bad their credit rating is. Companies in this financial situation must pay bond buyers a higher coupon rate, running from 1 to 8%.

If You're Worried About a Company Going Out of Business - Diversify

Books and articles on bonds often tell you that bonds are less risky than common stocks because if a company goes out of business, bondholders have rights before shareholders.

This is technically true, but in real-life terms, it's a lawyer-ish technicality. When a major corporation goes out of business, it's only the lawyers and the major creditors (such as banks) who win. The major creditors have ensured that their loans to the company are senior to ordinary bondholders. And the entire process drags on forever. You will get pennies on the dollar, and it'll take years.

For all practical purposes, you won't be any better off than the common stock shareholders who lost everything right away.

And if the company is "bailed out" by the company, bond holders may be cut out of the deal as they were with General Motors.

Anyway, it doesn't make sense to me to choose investments based on what would happen if the company goes out of business. Yes, it can happen -- that's why I preach the gospel of diversification, which is your best defense against it.

Some corporate bonds are secured by a specific asset, such as a particular airplane. This makes them seem safer from the risk of default than a general obligation bond, but in reality, a bankruptcy judge is probably going to let the plane keep flying if it's necessary for the company to stay in business. If you do have to take possession, you'll be just one of many bond owners with an ownership interest in that airplane (unless you're rich enough to have financed the entire aircraft by yourself), plus there may be no market for that model of used aircraft.

Many Corporate Bonds Have Call Provisions

Just in case you get excited because you own some corporate bonds paying 7% when the Federal Reserve lowers interest rates to 3%, don't party too hardy. Better remember that the corporation is paying a lot of smart people a lot of money to keep the corporation from losing money, so take a look at the fine print of your bond.

Chances are, your bond can be called. That means, the corporation can buy the bond back from you whenever it wants to, just by sending you a check for the principal plus any accrued interest due.

Will the corporation do this to you when the bond is paying BELOW market interest rates? Of course not. That would cost them money they'd have to borrow at prevailing market interest rates, so they'd lose money.

But will the corporation do this to you when the bond is paying ABOVE market interest rates? You bet your sweet bippy they will!

Because that will save them money. Why should they continue to pay you 7% a year, when they can pay you off with money they borrow at the current market rate of 3%?

That you'd rather continue to receive 7% a year rather than have to reinvest your principal for 3% per year, is of no concern to them.

Some bonds are freely callable, which means they can be called at any time. Other bonds are deferred callable bonds, which means the company cannot call them away from you before a certain period of time has elapsed - for example, five years.

This damned if interest rates rise (because the market price of your bond goes down), damned if interest rates go up (because your bond is called away from you) does limit the value of investing in corporate bonds.

Most corporate bonds are issued in $1000 denominations.

Although the bond market as a whole is huge (over $15 trillion just in the U.S.), the market for individual corporate bonds issues can be quite illiquid. Many corporations have many separate bond issues outstanding from the past 20 years, and keep issuing new ones. There's often no great demand for issue E of XYZ Inc., from 2001. Those bonds may not trade for months.

Plus, the bond market is decentralized, relying on individual bond traders, who mark the price up when they sell to you, and mark it down when they buy from you.

Don't Touch Convertible Bonds With a 10-Foot Pole

Some corporate bonds are convertible bonds. This means that under certain circumstances they can be converted into common stock. The terms can vary, but is often a price about 20% above the market price of the common stock at the time of issue of the bonds, and this remains fixed. Convertible bond holders can convert their bonds into stock at any time, but obviously there's no profit until the stock price has risen at least 20%.

These details can vary, and they enormously complicate valuation of the convertible bonds. Their market value is affected by everything that affects bonds - prevailing interest rates, the credit worthiness of the company and so on, and also by everything that affects common stock prices: the company's current stock price, its business prospects, the stock market as a whole, the economy, and so on.

To properly value convertible bonds takes a software program more complicated than putting a man on the moon.

Since the profiting from convertible bonds really requires the attention of a full-time professional, and since it involves requiring being right about many random factors (interest rates, stock market prices, and so on) I doubt whether the professionals really make money from trading convertibles.

The "trick" to profiting from convertibles is to make money through the conversion, which means realizing a capital gain through an increase in the common stock's price, so they're not really appropriate to income investing. If you're psychic enough to know that a company's stock price is going to rise soon, why not just buy the common stock? Playing that game is what this book is NOT about.

If you want bond interest from a company, buy their bonds. If you want stock dividends from a company, buy their common stock.

If you want to invest for capital gains, buy another investing book.

Outside the U.S. -- companies in Europe, Canada, Australia, Asia and other continents also issue bonds to raise money. Many of these bond issues will be rated by Moody's, Fitch, Standard & Poor's or your local bond rating service.

I know of no country with an investor-friendly bond market, so you will still find these bonds expensive.

The world bond market is fairly efficient, so don't expect to find any bargains in your backyard. The interest paid on corporate bonds is fairly equivalent throughout the world.

It is advisable for U.S. investors to buy some foreign bonds, and for those of you outside the U.S. to buy bonds from outside your own countries, as a currency hedge.

That is, when the U.S. dollar goes down (which has been its general direction for years now), it's a good idea to own yen, sterling, euros, Australian and Canadian dollars.

When your currency goes down, it's a good idea to own another currency, which may be going up.

Corporate bonds share the general qualities of all bonds.

Corporate bonds do have higher yields than Treasuries or municipals. You must be careful you don't buy corporate bonds that yield too much, though -- that means their credit rating is low. That means they're "junk bonds."

BOTTOM LINE:

On the whole, corporate bonds have a higher yield than other bonds.

Next: how to buy corporate bonds at minimal expense.

Chapter Thirty-Five

Direct Access Notes (DANs), InterNotes and CoreNotes

Starting in 1996, some major corporations and government-sponsored enterprises decided to organize offerings of their bonds to small investors.

They know it's difficult and expensive for small investors to buy corporate bonds from bond dealers.

These companies include: IBM, Dow Chemical, Prudential, Daimler-Chrysler, John Hancock, Caterpillar, Bank of America, Freddie Mac, Boeing, Citigroup, Sears and GE.

The bonds are offered in the normal denomination of $1000, but unlike dealing with typical brokers, small investors can buy just one (or more).

You can buy only new bond offerings. They are direct from the issuer. These are announced every Monday, and those bonds are available for one week.

Bonds can be callable or noncallable, have different maturity dates, have different coupon rates, and have different interest payment schedules.

You should also understand that the different issuing companies have different credit ratings. Some are riskier than others.

Because selling these kinds of bonds on the secondary market could be expensive for your estate, if you happen to die before the bonds mature, most of them offer a survivorship feature -- they'll buy the bonds back from your estate at par value. This could be a great benefit for your survivors.

You can obtain more information from:

http://www.internotes.com/

http://corenotes.ml.com/

http://www.bondclass.com/Home/Corporates/Additional-Topics/Corporate-Retail-Notes/Direct-Access-Notes.aspx

Outside the U.S. -- I didn't see any citizenship or residency requirements on either of the above three websites, so I must assume that, so long as your money is good and available, they'll be glad to sell bonds to you.

Unfortunately, you can't buy these bonds online, you must go through their networks of brokers. So you must contact one of them.

There are European InterNotes. See:

http://eu.internotes.com/

These notes are a terrific deal for small investors. They allow you to buy individual bonds without the markup and expense and high minimum payments required by using a normal bond broker.

Also, they enable you to avoid the commonly recommended alternative to buying individual bonds -- bond mutual funds. Bond mutual funds actively buy and sell bonds. This causes a drop in performance (unless the fund manager is psychic enough to predict interest rate changes) and high transaction costs. If your manager does realize a profit from trading, you must pay taxes.

BOTTOM LINE:

DANs, InterNotes and CoreNotes are perfect for investors who want the advantages of owning actual bonds. They avoid the disadvantages of buying bonds through bond brokers, and the disadvantages of using bond mutual funds.

Next: your mayor wants to borrow money from you.

Chapter Thirty-Six

Municipal Bonds

Bonds are often issued by local governments to raise money. You didn't think that the taxes you pay to your city and county were enough money for them, did you? Bonds help local governments pay for schools, road repairs, sports stadiums and so on.

Some muni bonds are backed by a specific revenue source (such as a toll bridge). Others are general revenue bonds, backed by that government's full faith and taxing power. General revenue bonds are therefore generally considered less risky. A flood may wash away a toll bridge, but the county government continues to collect property taxes.

In practice, however, a local government's taxing power may be limited by frustrated voters -- so bonds backed by an asset that more than pays for itself may be less risky than general obligation (GO) bonds.

The Biggest Attraction to Investing in Municipal Bonds

To encourage people to invest in local governments, the United States federal government has made the interest you receive from municipal bonds tax-free. Therefore, the yield that such bonds pay is generally lower than Treasury bonds and corporate bonds.

Therefore, in deciding whether or not to invest in muni bonds, you have to adjust their interest rate by your marginal tax rate. The higher your tax rate, the more advantageous to you these bonds are. Therefore, they are most popular with high income investors with a high marginal tax rate.

If you live in a high-tax state, municipal bonds issued in your state may be free from state taxes, so munis are particularly attractive to wealthy people living in such states as New York and California, so long as they buy munis issued in their own state. (However, a few high-tax states do not allow deductions for investing in munis issued in that state, so check with your financial advisor or other knowledgeable source before buying.)

Sometimes Congress considers repealing the federal tax-free status of municipal bond interest, and I can't promise you that it never will.

My theory is that it never will, because such proposals immediately draw fire from 50,000 U.S. mayors who tell the representatives that the repeal of the tax-free status of municipal bonds would bankrupt their cities and counties. Also, mayors tend to be politically active and influential members of their local Democratic or Republican organizations -- that is, the very people that members of Congress need the support of to win re-election.

Plus, repealing the tax-free status of municipal bonds would anger a lot of wealthy people – many of whom both vote and donate to political candidates.

The formula for determining the taxable equivalent of municipal bonds is:

Taxable Equivalent Yield = Tax-Free Yield / 1 - Tax Rate

Thus, if a muni bond's tax-free yield is 1.7% and your marginal tax rate is 28%:

TEY = 0.017 / 1 - 0.28

TEY = 0.017 / 0.72

TEY = 2.36%

Therefore, if you can buy ordinary bonds (that is, with taxable interest) with yields higher than 2.36%, you're better off doing that. If your only alternative is bonds that pay under 2.36%, you're better off buying the muni bonds.

Let's say that your state's income tax rate is 6% and you're considering buying a municipal bond issued by your state, so the interest payments are tax free.

Your total tax rate is now 28% + 6% = 34%

TEY = 0.017 / 1 - 0.34

TEY = 0.017 / 0.66

TEY = 2.57%

Therefore, you're better off buying bonds with taxable interest if you can get a yield of 2.57% or better. If not, you're better off buying the municipal bond from your state.

This tax-free status of municipal bonds means they are the one bond market not dominated by institutions. Institutions don't pay taxes anyway, so they don't need the tax savings muni bonds offer.

Credit Ratings Are Important

The other important issue regarding municipal bonds is the credit worthiness of the government or government agency issuing them. Local cities and counties are not as powerful as the federal government.

In 1975, New York City defaulted on some of its bonds.

Cleveland Ohio has also defaulted.

In August 1981, Moody's Investor Services cut the credit rating of The Washington Public Power Supply System (WPPSS), leading bond underwriters to demand immediate repayment of interest and principal. WPPSS did not have the cash to oblige.

In December 1994, Orange County California surprised the country by declaring bankruptcy and defaulting on their bond obligations, because it lost $1.6 billion in its investments.

Muni bonds are rated by Standard & Poor's and Moody's much like corporate bonds.

However, you can't take their ratings at face value. That's because most local governments now have their municipal bonds insured. When they do so, the credit rating of the insurance company becomes the credit rating of that issuance of municipal bonds.

Therefore, officially, municipal bonds are as good as the insurance company's financial backing, because if the local government fails to make the interest payments or the final return of principal, the insurance company will make this for them.

This is fine as long as the insurance companies themselves are financially sound and in business. So long as local government bankruptcies remain isolated incidents, there won't be any problem.

However, realize that if there's ever a general financial collapse or overall decline in the United States economy, that the tax base of these local governments may erode to the point that many of them can't meet their obligations -- at the same time. This could overwhelm the financial resources of the insurance company.

In that event, you'd be S*O*L.

Officially, municipal bonds rated AAA because of insurance are just as credit-worthy as municipal bonds rated AAA because the local government issuing them rates that AAA on its own merits.

Unofficially, bonds rated AAA without insurance are considered less risky.

Although municipal and corporate bonds are evaluated by the same credit ratings, municipal bonds are considered less risky than corporate bonds of the same credit value.

Standard & Poor's did a study of a 15 year period that discovered that an A rated municipal bond was 1/10 as likely to default as an A rated corporate bond.

However, the study also found that some sectors of the muni bond market have very high default rates: housing, health care and industrial development.

Most municipal bonds are issued in $5000 denominations.

Outside the U.S. -- I don't know, but I'm pretty sure that many municipality and other local governments around the world issue bonds. Countries, cultures and languages can be different -- but all governments want more money.

However, the mechanics of investing in your local version of muni bonds may be different. And I don't pretend to know about tax laws throughout the world. So check with a local broker or financial advisor.

Municipal bonds share the strengths and weaknesses of all bonds.

Municipal bonds can pay decent amounts of income on a post-tax basis. Their yields are lower than other bonds, but that's because their interest is not taxable by the federal government. If you're in a high tax state, you can also buy munis issued within your state that are not subject to state taxes (not true of all states). The higher your tax bracket, the more municipal bonds are worth to you.

It could be argued that municipal bonds meet basic human needs.

Municipal bonds are backed by local governments and by specific revenue-generating projects. People do need highways, schools, libraries, police departments and other aspects of local government. They don't choose to pay for these on a daily or monthly basis as they do with food and utilities, but as voters and taxpayers they, on the whole, accept the necessity of some form of local property and sales taxes to cover these items.

Despite general frustration over the amount of taxes we pay, and occasional "tax revolts," we are not going to transform our country any time soon into a libertarian paradise.

Since muni bonds must be bought from brokers who charge you a high bid-ask spread if you don't have 7 figures to spend on buying bonds, they are expensive to buy.

BOTTOM LINE:

Municipal bonds are a good investment for the wealthy, especially those living in most states with high income taxes.

Next: thinking you'd like to invest in mortgages?

Chapter Thirty-Seven

Mortgage-Backed Securities

Some of the government-related agency bonds are related to mortgages, such as those from the Government National Mortgage Association (GNMA) -- better known as "Ginnie Mae." That's a U.S. government agency within the Department of Housing and Urban Development.

These are "pass through" securities. Mortgages from people buying their homes are pooled, and you receive your share of the money they pay.

These are a huge percentage of the total bond market -- over $2 trillion dollars worth in 2001, before the beginning of the bubble in U.S. house prices.

GNMAs are primarily intended for institutional investors, since the minimum amount is $25,000. However, you as an individual investors may well see pitches for the closely-related Freddie Mac (Federal Home Loan Bank) or Fannie Mae (Federal National Mortgage Association), derivative products such as CMOs, or mortgage-backed securities mutual funds. Freddie Mac and Fannie Mae bonds were not explicitly backed by the full faith of the U.S. government until the government had to take them over in September 2008. It'd been widely believed for many years that in the event of a crisis most politicians would agree Fannie Mae and Freddie Mac were "too big to fail," and would therefore vote to use taxpayer money to support them. Therefore, they had an implicit credit rating of AAA.

Now that we're in the financial crisis, we've learned that the belief in an implicit guarantee was justified. U.S. taxpayers now have to bail them out.

GNMAs do have the unconditional backing of the U.S. government, and usually pay monthly checks. Plus they sport high current yields -- they pay higher interest rates than Treasuries. Sound interesting? If so, please read on!

If you are or have ever paid on a mortgage, you should know that each monthly payment, although the same amount of money, consisted partly of interest and partly of a steadily increasing amount of principal -- that is, you are slowly paying off the loan balance.

As the holder of a mortgage-backed security, you're on the receiving end of those payments. Each monthly check you receive consists of both interest and principal.

Mortgage-Backed Securities Have Two Main Risks

1. The home owners don't make their monthly mortgage payments.

This is credit risk. The books will tell you that the credit risk for first home mortgages is low. As I write, however, the world financial markets are threatened the large amount of subprime mortgage backed securities.

If a home owner falls too far behind in their monthly payments, the bank will foreclose on their home. Now, instead of receiving a portion of their monthly payments, you own a portion of an empty house.

Foreclosures are currently very high rates. And many more homeowners are behind in their payments.

2. The home owners pay off their mortgages.

Home owners refinance their loans to take advantage of lower interest rates. for various reasons, they sell their houses. They inherit money, win the lottery or listen to Dave Ramsey and pay their mortgages off.

When this happens, your principal is returned to you, and you get no more interest income from that loan.

The fate of each GNMA bond is unique – it reflects the behavior of the home owners represented by each particular bond.

Because you do get capital returned to you, these bonds are not strictly for income, and so I can't recommend them. Depending on mortgages is too volatile.

Even if all the home owners simply made their payments on time, each of your monthly checks contains both interest and principal. The principal should be reinvested per Principle 2, but how can you reinvest it when you receive it back in small chunks on a month by month basis?

Collateralized Mortgage Obligations (CMOs) from the Collateralized Mortgage Association are another form of bonds based on mortgages. They're also known as REMIC (Real Estate Mortgage Investment Conduit). Unless you're a full-time professional, stay clear of these.

They have been restructured so that you buy "tranches" of them. The lower tranches get paid off first.

Who do you think will get first choice of tranches? An institution spending $10 million dollars -- or you?

There are multiple variations of CMOs. We don't need to go into them.

You can also buy bonds backed by other forms of debt, such as credit cards. If mortgages, which are backed by a physical house which is needed by people to live in, are risky -- what about credit cards? If you have enough money to pay your mortgage or your Visa card, but not both, which one do you pick? Do you force your family to live in the street to make Visa happy?

These bonds do generate a fairly high yield, but actual receipt of interest payments is erratic. Interest goes down as homeowners make each monthly payment and owe slightly less on their mortgages. And when homeowners pay off their mortgages, you lose all the interest on that principal.

BOTTOM LINE:

If you want to have more income by investing in home mortgages -- pay off your own house loan.

The risk -- danger -- associated with these loans is very high. If you don't believe me, just look at the headlines from 2008.

This type of investment almost brought down financial markets around the world.

Enough said about them.

Next: the term of a bond is important.

Chapter Thirty-Eight

Short-Term, Intermediate-Term and Long-Term Bonds

Bonds are also classified based on the length of their life, from issuance to maturity.

This complicates the discussion of bonds, since all types of bonds can be short, intermediate and long term. So you can have short-term Treasuries, intermediate-term corporates and long-term municipal bonds, and the effects of their terms interact with the aspects of each type of bond.

Short-Term Bonds

Short-term bonds have a maturity of from one to three years. These are considered the least risky bonds, because there's so little time for something to go wrong.

Also, since interest rates generally don't change at lightning speed (though there have been exceptions), short term bonds are not as likely to go far up or down in value due to changes in prevailing interest rates during their lifetime. That's not a consideration to us, since we're after interest income, not capital gains. Plus, we recognize that we can't predict where interest rates are going.

Because they're the least risky type of bond, short-term bonds pay the lowest yields.

Therefore, short-term bonds are most suitable for people who are saving for a particular short-term need, not for retirement or even for current income.

For example, if you have a son or daughter starting college in two years, you might want to buy a bond that matures in two years with the money you've saved up to send them -- assuming you'll get a higher interest rate than if you simply put the funds into a money market account.

Intermediate-Term Bonds

These have a lifetime of from three to fifteen years.

In fifteen years, a bond issuer can meet cash-flow challenges, so these bonds have a higher credit risk.

Plus, in fifteen years, interest rates can go up and down a lot, so they're considered risky by the financial markets that buy and sell for capital gains.

Because they're riskier than short-term bonds, they pay a higher coupon rate.

Therefore, intermediate-term bonds are more suitable for people who want higher incomes from their bond portfolios.

Long-Term Bonds

These bonds have maturity dates from fifteen to thirty years out.

Because anything can and sometimes does go wrong in this amount of time, long-term bonds are the most risky.

So, does that mean that long-term bonds pay the highest yields?

Usually, that's true.

BOTTOM LINE:

1. Short-term bonds - not for us long-term income investors.

2. Intermediate-term bonds -- best for corporate and municipal bonds.

We want a higher yield than what's available through short-term bonds. We don't care about fluctuations in market rates of the bonds we already own, but we do care about credit risk. In time, even AAA rated companies and local governments can have cash flow problems.

3. Long-term bonds -- Treasury bonds

Why not take the extra yield, meager though it may be? We don't care about the interest rate risk. Treasuries have no credit risk.

If you have enough money, it's actually best to diversify Treasuries by their term, to reduce reinvestment risk. Buy some intermediate-term and some long-term Treasuries.

That way, we may capture higher yields in the future.

Next: bonds that keep up with inflation.

Chapter Thirty-Nine

Treasury Inflation Protection Securities (TIPS) and I Bonds

One of the accomplishments of the Clinton administration was the issuance, starting in 1997, of TIPS. These are government-issued bonds that are deliberately designed to protect you from inflation.

When they're issued they have a normal par value of $1000, with a low market rate of interest. Every year until maturity, the principal is increased by the amount of annual inflation - the Consumer Price Index for Urban Workers (CPI-U).

Thus, if inflation is 3.5% in its first year, after that year the principal amount of a $1000 face value TIP bond becomes $1035, and your interest payment is the rate times $1035 instead of $1000.

The interest payments are made every six months.

You Do Pay for This Inflation-Fighting Guarantee With a Small Yield

One disadvantage to these bonds is that their interest rate is fairly low, to pay for this inflation protection. Thus, if inflation remains low during the lifetime of the bond, you'd have done better to buy another type of bond.

An ever bigger disadvantage is that you must pay federal income taxes on the interest and the inflation adjusted amount - even though you don't actually receive the cash for them until the bond matures, which could be 20 years from now.

Therefore, in the example above, you would have to report that $35 increase in your bond's face value on your tax return, and pay taxes on it as well as on the interest you received.

But notice that $35 is not in your pocket - you won't actually receive it for another 19 years.

It may seem unfair to pay taxes on money you won't receive for up to 19 years, but that one of the prices you pay for inflation protection.

Investors Not Yet Retired Should Holds TIPS Only in Tax-Deferred Retirement Accounts

Therefore, if you are still saving for retirement, you should hold TIPS only in tax-deferred accounts such as IRAs. If you're already retired and need the interest payments to live on, there is a way to own TIPS outside a tax-deferred account without paying taxes on the phantom income. I'll cover that when I give specific investment suggestions.

In the (unlikely) event that inflation actually goes down during the period you own TIPS, you'll receive the full par value at maturity. You are not penalized by deflation.

TIPS are issued with a $1000 par value. Their interest payments are excluded from state and local taxes.

Other entities are getting into the inflation-protection bond business, but be careful. One of them is Freddie Mac (mortgages) and another is the Goldman Sachs Group, which in September 2008 had to go from being an investment bank to a bank holding company. Sallie Mae (student loans) is another government-related agency that issues some adjustable rate bond issues.

Outside the U.S. - You can buy U.S. TIPS the same as Treasury bonds, using the same website (http://www.treasurydirect.gov/) and telephone number: 1-304-480-7955. But unless you can buy them for a tax-deferred account, better check your local tax laws. You don't want to pay taxes now on income you won't receive for many years.

Also, check with your own government. They may have your own equivalent of TIPS.

TIPS switch the weaknesses and strengths of other bonds.

They offer inflation protection, but at the cost of reducing the amount of income they pay out.

I Bonds

To help people save for retirement despite inflation, the U.S. government also sells I-series savings bonds.

I Bonds come in denominations of from $50 to $10,000, but you're limited to buying no more than $30,000 per year.

They have a fixed coupon rate that's set when they're issued, plus every 6 months the government adds to this based on the rate of inflation.

If the cost of living actually goes down, the value of the I Bond remains at its pre-deflation level.

Their maturity is set for 30 years, though you can cash them in any time after six months (but you pay a penalty of three months' interest if you cash them out before five years). They don't trade in the secondary market.

They have one big advantage over TIPS -- you don't realize the interest income until you cash them in. Therefore, you don't owe any taxes until then. They're exempt from state and local taxes.

BOTTOM LINE:

TIPS are a vital part of every income investor's portfolio, since they give you a guaranteed real rate of return -- that, they fight inflation.

I Bonds are almost perfect income investments -- except that they don't actually pay income! They are therefore not suitable for investors who need current income. They are good for people who are still saving for retirement.

Next: a high-yield investment.

Chapter Forty

Preferred Stocks

The various categories of preferred stocks can get complicated.

First of all, I am distinguishing between "true" preferred stocks (you could perhaps call them "old school" or "classical" preferred) and the newer, "trust" preferreds.

True Preferred Stocks

Technically, true preferred stocks are a kind of stock -- that is, they represent equity in the company that issued them.

In practice, they are more like a kind of bond, though one the company often never has to pay off -- unless it wants to . . . when it's good for the company to do so, which means when it's a bad deal for you.

Say a company needs to raise some cash, but they don't want to upset current common stock shareholders by issuing more shares of common stock. Issuing more shares of common stock dilutes the value of those shares already outstanding. That's because the company's total value isn't any higher just because it issues more shares of stock. When additional shares are issued, each outstanding share becomes a smaller percentage of that total value.

The other common alternative is to sell bonds. However, bonds are straight out debt, and maybe the company already has too much debt. Issuing more debt may make its balance sheet look bad, and that could lower its overall credit rating.

It's similar to your personal finances. If your mortgage payment plus car payment plus minimum credit card payments plus student loan payments and so on add up to a high percentage of your income and net worth, you'll have a lower credit score than somebody who doesn't owe so much money in proportion to their income and resources.

So what can this company do to raise a lot of money? They can issue preferred stock.

Preferred Stock is a Debt That Need Never Be Paid Off

Since preferred stock is not common stock, it usually does not come with voting rights (not that voting at annual meetings is of much value to us small investors) and its value does not rise and fall as common stock shares do. It is technically equity, but does not dilute the equity of common stock shares. Preferred stock owners do not share in the growth of the company.

Since preferred stock is not a bond, it does not added to the overall debt of the company -- technically.

In practice, preferred stock is a form of junior debt that the company never has to pay back.

The dividends on preferred stock must be paid before any dividends are sent out to common stock holders.

The company issues so many shares of the preferred stock (1 to 2 million shares). Usually, the face (par) value of each share is $50 or $100. As with bonds, the company is obligated to pay the fixed amount of dividends on each share. Unlike bonds, there is no maturity date, so these shares don't have to be paid back. That's the feature that makes preferred stock legally equity instead of debt -- the company doesn't have to ever pay the money back to you, though it is of course supposed to pay you the dividends on it.

If business is tough, it can decide not to pay scheduled dividends on preferred stock, but this is a huge red flag to both creditors and investors signaling serious financial difficulties, so it's not something a company does on a whim.

If a company does have poor cash flow one year and can't pay dividends to preferred share holders, the obligation accumulates from year to year. When business picks up, it has to repay preferred share owners all the past dividends due.

Preferred Stock is High Income for Now

Basically, you're paying for an ongoing stream of income (often "perpetual") that's fixed at that percentage rate. The money paid to you is called dividends, but in practice it's more like interest, since it's fixed at the set rate. Unlike dividends on common stock, it never grows.

However, dividends on true preferred stock do qualify for the 15% tax rates (as long as the 2003 Bush tax cuts remain in effect) -- unlike bond interest.

Most preferred stock issued these days is callable, usually any time after 5 years. That means that if overall prevailing interest rates go substantially lower, the company can buy back your shares of preferred stock. If it still needs the cash, it can then issue new shares of preferred stock at a lower interest rate.

Obviously, this costs you the income that's earning a higher than prevailing interest rate, but saves the company money. Owning preferred stock means that you face reinvestment risk more than 5 years after their issue date.

If the company goes out of business, preferred stock holders have a lower claim to company assets than bond owners, but a higher claim than common stockholders. Let's hope that is never important to you -- invest in companies that aren't at risk of bankruptcy.

For all practical purposes, if you own investments in a company that's liquidated, you can kiss your money goodbye whether it's in bonds (you might get pennies on the dollar a few years later), preferred stock or common stock.

The market prices of preferred stocks vary with prevailing interest rates and the credit rating of the issuing company. In effect, as an investment, preferred stocks are much the same as bonds.

And you buy preferred stock pretty much for the same reason as bonds -- because the current yields are much higher than you can get from stock dividends.

You Can't Profit Much From Preferred Stock, Because They're Called Away From You Just When They're Worth More Money

However, the market price of preferred stock shares usually doesn't go much over the par value, even if interest rates fall a lot, because of the call risk (especially when they're five or more years old).

In the United States, true preferred stock is usually issued only by financial institutions, REITs and utilities, for regulatory reasons. That's because paying dividends is not a tax deductible expense for other companies. They prefer to pay interest on bonds, if possible, for the tax deduction.

Up until 1993, few individuals bought preferred stock because yields weren't high enough to justify the transaction costs. The main market consisted of corporations, because the law exempts them from paying taxes on 70% of the dividends they receive. We mere people don't get that break.

(If you own a C corporation, check with your advisors about buying true preferred stock through your corporation. It must be a C corporation, though -- not an S corporation.)

Also, as with bonds, many companies have many different issues of preferred stock, perhaps dating back many years. They differ only by date of issue and interest rate of dividends paid.

Given enough time, almost anything can go wrong. That's why the long terms of preferred stock (forever, 30 to 50 years, or until you really want to keep the preferred stock shares) is itself a risk. Good companies today can eventually become failing companies.

"Trust" Preferreds

In 1993, U.S. companies became able to issue preferred stock through a specially set up trust that issues them as bonds.

This is an accounting technique for issuing preferred stock as debt instruments. These trust preferreds are technically debt instruments, so the payments can be deducted by the companies as interest, but otherwise have the characteristics of preferred stocks.

But since the dividends from trust preferred are tax deductible by the issuing companies, they're countable to you as ordinary income, not qualified dividends under the 2003 tax law -- which the Democratic politicians want to allow to get rid of anyway.

Interestingly, although dividends on trust preferreds is counted as a form of tax-deductible interest expense on the company's tax return, the shares of trust preferreds are still considered a form of equity on the company's balance sheet.

The Best of Both Worlds -- For the Company

Thus, with trust preferreds the company gets the best of both worlds -- the tax-deductible expense advantage of bond interest, along with the looking good to investors and credit ratings advantage of being equity on their balance sheet.

Trust preferreds are usually issued with a par value of $25. Dividends are usually paid quarterly.

Because the market pricing of preferred stock is complicated by interest rates, credit ratings and so on, I advise you not to buy outstanding shares in the secondary market. Many of the issues are not very liquid. That is, they don't trade very much. Everybody who wants them (mostly other corporations) already owns them. Most issues are too small for the large institutions.

That means to buy them now, you'd have to pay a high bid/ask spread.

However, preferred stocks do trade on established stock exchanges, so although they're relatively expensive, because of the lack of liquidity, it's still a lot easier and cheaper to buy individual shares of preferred stock than individual corporate bonds.

The best strategy for individual investors is to buy newly issued shares of preferred stock. You'll pay the $25 par value for round lots of 100 shares, plus a commission to your discount broker.

There are mutual funds of preferred stocks, but just as with bonds, their performance is diminished by managers attempting to time the market and predict interest rates.

Unfortunately, there is no index of preferred stocks, so there's no simple and easy way to buy a broad range of them. There are closed-end funds that hold preferred stocks, but they are actively managed, use leverage to boost yields (it works when it works, but when it doesn't work, you lose more money), and also invest in other types of securities.

Convertible Preferred Stock

All of the above describes straight preferred stock. Some preferred stock is called convertible, because under certain conditions it can be exchanged for a certain number of the company's common stock.

Since convertible preferred stock can become common stock, figuring out the fair price for these securities is highly complicated. Their market prices are affected not only by interest rates, but by the market price of the common stock shares.

Since convertible preferred stock contains this additional benefit, its price tends to be higher than straight preferred, and therefore its yield is lower.

But what you're paying for is the opportunity to buy common stock and see its market price go up.

In other words, with convertible preferred stock you pay extra for the chance you'll get some capital gains, in addition to some current income.

You can't compete in the convertible securities marketplace against full-time experts, often employed by institutions. You are guaranteed to overpay for preferred convertible stock.

I say -- go for income. Buy straight preferred stock.

Weaknesses:

1. No inflation protection.

Because preferred stock yields remain constant, their purchasing power steadily declines.

If prevailing interest rates in the economy actually go down, the company will probably call your preferred stock issue.

Strengths:

1. Income.

Preferred stocks dividends are usually higher than bond yields.

BOTTOM LINE:

Preferred stock is good for current income. But it has too many disadvantages to make it more than 5% of your portfolio. For all practical purposes they're bonds that may never be repaid.

Next: Fixed annuities explained.

Chapter Forty-One

Fixed Annuities

"Because undue longevity is a risk, not a certainty, it is an event that should be insured against rather than saved for."

-- Jeffrey K. Dellinger THE HANDBOOK OF VARIABLE INCOME ANNUITIES

An annuity is a contract for a life insurance company to send you monthly payments for either a fixed length of time (such as 20 years) or for the remainder of your life.

A "fixed" annuity means that the monthly payment amount remains the same -- although, thanks to clever marketing, there are annuity products that do go up in set amounts.

You start out by paying the annuity company a lump sum amount of money. Or, you can send them money over time, using them as a form of savings account.

The annuity company (often a life insurance company) pools that lump sum payment with the money it's gotten from other annuitants, and invests that money on your behalf.

Deferred Annuities -- You Choose Not to Receive Any Checks Yet

If you choose to wait until you start getting that stream of monthly payments, you've got a deferred fixed annuity. In effect, it is like putting money into a savings account.

If you want money right away, the annuity company sends you a check every month. That's an immediate fixed annuity.

This is not a bad deal, especially for people who have saved up small amounts of money, or people who have received large lump sums (for example, from inheritances, insurance settlements or even lotteries) but who don't want to manage the money themselves. Maybe they lack the knowledge, the capability, the discipline, or just don't want to make the effort.

When you tell the annuity company how much money you want to annuitize (that is, turn into a fixed monthly payment for life), the annuity company:

1. Makes a statistical calculation of how much longer you're expected to live, based on your current age and other factors. (This is why life insurance companies sell annuities -- they already have a tremendous amount of statistical actuarial data on life expectancies.)

2. Estimates how much they can expect to make by investing that money in fixed income investments such as bonds. (They don't speculate with it.)

3. Performs a financial calculation of how much income that your lump sum will make on a monthly basis over the course of the number of additional years you are expected to live.

4. Subtracts some money to pay their expenses and to make a profit.

5. Agrees to pay you that monthly amount of money, for the rest of your life. That's your minimum guarantee.

For couples, the company can make a joint estimate of your combined life expectancies, and make payments to both of you until one of you dies, then pay the survivor until they die.

As mentioned, you can also do this same process for a set period of time, such as 10 or 20 years. In that case, the company's calculations are easy because they don't have to come up with an estimate of when (on average) you're likely to die.

If you do die before the set period of time is up, the company will continue to make the monthly payment to whomever you've designated as your beneficiary.

However, I'm not sure why people do that, unless they're sure they're going to die before the set period is over, but want to make certain that their designated beneficiary receives some income after that.

Advantages of Fixed Annuities

You're guaranteed the agreed-upon monthly income for the rest of your life.

The monthly amount is relatively high because:

1. The insurance company can invest in fixed income securities with greater sophistication and cost-effectiveness (due to their size) than you can on your own.

2. Because your money is pooled with other people's money, the life insurance company can afford to pay you what it'll take to spend all your money based on your average life expectancy age.

See, if you retained control of that money, you couldn't spend as much per month, because you'd have to assume you are going to live to be 100+. If you mishandle your money and investments, it's possible to outlive your savings and therefore depend solely on your pension (if any) and Social Security.

But the life insurance company may have 100,000 annuitants. Because of their statistical actuarial tables, they know that of the people now aged 65, how many are going to die within one year, and how many are still going to be going strong at 105.

Of course, they don't know precisely which individual is going to die while snorkeling in the Bahamas one week after they write a check for their lifetime annuity or which particular individual is still going to be playing golf at 105. It doesn't matter to the life insurance company. They know, on average, how many people are going to die before their life expectancy, and how many will people will not die until after their life expectancy.

The life insurance/annuity company can therefore pay everybody based on that average life expectancy.

There're Two Ways to Lose With Fixed Annuities:

1. Die before your life expectancy age.

2. Die after your life expectancy age.

If you're one of the one-half of your age group who dies before the average age, you'll get less money than the average. Therefore, if you have a terminal illness or other severe poor health, fixed annuities are not for you.

If you're one of the one-half of your age group who dies after your average age, then you receive more money than the average.

However, you're then faced with the risk of inflation reducing the purchasing power of your fixed monthly payment.

The monthly amount that helps you live comfortably right now may not be enough to scrape by on 30 years from now.

Whom Fixed Annuities Are Best For

That's why I said that fixed annuities are especially good for people with small lump sums and large lump sums.

If you have a small lump sum, turning it into a fixed annuity can guarantee you some return on that money for the rest of your life. It may not buy very much, especially forty years from now if you live that long, but it'll still be something over and above Social Security. And if you tried to manage it yourself, you'd either spend it all or receive only a very small income from it.

If you have a large lump sum, turning it into a fixed annuity can provide you with a large monthly income that will still buy a lot even after 40 years of inflation have eroded the purchasing power of that income.

It is possible to buy fixed annuities that go up a particular percentage every year. Understand this, however -- you're paying for this through a lower initial payment. The annuity companies don't give out any free benefits.

Now, understand that when annuity companies speak of income that's "guaranteed" for life, that guarantee comes from them -- it's not backed by the government, Fate, the Stars or God. That guarantee is only as good as the financial condition of the life insurance company making the fixed annuity contract with you.

Therefore, you should check out the credit ratings of the companies you are considering. Use:

1. AM Best -- http://www.ambest.com/ratings/guide.asp

2. Weiss -- http://www.weissratings.com/products_lh.asp

Also, keep in mind that once you turn over that lump sum money, you don't own it anymore. Whether you collect your annuity for one year or forty, that money is gone. Therefore, you can't leave that money to your heirs.

The portion of your monthly payments that consists of interest from investments is taxable as ordinary income. The portion of your monthly payments that is considered a return of principle (the money you originally paid to the annuity company) is not taxable.

Weaknesses:

1. No inflation protection.

Your income is "fixed" -- so its purchasing power will decline as the cost of living rises.

Strengths:

1. You can receive a monthly income that's higher than you could obtain by yourself.

BOTTOM LINE:

Fixed annuities are good for people with small savings, to get some benefit from those savings throughout their lifetimes. Because otherwise they'd be likely to spend all their money before they die.

They're also good for people with lots of money, who can convert it into a spendable income that's large enough (because they're starting with such a high amount) to enable them to live comfortably for the rest of their life -- without having to manage their overall portfolio, and who don't want to leave an inheritance.

But since you do lose control and access to your money, you should not annuitize all your savings. Keep some cash on hand for unexpected needs.

Besides, someone has come up with a solution to the inflation problem faced by fixed annuities. What if your annuity could be invested so that its value went up along with inflation?

Next: What if you could get the guaranteed for life income of a fixed annuity combined with the inflation protection offered by investing in stocks and other investments?

Chapter Forty-Two

Variable Annuities

Variable annuities are, without a doubt, the most misunderstood and misinterpreted investment vehicles widely bought by investors. They have aspects that make them different and more complicated than other forms of investments, and can come with or without a wide variety of features that can make buying one a chore -- because you must choose among a bewildering array of options.

My own introduction to variable annuities was through my mother. She'd had a lot of stock in a company that got bought out by another one. She'd told me that her broker had put the money she got from the sale of the stock into some "funds." I assumed they were regular mutual funds. They had names unfamiliar to me, but with over 8000 mutual funds on the market, that didn't surprise me.

When I first looked at one of her fund statements, I was surprised to see that it listed about 30 different mutual fund names. It seemed to be a "fund of funds."

Turns out it was something I'd heard of, but knew nothing about -- a variable annuity.

Every year, Americans put lots of money into variable annuities (According to THE WALL STREET JOURNAL, by the end of 1997, annuity contracts had $1.2 trillion - yes, trillion with T -- invested in them. In 1998, another $100 billion was deposited into them) -- yet the financial press usually ignores or smears them.

Most Financial Writers Hate Variable Annuities

One (otherwise) great financial writer, Burton Malkiel, in A RANDOM WALK DOWN WALL STREET looks down his nose and sniffs, they're mutual funds in a life insurance wrapper. That's not an exact quote but it's close enough. He doesn't bother to explain what he thinks is wrong with mutual funds in a life insurance wrapper.

Unlike stocks, mutual funds and even bonds, there are few books available on variable annuities. Many investing books don't even mention them.

Here are the 3 best books currently available on variable annuities:

GUARANTEED INCOME FOR LIFE: How Variable Annuities Can Cut Your Taxes, Pay You Every Year of Your Life, and Bring You Financial Peace of Mind by Michael F. Lane is the best book for us ordinary investors, yet that one still left me unsatisfied.

THE HANDBOOK OF VARIABLE ANNUITIES by Jeffery K. Dellinger costs about $100 and is aimed at financial professionals. You can get useful information out of it, if you read around the many pages of complicated equations. If you want to understand the actual numbers, you'll need a doctorate in Math combined with specialized knowledge of actuarial symbols.

INVESTING WITH VARIABLE ANNUITIES by John P. Huggard also costs about $100, but it doesn't include 300 pages of complex math. It's aimed at brokers/dealers, but can help you sort out what variable annuities can do for you. He compares them to investing with load mutual funds, and makes many excellent points.

Unfortunately, all of the above are also somewhat behind the times -- they don't cover the latest annuity options and benefits.

Therefore, I decided to explain variable annuities to you in a way that you can understand -- and, most importantly, use to decide whether or not they are useful investments for you.

Frankly, they're usually sold to people who shouldn't be buying them.

The Origin and a Brief History of Variable Annuities

In the section on fixed (or "straight") annuities, you learned that you can let an insurance company pool your money with money from many other people, and pay all of you a fixed monthly amount until you die, based on your actuarial life expectancy and the return the life insurance company can achieve from investing your money.

Fixed annuities are good for allowing people to have a "guaranteed income" for life -- but they do not keep up with inflation.

In 1952, someone at the College Retirement Equities Fund (CREF) got the idea of allowing annuity customers to invest in the stock market with their money, so it would grow along with or perhaps even more than inflation. Since the annuity's returns would vary along with the market's ups and downs, these were called variable annuities.

In the 1970s, the "investment annuity" started. This allowed customers to buy and sell stocks and bonds inside the annuity on a tax-deferred basis.

In those days, you could pick and choose your own stocks and bonds. Unfortunately, the government realized that it was losing a lot of taxes on capital gains taxes, so it changed the law. Now, the money you place into an annuity must be controlled by a third party, such as a professional money manager.

The Money Inside Your Variable Annuity Account is Segregated From the Company's Money, So You Can Get It Back Even If They File Bankruptcy

This money used to go into one "subaccount," where it was managed by a professional money manager. It was named "subaccount" because your annuity contract in its entirety is an account within the annuity company, and so your money under their management is under the overall company account.

Having your annuity contract set up as a separate account may seem like semantics, but it provides a measure of protect for you in case the life insurance company that issued your annuity goes into bankruptcy.

By law, it's supposed to keep enough reserve money in your account to cover its obligations to you. This money is kept separate from the annuity company's own cash money.

By law, you have first claim on all the funds in your account, even though the company itself owes more money than it can pay. You have the right to your money. Legal proceedings might freeze it for a time, so you should still choose a company with a high credit rating, but eventually you should get your money back even if the company gets into big financial trouble.

(By the way, this is NOT true of fixed annuities. The money paid to you every month comes out of the company's general account. If you have a fixed annuity with an annuity/life insurance company that goes into bankruptcy, you're just one more creditor listed in the bankruptcy proceedings. If you're lucky, in five to ten years you might get 10 cents on the dollar.)

Subaccounts

About 1980, annuity companies began spreading out the financial oversight for variable annuity funds to different managers, including those already managing mutual funds. So now most annuities offer a wide variety of subaccounts which are essentially licensed to the annuity company versions of name-brand mutual funds.

Unfortunately, this means that these subaccounts also have most of the problems associated with open-ended, mutual funds.

People Use the Term "Variable Annuity" to Mean Different Stages of the Contract, Which Partly Explains the Confusion Associated With Them

What makes them more confusing, is that people use the term "variable annuities" to write about them at various stages of the contract.

So let's break down the basics, so you can understand them, one at a time.

Saving Money for Your Future Retirement

1. You put money into the variable annuity contract, but don't withdraw any money.

This is often referred to as the "accumulation phase." It normally applies to everybody taking out variable annuity contracts before age 59 1/2 (that's the government's set age for when you can start to withdraw money from a tax-deferred retirement fund without penalty.) -- and after, because you may be a late starter.

So here we're talking about people who are still working. They're in their 20s,

30s, 40s, 50s or 60s. They still get a paycheck or have their own business. They want to save money for their future retirement.

They have chosen to use a variable annuity contract as one way to save money for their retirement.

OK? Read that over again -- in the accumulation phase, variable annuity contracts are a way to save money for retirement. You put money in. You don't take any money out. You're not retired yet -- you're still working and earning.

We'll talk about why you might want to do this, and what's involved, later on.

Taking Money Out, and Maybe Putting Some In

2. You take money out of the variable annuity contract. You might also put more money into it.

This "withdrawal phase" can begin at age 59 1/2 (again, this age was set by the government -- if you withdraw any money before age 59 1/2 you must pay a 10% penalty on your profits, same as with an IRA) or at any later date you choose.

You've already put money into the annuity contract. Maybe you've been accumulating money in it for many years. Now you want to take some out.

But that doesn't mean you can't also put some in.

Maybe you're retired and you withdraw $1000 a month from your annuity to pay your monthly expenses. One day you win the lottery. You can put that money into the annuity, and keep withdrawing money every month or whenever you choose.

My mother didn't even buy a variable annuity contract until she was past the usual retirement age. It's the investment vehicle her broker put her in after a company takeover forced her to sell much of her stock.

She takes money out. And sometimes, when she has it, she puts money back in.

Begin Receiving Monthly Checks for Life

3. You give up ownership of the money you have in the variable annuity contract, in exchange for a stream of monthly checks for a set period. Usually that set period is for the remainder of your life, or for both of you if you're a married couple. However, just as with fixed annuities, you can choose to make it 10 or 20 years or other precise figure, though I don't know why you'd want to. (That's like betting you're going to die before that period is over.)

This process is called "annuitization."

You're allowing the annuity company to take all the money you have in the contract, and then figure out how much you should get a month until you die -- using their actuarial tables to figure out your average life expectancy.

This annuitization is much the same as for fixed annuities.

There is one key difference which makes "variable" annuities VARIABLE -- that is, the monthly checks are NOT the same. They can and do go up and down based on how your money is invested.

Variable Annuities Invest Your Money In Subaccounts That You Choose, so Your Income Is Not Fixed and Therefore Your Purchasing Power is Not Automatically Eroded Away by Inflation

When you pay money to an annuity company for a fixed annuity, the company invests it in fixed-income investments that the company believes will earn enough money to allow it to pay you the monthly check, plus make a profit for the company. They use sophisticated asset liability management techniques, financial models and software to control the risk.

In exchange for that fixed monthly check, you have given up all control over your money.

In an economically perfect world, this would be enough to guarantee you financial comfort for life.

Alas, this is not a perfect world in any way -- certainly not economically. Since the end of World War 2, modern economies have had to deal with inflation.

That is the great disadvantage of fixed annuities. A fixed income is good only for a few years. Eventually, its spending power goes downhill. Instead of steak and champagne, a few years later your annuity check buys you only hamburger and beer.

Wouldn't it be great to have an annuity that gives you a guaranteed income for life -- but one which keeps pace with inflation?

That's the promise of variable annuities.

Every variable annuity company gives you the opportunity to place your money into many different types of investments. Not just conventional fixed income investments such as bonds, but stocks and more.

The idea is that by having your money in different types of investments, these investments will grow in market value, allowing the annuity company to periodically raise your monthly checks.

These different types of investments are put into "subaccounts." In the subaccounts I've seen listed in my mother's funds, they all had the names of mutual funds, most of them well-known.

If you have your money in various stock mutual fund subaccounts, and the stock market goes up, so does your money inside the variable annuity contract.

Of course, if the stock market goes down, so does your income.

Variable annuity contracts ARE called "variable" for a reason.

All right, let me explain how variable annuities work, and why you might one to invest in one, by going back to the phases.

1. The Accumulation Phase

In this phase, the still-working investor is putting funds into the contract, but not taking anything out.

Why invest money into a variable annuity when you can't take it out?

Because the money earned in variable annuities is tax-deferred.

Yes, variable annuities are a tax-deferred way to save money for your retirement, much like a Roth IRA.

That is, unlike conventional IRAs where taxes on the money you place into the IRA are tax-deferred, with a Roth IRA you pay taxes on your contributions, but as that money earns more money inside the Roth IRA, those dividends and interest all tax-deferred. When you withdraw the money, you don't have to pay any taxes.

So you must pay taxes on the money you place into a variable annuity contract, but the money it earns inside the variable annuity contract is tax-deferred. You do have to pay taxes when you eventually withdraw the interest and dividends, but for years they've been growing and compounding without taxes. (But not on your initial contributions, which you've already paid taxes on.)

If you read the conventional financial magazines and books, you know that for 30 years they've been beating the drum to encourage Americans to use these tax-deferred accounts to the max.

Put that $2000 into your IRA!

Take the maximum allotment your 401(k) plan allows!

Variable Annuity Contracts Allow You to Shelter Earnings On Income Without the Contribution Limits Imposed on Tax-Deferred Accounts

IRAs have strict limits. It used to be $2000. In 2007 it was $4,000 for people under 50 years old, $5000 for people over 50. In 2008 it went up to $5000 for people under 50, $6000 for people over 50.

Roth IRAs have the same limits, but are closed to individuals who make over $110,000 per year -- and your eligibility begins to be closed out at $95,000 (Adjusted Gross Income). For couples, eligibility for Roth IRAs begins to be closed out at $150,000, and couples making over $160,000 may not contribute to a Roth IRA.

401(k) plans allow you to invest up to $15,500 (people over age 50 can make a $5000 "catch up" contribution). The 401)k) maximum amount will go up to $16,000 in 2008. That's much more generous than IRAs, but is still not a lot of money for people who want to make sure they enjoy a prosperous retirement.

Yet how many of you have ever read the same advice regarding variable annuities?

Me neither.

Isn't that odd? The mainstream financial writers place such great importance on $2k-5K IRAs and the 401(k) tax deferral opportunities -- and they're right to encourage us to contribute the max to these accounts -- but don't tell you about the tax deferral opportunity you have with variable annuities.

What do you think is the limit the government places on tax-deferred contributions to variable annuities? $5000 as with IRAs? $15,500 as with 401(k) plans?

There's NO LIMIT!

A variable annuity contract is a NO LIMIT way to defer paying taxes on the income generated by your retirement investments.

With variable annuity contracts, you not only can put in unlimited amounts of money, you have it compound inside the contract on a tax-deferred basis.

Let's say you're a plant manager or head accountant or whatever -- you have a good job. Your spouse has a good job. Together you make $165,000 or more. You live well, and you want to live well in retirement. You are contributing the max to your 401(k) plan. You each contribute the max to an IRA.

But you still have more money you want to save for retirement. You make too much money to contribute to a Roth IRA. What do you do?

Variable annuities are especially good for you -- the affluent investor who's already maxed out your other tax-deferred contributions, yet still has more money you'd like to save for retirement.

Once you have maxed out your available tax-deferred accounts, you have only two options:

1. Invest money outside of tax-deferred accounts

2. Take out a variable annuity contract and add funds to it as you can.

If you choose Number 1 (as most people do), you can make money (especially if you follow the advice in the rest of this book), but you'll still have to pay taxes on the earnings.

If you put money into actively managed open-ended mutual funds (as most people do), you will have to pay taxes on capital gains (even if the fund later on loses money) and income distributions, even if you reinvest them.

If you put money into individual investments such as stocks and exchange traded funds, you'll have to pay taxes on the dividend income you receive. If you are foolish enough to buy and sell them, you'll have to pay taxes on the capital gains you realize.

If you choose Number 2, you can place your money into various stock and bond subaccounts. All capital gains and income that these subaccounts make stays inside the annuity contract -- tax deferred.

All the benefits of tax-deferred compounding that the mainstream financial writers have beaten into your head for the past 35 years -- you get with variable annuities.

It's true you don't get a tax deduction for the money you put into the variable annuity, but that's also true for Roth IRAs.

And it's also true that unlike Roth IRAs, when you withdraw variable annuity earnings you'll have to pay taxes on them at your ordinary tax rate -- but because they've been compounding an a tax-deferred basis for years, you'll have more earnings than you would if you'd put your initial contributions into taxable accounts, and more money leftover after paying taxes.

That's the goal -- to have the most money left after paying taxes.

Variable Annuities Are For Long-Term Investing, For Your Retirement

Be very clear on this point, however -- this phase is only for long term investing.

The first reason that many financial writers don't like variable annuities is that a large majority of of them are sold to customers by brokers -- and the commissions are a high 5-7%.

Brokers respond to this by saying that they deserve higher commissions on sales of variable annuities, because they require a lot more time and effort, to explain variable annuities to the people who would most benefit from them.

After researching variable annuities and struggling to understand them until I thought my head would explode, I can sympathize with this argument.

However, it's also true that I believe that broker commissions are largely unnecessary.

I'd much rather that you educate yourself (by reading this book), then -- if you think variable annuities are right for you -- check out some companies and find one that's reasonably priced. Shop around.

Variable Annuity Expenses

Subaccount management fees can run as high as 2.5%, even though these subaccounts don't have as many expenses as ordinary mutual funds. (That is, they don't send out monthly statements. They don't maintain a staff to answer a 24 hour 800 number customer service line. And so on. They do have many of the same record keeping and transaction expenses.)

As you may recall, according to Morningstar, the average retail mutual fund charges an annual expense of 1.33%. Also, you should recall, retail mutual funds have other operational expenses, especially trading expenses, that are NOT disclosed in the prospectus. According to a study by Wake Forest University, the University of Florida and the Zero Alpha Group, these expenses average an additional 1.25% per year.

Thus, retail mutual funds cost you an average of 2.38% -- and variable annuity subaccounts are clones of these funds.

However, you can find variable annuities where the subaccounts pass on their expense savings and charge less for subaccounts than for the equivalent public mutual fund.

Variable annuities also have an expense that's unique to them called M & E - Mortality and Expenses, which is often about 1.25%, but can be less or more. Since there are also administrative fees, these are often grouped together as M & E & A. (The Administrative fees may be around 0.15% per year in addition to the 1.25% M & E.)

If the contract doesn't charge you that 0.15%, there's probably an annual account fee of about $25-$35. (May be waived for contracts over a certain amount, such as $100,000)

The M & E charge is in effect the premium of the life insurance aspect of the variable annuities. This is what tends to make it confusing, plus it attracts criticism.

Your variable annuity contract is insured for the amount the money you put into it. If you died at this point, your beneficiary would receive the market value of the contract, or what you originally put in -- whichever is greater.

How a Traditional Basic Variable Annuity Contract Death Benefit Works

Let's say that you have put $100,000 into your variable annuity over the years, then one day you die.

1. If the market value of the contract has fallen to $70,000 (say, because of a stock market crash) -- your beneficiary would still receive $100,000.

2. If the market value of the contract has risen to $130,000 -- your beneficiary would receive $130,000.

If your money was in any other kind of account, your beneficiary would receive the market value -- no more and no less.

This is a form of life insurance, and it's part of what makes variable annuities more expensive than other types of investments.

I've seen this benefit criticized because it's highly unlikely that it'll ever be used.

I have two responses to that:

1. Stock markets crash.

We learned that lesson in 1929, 1973-1974, 1987, 2000-2002 and 2008. Or did we? Some financial writers still assume that when you put money into the market today that it's inevitable the market price will be higher tomorrow.

Often true, but not always.

I've stressed throughout this book investing for income, not capital gains, partly for this reason. And that's what I continue to tell you to invest for while you're alive. But if you die, the market price of your investments will be important to your heirs. (So you should also leave behind a copy of this book, so they'll benefit from investing for income.)

2. Death happens.

Maybe the odds are good you won't die for many years, but none of us knows for sure whether we'll be here tomorrow. If you're the unlucky one who dies during a bear market, do you want your spouse and children shortchanged?

The variable annuity company's M & E and other fees do add a layer of fees onto the management fees you pay to the mutual fund companies for your subaccounts. However, these fees allow you to accumulate investment earnings on a tax-sheltered basis.

Also, some variable annuities offer more complicated plans. You can find contracts that will insure your account for the greatest market value it's ever held.

Another Possible Type of Death Benefit

Let's say you put $100,000 in such a contract in 1998 and by early 2000 it was worth $180,000. But by 2002 it had crashed to $50,000 -- and that's when you died. If you had this provision (insured at the highest market value ever reached), your beneficiaries would receive $180,000.

Your Heirs Will Owe Your Unpaid Taxes on the Profits They Receive

Anti-variable annuity financial advisors will tell you that you are hurting your heirs by putting money into a variable annuity. That's because when you die, they must pay ordinary taxes on the money they withdraw from the annuity -- just as you would if you were withdrawing it while still alive. Plus, they must pay estate taxes on what's left.

The ups and downs on this depend on a lot of variables, but for most investors, it's not critical. That's because the money you put into a variable annuity grows tax-deferred while it's in there -- so at your death, your heirs will pay taxes on far more money than if you'd placed it in mutual funds and had to pay capital gains taxes every year.

Plus, if you die during a bear market, your heirs will receive a lot more cash than if you'd put your money into stocks or mutual funds.

Nobody Knows What Estate Taxes -- Or the Mutual Funds "Step Up" Basis Provision of the Law -- Are Going to Be After 2010

Federal law regarding estate taxes is up the air. As I write, they're scheduled to be eliminated in 2010 -- but reinstated in 2011. The current U.S. political climate seems to favor Democrats, but as millions of baby boomers become concerned about their retirement and how much money they'll be able to leave to their heirs, political pressure may force the politicians to stop taxing the dead.

Plus, a few years ago, Congress began eroding the "step up" basis in stocks and mutual funds. That is what allows heirs who inherit mutual funds to use their value at death as their cost basis. This is what saves them from paying the taxes heirs of annuities must pay.

Now, this step up is limited to $1.3 million. That may seem like a lot to you, but many baby boomers are going to receive and pass on inheritances of that much or more.

And many tax experts believe that Congress is going to continue to chop away at the step up basis for inherited stocks and mutual funds.

So my point is -- you can't make plans for the future of estate taxes, because nobody knows what's going to happen . . . in 2010, and especially not in 2020 or 2030.

Variable annuities don't go through probate, so that's an advantage to your heirs.

The Earnings Enhancement Benefit Rider Can Pay Your Heirs' Taxes for Them

Besides, you can now add a rider to many variable annuities called the Earnings Enhancement Benefit (EEB). If you die, this would pay the income taxes for your beneficiary. This could prove a greater benefit to beneficiaries than the step up basis of stocks and mutual funds.

You Can Help Your Heirs Avoid Estate Taxes By Giving Them a Variable Fund While You're Still Alive to See Their Gratitude

Also, with variable funds you're allowed to give them away while you're still alive -- and the beneficiary receives a step up in basis.

For instance, a few years ago you bought a variable annuity for $150,000 and its value is now $200,000. You can give it to your son or daughter, and their cost basis is stepped up to $200,000 -- though you must pay taxes on the $50,000 increase for the year you give this gift.

This is obviously limited by your ability and willingness to gift the annuities while you're still alive, plus your ability and willingness to pay the required taxes, but for high net worth people who will still have plenty of money to live on, it's a good way to help their children or other heirs while they're still alive . . . so they can see the good their gifts bring and receive appreciation from the recipients.

Back-end Surrender Charges

Conventional variable annuities have a back-end surrender charge for early withdrawals. These vary, but the typical contract will charge you a penalty for withdrawing more than 10%-15% of your money within the first 6-8 years. Some contracts have back-end surrender charge periods as long as 10 years.

Typically, if you close out the contract in the first year, you're charged a 7% penalty. 6% in the second year, and so on until there's no penalty at the end of 7 years.

Beware of Rolling Back-End Surrender Charges

Also, something to avoid -- rolling surrender charges. This is where you're charged a surrender charge not just for the initial money you deposit into the contract, but every deposit starts a new surrender period.

For example, the rolling surrender charge period is 10 years. You took out a contract with $10,000 in 1990, and put in another $10,000 in 2001. You can withdraw the initial $10,000 without a back-end surrender charge, because it's now been 11 years since you put it into the contract. But until 2011, you cannot withdraw the second $10,000 without a back-end surrender charge.

Avoid variable annuities with rolling back-end surrender charges.

It's fair to ask you to tie up your money for some years -- as I keep repeating, variable annuities are long term investments -- but it's not reasonable to tie up every additional contribution you make once you've taken out the contract.

Beware of Back-End Surrender Charge Periods That Are Too Short!

Some companies are now offering "L-Share" Annuities, which means that they've shortened the surrender charge period to only 3-4 years.

This sounds good, but there's no free lunch when you're buying annuities (some meals are cheaper than others, but none are free!). To pay for this, they typically charge you a higher M & E & A figure. Therefore, your contract's performance will suffer. Also, they often pay a higher commission to the broker who sells them.

Remember -- variable annuity contracts are long term investments for your retirement. You should not be withdrawing money from them before retirement.

Therefore, paying higher M & E & A fees out of your account for a "benefit" you should not use doesn't make sense.

Beware of Contracts With No Defined End of Term

Some variable annuities now have NO defined "end of term." Maybe they tell you that you must keep your money in the contract for 10 years. What they don't tell you is that even after 10 years, you can only take out your money over a 5 year period.

This is usually associated with variable annuities with "bonuses." Remember -- whatever they seem to be giving to you up front, they're taking from you somewhere else. Probably on the back end.

My advice -- don't accept any contracts with no defined end of term, and fire any broker who tries to sell you one.

Catastrophic Clauses

Good variable annuity contracts allow you to get out without a surrender charge if you have to go into a nursing home or you're diagnosed with a terminal illness expected to result in death within a year.

Switching Funds From One Subaccount to Another

When you are in this accumulation period, you can switch your money from one subaccount (mutual fund) to another without any transaction fees (though the annuity company may have limits on how often you can do this).

I don't see this as a great benefit, for the reason that the markets are efficient (or at least unpredictable), and if you go switching from stocks to bonds or vice versa because of your guesses about where those markets are going, you're trying to time the market, and if you do so, you'll eventually lose money.

Income Investing Secrets

That's playing roulette. You can make a bet and win -- but it was good luck, not your skill in predicting where the ball would land inside the roulette wheel. Eventually, if you keep playing, you'll lose.

However, it's also true that it's cheaper to do this inside a variable annuity than with nonqualified mutual fund accounts. If you switch your money from one mutual fund to another, even within the same fund family, it's a taxable event. You'll owe a capital gains tax if you made a profit. Plus, many families will charge you a service fee for making the switch.

Variable Annuities Save You Paperwork

Keep in mind also that with nonqualified mutual funds, you must do a lot of record-keeping. Since you have to pay taxes on capital gains distributions and dividends even if reinvested, you must keep all your statements so that you or your tax professional (who of course will charge you for this additional work) can figure out your taxes -- maybe years later.

You Must Choose At Least 5 Subaccounts

The IRS is concerned that investments in variable annuities be diversified, or they're taxable.

To meet U.S. IRS tax-deferral status, variable annuities must meet the diversification rule:

1. No more than 55 percent of the value of the total assets of the account is represented by any one fund;

2. No more than 70 percent of the value of the total assets of the account is represented by any two funds;

3. No more than 80 percent of the value of the total assets of the account is represented by any three funds; and

4. No more than 90 percent of the value of the total assets of the account is represented by any four funds.

So you must have at least 5 subaccounts.

Switching Subaccounts to Rebalance Asset Allocation

The annuity contract may require you to switch your money around to rebalance your portfolio.

As I wrote earlier, I'm skeptical of the benefits of continually re-optimizing asset allocations. I believe in asset allocation, but only in the sense of setting up a diverse portfolio from the beginning, or as you can afford to buy more and different types of securities.

Still, rebalancing your portfolio inside of a variable annuity at least does not cost you any transaction fees, as it does outside the shelter of tax-deferral.

Besides, you must rebalance to make sure the subaccounts always meet the IRS diversification rules.

Choosing Actively Managed Subaccounts Will Cost You Money

One problem with variable annuity contracts at this stage, is that the subaccounts are often actively-managed mutual funds. Therefore, you do pay management fees to the mutual fund companies for your subaccounts. Of course, all such fees subtract from overall investment performance and should be minimized (per Principle 7).

Plus, if you choose subaccounts of actively managed mutual funds, then your overall performance will pay for the manager's mistakes. Various academics studies suggest that, on average, active management costs investors about 1% a year.

(That may be a too-generous figure. I just discovered the results of a study by Mark M. Carhart, published in the March 1997 Journal of Finance. He analyzed the performance of 1892 equity mutual funds for the period 1962-1993. On a pretax basis, these funds underperformed the market on average by 1.8%. The only fund managers who didn't perform by chance, in the long run -- were the ones who did the WORST . . . the really lousy managers stayed lousy.)

And remember that this 1% is compounded over the years. At the end of 20 years, your final balance is reduced by 17%.

For these two reasons, I urge you to buy only variable annuity contracts that offer index mutual funds and a wide variety of income mutual funds -- such as those paying high stock dividends, TIPS bonds, Treasury bonds, REITs and utility index funds.

Unfortunately, you're not likely to find funds devoted to the more "exotic" high income investments mentioned in this book, such as Canadian royalty trusts and master limited partnerships. It's possible that some subaccounts will have bought some of these, however.

The good news is that tax-sheltering mutual funds inside the variable annuity contract means that you don't have to pay taxes on the capital gains. Still, it's a good idea, for the sake of your overall performance, to minimize exposure to a fund that has a lot of capital gains.

That indicates active trading. That indicates you're losing money.

Hopefully the Law Will Someday Allow Us to Invest in Subaccounts that Hold Exchange Traded Funds

While thinking about the disadvantages of subaccounts for variable annuities (since I don't like actively managed mutual funds), I wondered if any variable annuity companies were using exchange traded funds now for their subaccounts instead of mutual funds.

I'm not the first one to have that idea -- Google led me to a page on a site of proposed patents where somebody else described the same idea.

However, it would possibly be illegal as the law now stands, since the government no longer allows variable annuity owners to use that contract to tax defer the buying and selling of individual securities, which exchange traded funds are. So for now, we're stuck with subaccounts/mutual funds.

Maybe this law will be changed someday. Although exchanged traded funds are technically individual securities, they represent ownership interest in a group of securities. They have low expenses and because they own shares based on public indexes, they're far more transparent than mutual funds.

You Should Have Funds in a Money Market Account Outside of Your Variable Annuity, Not Inside It

One last note about subaccounts: Variable annuities include a subaccount that's a money market fund account.

Money market funds are good for earning a little interest on money you need to keep safe for the short term. They're good for money you want to keep on hand for emergencies (most financial advisors tell you to keep enough money on hand to meet 3 to 6 months of your basic expenses, in case you're laid off or have another problem.)

They're also good for "parking" short term money such as the cash you're saving for a downpayment on a new house, for an upcoming vacation, a medical or dental expense, and even for a child's college tuition.

It makes no sense to me to put your long term investment money into a money market fund. You get neither growth nor much in the way of income.

Keep your variable annuity investment money in subaccounts that will either grow (an S&P index fund, for example) or pay good income (an intermediate, investment grade corporate bond fund, for example).

This book is about long term investing, not short term get rich quick trading.

Equity Indexed Annuities (Index Annuities or Fixed Index Annuities)

Some annuity products have come on the market that supposedly are based on the performance of an equity index -- that is, a stock market index such as the S&P 500.

Don't get too excited, however. Although they won't go down if the stock market does (which happens on average 1 year out of 3), these are usually capped to the upside. So if the stock market has a good year such as it usually did in the late 1990s, and goes up 20%, your annuity will probably go up just 10%.

During the market's down years, your annuity doesn't go down, but it doesn't go up either. If you had some money in bonds or even a money market account, it would earn some interest.

So you're really not taking advantage of the potential of the stock market. You don't suffer in the down years, but you won't go up as much as the market in the up years. And it's in the up years that the market makes most of its gains.

Variable Annuities are For the Long Term

Variable annuities are more expensive in some ways than mutual funds. They have their advantages, but these take time. Michael Lane says 10 to 15 years. Another writer says 25 years.

Let's sum up --

1. ACCUMULATION PHASE

1. Invest money -- in lump sums or gradually over time.

2. Money is held in subaccounts which are essentially mutual funds.

3. Your overall performance is the sum of the performance of the subaccounts you place your money into. (It's your choice.)

4. All returns generated by the subaccounts are tax-sheltered.

5. Your contract is insured so that if you die at this stage, your beneficiary will receive at least what you paid in, even if its market value is below that. (Or even more, if you choose a plan with more life insurance coverage.)

Advantages

1. Your investments are growing tax-sheltered.

2. Unlike all other tax-deferred vehicles such as IRAs, Roth IRAs, 401(k) plans and so on -- there's no limit as to how much money you can invest in a variable annuity.

3. Your investment's value is insured for the original amount, or more (depending on the terms of the contract you take out).

4. In some states, variable annuities cannot be attached by creditors, so they offer a degree of asset protection that other tax-deferred accounts don't. Last I saw, these states include Arkansas, Florida, Michigan, New York, North Dakota, Ohio, Oklahoma and Texas, but I can't guarantee that list is complete and accurate when you read this. Therefore, you should check with a local financial advisor for the applicable law in your state.

This benefit could be especially important if you're a doctor, lawyer or other professional at high risk of being sued.

5. Your investments are connected to financial market performance -- when stocks and bonds go up, your variable annuity contract goes up in value.

6. Unlike IRAs and other tax-deferred accounts, you can contribute to variable funds with non-work related income. Inheritances, prizes, proceeds from sale of a business or house, and so on.

Disadvantages

1. You don't get a tax deduction for money placed into a variable annuity contract. But that's true of all money invested outside of retirement accounts. And if you invest it outside of a variable annuity, you're also going to pay taxes on the income!

2. Subaccounts are mutual funds, so you pay some fees and lose performance if you put your money into an actively traded mutual fund, and you can't invest in certain types of income investments not covered by mutual funds. But you defer paying taxes on realized capital gains.

3. You pay for a form of life insurance you may not want. Especially if you don't have a family to leave money when you pass away.

4. The additional expenses make variable annuities expensive in the short run. But they're intended as long term investments.

5. The government forces you to invest in subaccounts/mutual funds rather than select individual securities. Even, apparently, individual securities that are proxies for index funds -- that is, exchange traded funds, which didn't exist in the 1970s.

6. Your annuity's performance goes along with that of the markets. If stocks and/or bonds crash, so does the market value of related subaccounts inside your variable annuity contract.

Are These Investments Right For You?

People for whom variable annuity contracts -- accumulation phase -- may be good for:

1. People who have maxed out their retirement account contributions but have more money they'd like to invest for retirement so it grows on a tax-deferred basis.

2. People who have received large lump sums of money (inheritances, life insurance proceeds, sales of houses, forced sale of investments, sale of a business, lawsuit settlements, lotteries or other prizes) and who want to invest it for their retirement so it grows on a tax-deferred basis.

3. People who are determined to ignore the proven Efficient Market Hypothesis and think an actively managed stock mutual fund can beat the market, but are smart enough to want to avoid paying taxes on the inevitable capital gains generated by the fund's turnover. (Such believers in capital gains probably aren't reading this book!)

4. People who want to use rebalancing of asset allocation to keep their savings growing, and want to avoid paying taxes on the capital gains generated by these transactions.

This could legitimately include many retired people who have a nest egg saved up, but who don't want to annuitize it because they want to leave money to their heirs.

5. People at high risk of being sued, if they live in states that protect variable annuities from creditors.

However, the majority of people who buy variable annuities are near or in retirement.

2. ACCUMULATION/PAYOUT PHASE

The Accumulation phase is easy to understand. You put money into subaccounts.

Now, what about getting money out?

In theory, when you retire, you're supposed to turn over all the money to the life insurance company in exchange for a guaranteed lifetime income.

However, you don't have to take that step.

According to RoxAnn Klugman in THE DIVIDEND GROWTH INVESTMENT STRATEGY, only 5% elect to annuitize their money. She claims that the other 95% withdraw it all in a lump sum.

I don't know where she got those figures. I suspect that a large number of those 95% don't close out the annuity contract. I suspect that many do what my mother does -- they take systematic withdrawals, but keep the rest of their nest egg growing on a tax-sheltered basis.

If they receive a large lump sum, they can even add it to the annuity.

That's why I call this section the Accumulation/Payout phase.

The payout is the most important part, but you can still accumulate.

Don't Withdraw Money From a Variable Annuity Before You Turn Age 59 ½, Unless You're Disabled

As with all tax-deferred accounts, the government imposes a 10% penalty for withdrawals from annuities prior to age 59 1/2 or disability.

(I'm not sure how the IRS and retirement laws define "disability" in this context. If the government wants to be consistent, it'd require a finding of disability under the rules of the Social Security Administration, which can take anywhere from two months to two years or even more, to make a final determination. But since when has the government always been consistent? Also, if the person is not insured for Social Security benefits, the Social Security

Administration won't make a disability decision on them. Possibly the IRS has a less difficult standard.)

Most variable annuity companies allow you to withdraw up to 10%-15% of the annuity's value without imposing a surrender charge. Make sure that yours allows this, or more.

Investment Profits You Withdraw Are Taxed At Your Full, Ordinary Tax Rate

When you do withdraw funds from your variable annuity contract, it's important to understand that the money that represents an increase over your original contribution will be taxed at your full, ordinary tax rate.

This is another point that critics of variable annuities love to write about.

If you buy some stock today and sell it for a profit over a year from now, the profit is taxable at the long term capital gains rate of 15%.

But if, instead of buying stock you put money into a variable annuity, and a subaccount money manager buys some stock and then over one year later sells that same stock for a profit, and you withdraw the money, the profit is taxed at your ordinary tax rate, which will be higher than 15% unless you have a very low income -- which most variable annuity owners don't.

Many financial writers like to point out that variable annuities force you to pay higher taxes on realized capital gains.

My obvious answer to that is -- I'm against investing for capital gains in or out of tax-deferred vehicles.

Since variable annuity subaccounts are open-ended, actively traded mutual funds, they are going to realize capital gains, and if you withdraw that money, you will pay taxes it at your ordinary tax rate instead of the lower capital gains.

If you made those same capital gains outside of a variable annuity, you'd pay only the lesser rate of 15%.

If you do put money into a variable annuity contract, I suggest choosing subaccounts that focus on income instead of capital gains. (Other writers also point out that by maximizing income from your annuity subaccounts, you're taking maximum advantage of the tax-deferral.)

If you have money outside of your variable annuity, I suggest focusing on income instead of capital gains. That's the point of this whole book.

If you do put money into a variable annuity's subaccount whose manager realizes capital gains, at least you will not have to pay taxes on them until they are withdrawn. The capital gains can be reinvested and compounded free of taxes -- until you withdraw it. In the long run, this means more money for you.

Again, variable annuities work best as long term investments.

Mutual Funds Make You Pay Capital Gains Taxes Against Your Will -- And Often They're Short-Term, Not Long-Term . . . No Matter How Long You Have Owned Your Fund Shares

Also, I can't resist pointing out that investors in non-tax-deferred, open-ended, actively traded mutual funds often pay capital gains taxes involuntarily. That is -- because the mutual fund manager sold stocks for a gain, and the law demands that the mutual fund shareholders must pay taxes on them.

And this is true even if the fund's value has decreased!

With variable annuities, you have control over when you have to pay the taxes, by controlling when you withdraw money from the contract.

Also, I must point out that the capital gains realized by many mutual funds are short term, not long term. That is, the mutual fund held the security for under a year before selling it.

Many people have the mistaken idea that, if they own mutual funds for over one year, that all capital gains realized within the fund are taxed at the long-term rate of 15%.

Not so!

You pay taxes on capital gains realized within your mutual fund based on how long the mutual fund held those particular securities -- not on how long you've owned the shares of mutual funds.

Let's say you've owned an actively managed equity mutual fund for five years.

If your mutual fund manager buys Microsoft today and sells it next month for a $10 per share profit -- you must pay taxes on that capital gains at your full, ordinary tax rate, because the fund held those shares of Microsoft for less than one year.

When the mutual fund realizes short-term capital gains, you the mutual fund owner must pay taxes at the short-term capital gains rate -- that is, your ordinary tax rate.

How long you have owned the mutual fund shares doesn't matter.

Annual Taxation of Mutual Funds (Outside of Tax-Deferred Accounts) Costs You More Than a Variable Fund's Expenses

According to Arthur Levitt, former Chairman of the Securities and Exchange Commission, studies have shown that annual taxation of mutual funds reduces returns on the average of 2.5% to 5.5%. The SEC itself made a study that showed the figure on average was 2.5%.

So paying your ordinary tax rate on withdrawals from variable funds is often not as expensive as financial writers like to argue. Remember, you've not paid any taxes on capital gains or income on these subaccounts since you put the money into the fund.

It's not widely known, but when you purchase mutual funds late in the year, you must pay capital gains taxes on the sales of securities the fund made throughout the year -- even though you didn't own the fund during that period!

What's more, if a fund realizes a gain early in the year and then its value goes downhill, and therefore many shareholders sell their shares before the capital gains distribution, you are stuck with an increased share of the capital gains distribution!

You pay the capital gains distribution taxes for the former shareholders who bailed out earlier in the year!

Capital Gains Distributions From Your Mutual Funds Can Greatly Increase Your Other Taxes

Depending upon your tax bracket and other personal considerations, receipt of capital gains distributions from ordinary mutual fund can also affect your taxes in other ways, because they're affected by the amount of your AGI (Adjusted Gross Income).

By increasing your AGI, capital gains distributions from taxable mutual funds can cause you to lose tax deductions, tax exemptions, and tax credits; subject you to the Alternative Minimum Tax (AMT); prevent you from opening a Roth IRA; cause you to owe taxes on your Social Security income; and disqualify you from tuition assistance for your child's college education.

Plus, don't forget that you must also pay state and local taxes on those mutual fund capital gains distributions. And since many state taxes are based on federal taxes, the increase in federal taxes can increase your state taxes, over and above simply paying your state's marginal tax rate on the capital gains.

Until You Annuitize Your Variable Annuity, You Can Take Money Out and Still Put Money In

When you're putting money into a variable fund but not taking it out, it's called a deferred annuity.

Once you start withdrawing the money, it's an immediate annuity.

Of course, take out only as much money as you need to live on.

You can keep putting money into the annuity, especially when you receive enough money to make it worth your while. (An inheritance, proceeds from the sale of a house or business, a large insurance settlement, lawsuit funds, or you finally win the lottery.)

What you're doing, is you're living on some of your savings, while allowing what's left to continue to compound tax-deferred.

Plus, if you do receive some other money, you can still add that to your savings.

You can also do the same thing with an IRA or other retirement account - withdraw just as much money as you need, while allowing the remainder to continue to compound tax-deferred.

The difference is that the IRA has only the money you were allowed to place into it (for many years, the limit for one person was $2000) plus accumulated earnings.

Therefore, variable annuities are for savings that couldn't go into an IRA.

With an IRA, you are required to begin making withdrawals at age 70 1/2, or you'll owe a penalty to the IRS.

With a variable annuity, you may be charged a hefty penalty if you withdraw money before a certain period. This varies with each particular annuity company and contract.

When you shop around, you should choose an annuity with the least restrictive rules and penalties for withdrawing your money.

Do Be Careful -- Don't Run Out of Money

The big disadvantage to making systematic withdrawals is that if you take out too much and your subaccount investments take a nosedive, you could still run out of money.

A guaranteed income for life is the promise of the next phase:

III. ANNUITIZATION PAYOUT STAGE

Once you're sure you're done putting any more money into the annuity, you can continue to simply take it out as needed, or you can take the step of annuitizing your funds.

When you do this, the annuity company uses your age and gender to determine your life expectancy, based on its actuarial records. Then it figures how much of the funds in your contract can be paid to you each month.

What Can Cause Confusion is That You Don't Ever Have to Annuitize Your Variable Annuity Contract

Annuitization is always optional, never mandatory. This is not clear in many of the books and articles written on variable annuities. While you're in the surrender period, you can choose to simply withdraw up to 10% to 15% with no back-end surrender charge. Once past the surrender period, you can withdraw as much as you want. All of it, if you choose.

Once you choose to annuitize your money and begin receiving checks right away, this is an immediate annuity.

Immediate annuities can be fixed. They can also be based on stock market performance, and so are then called variable immediate annuities.

By the way, annuity companies do set maximum ages for annuitizing your contract. If you don't choose annuitization by that age (90, 91, whatever), you lose the option.

Advantages --

1. You and your spouse get a guaranteed income for life.

2. If you choose a variable immediate annuity, the monthly amounts vary, but when your investments do well, the monthly payments will exceed what you would have received from a fixed annuity, and will increase as the years go, so your spending power stays up with inflation.

3. Annuitized variable annuity contracts are not counted as a resource for qualifying for Medicaid. (However, there are legalities you must observe, so be sure to consult with a lawyer specializing in elder care before you must go into a nursing home.)

4. If you and your spouse live longer than other annuity recipients in your age group, you'll receive a higher monthly benefit. It will keep going up the longer you survive, because many of the people you used to share the investment returns with are no longer receiving it, because they're dead.

Disadvantages --

1. You have no more access to the money in your contract. (Though many companies now offer revocable annuitization.)

2. You cannot leave this money to your heirs, although you can structure the monthly payments so they continue to your heirs for a set period after you die.

3. If you die earlier than the average for your age group, you'll get less money.

Also, I should make clear that these annuities can be set up for couples. That is, the monthly income stream will continue for so long as one member of the couple is alive.

There are many possible variations -- you should discuss your particular needs and wishes with your financial advisor and the annuity company itself, to make sure your contract has the provisions and options you want.

There are other options, such as the "Life with Period Certain."

This means the insurance company will pay the monthly annuity for the longer of your life, or a specified period such as 5, 10 or 20. If you pick 20 years, for example, but you die after 15 years, the annuity continues to be paid to your designated beneficiary for five years after your death.

This way, you know you or your family will get the benefit of the annuity for at least the specified time.

There are no free lunches, however. If you choose a benefit beyond your lifetime, you'll pay in the form of a reduced monthly payout.

Be aware that to the annuity company, the present value of all options given to you are equal. So select the one that works best for you in your financial/personal situation.

Newer, Living Benefits of Variable Annuities

In the last few years, variable annuity companies have come up with many different benefits to sell to customers. Some are called "living benefits." In many contracts, if you sign up for any of these benefits, the company may require you to allow the company to invest in its subaccounts according to asset allocation and rebalancing procedures or even to totally give up control over your investment options. If they don't go that far, they'll often prohibit you from putting your money into an "aggressive," "high growth" subaccount. This lowers the risk that they can't afford to provide you with these benefits.

1. Guaranteed Minimum Accumulation Benefit (GMAB)

This guarantees that after a set number of years, usually 10, the account's value will be no less than the amount of premiums paid into the annuity.

This doesn't sound like it's worth paying any money for. Short of a disaster on the order of the Great Depression, after 10 years the market value of your account should exceed the net deposits plus accumulated earnings. (Though I can't rule out a repeat of the Great Depression.)

2. Guaranteed Minimum Withdrawal Benefit (GMWB)

This allows you to withdraw a fixed dollar amount per year regardless of subaccount performance, without annuitizing -- usually 7% of your net contributions.

Some options give you this benefit until your net contributions have been withdrawn. You can also choose to withdraw 5% for life.

Again -- this is regardless of subaccount performance.

This is almost like annuitization, without annuitizing.

If your subaccount investments have done really well, you can just withdraw that money. But if they're down, you can take advantage of this benefit.

The one disadvantage I see is that unless your subaccounts go back up in the future (hopefully they will), you will fall behind inflation. This is almost like a fixed annuity -- but there are options to step up the amount in the future, based on subaccount performance, so it is more flexible than a fixed annuity.

This benefit can also be taken out to cover your spouse.

3. Guaranteed Minimum Income Benefit (GMIB) -- also called a Guaranteed Retirement Income Benefit or Program (GRIB or GRIP)

After a set period (usually 10 years), the contract owner can annuitize using the greater of:

1. Actual contract balance

2. Net contributions compounded at a certain rate

3. Or highest contract balance as of any anniversary date

Here's the benefit: the more money you annuitize, the higher your monthly checks will be. Therefore, you want to annuitize as high an amount of money as you can.

If you choose to annuitize at a time when your subaccounts have their highest market value, then #1 above will be best.

If you choose to annuitize and your subaccount performance has been below what the company could have done for you, then #2 above will be your best choice.

If you choose to annuitize when your subaccount performance is below what is was at the last contract anniversary date (say, the stock market crashed just last week), then #3 will be your best choice.

The problem, of course, is that when you take out your contract now, you don't know how your subaccounts are going to perform over the next 10 plus years, or whenever you will choose to annuitize.

That's why this is a potentially terrific benefit.

In general, these living benefits obviously appeal to people's fear of poor investment performance -- that when they need the money in the annuity, the markets will be down. Two years ago it was easy to scoff at such fears. Now that the market's 14,125 October 2007 peak is just a distant memory, we better remember that what goes up can also go down.

#2 Guaranteed Minimum Withdrawal Benefit (GMWB) is a pretty good option for people who fear running out of money before they die, but who also don't want to lose total control of their funds, or who want to leave some funds to their heirs.

There is one disadvantage to this benefit over straight annuitization -- if you live longer than your actuarially expected age, your payments won't go up because other customers your age have already died. This will reduce the money paid to long-lived contract owners.

#3 Guaranteed Minimum Income Benefit (GMIB) may well be a good benefit for people who are going to annuitize but who're afraid the markets and their investments will be down when they do so.

Overall, I'm not so sure any of these benefits are worth giving up control of your subaccounts, although I like #2.

Personally, I'd look for a contract that will still allow me to choose income-oriented subaccounts. I have no interest in putting my money into "high growth" mutual funds, so they're welcome to exclude me from those subaccounts.

Be careful with these living benefits -- make sure you understand all the terms and conditions. Sometimes they are not as good a deal as they appear.

How You Can Exchange Your Current Variable Annuity for a Better Contract

What if you already own a variable annuity, but now see that it isn't the right one for you, or now you understand that there are cheaper and better ones -- what can you do?

The IRS, through tax code 1035, allows you to exchange your contract for another one, without taxation, as long as certain contract basics remain the same.

If the variable annuity contract you now own has you locked into an early surrender charge, that is still applicable, so you should wait out the end of the surrender charge period.

But if you can get out without paying a back-end early surrender charge, and want to change, you should check with a financial advisor about doing a 1035 code swap.

I would advise against swapping funds simply because you think or some broker tells you that another annuity company will have better "performance." Performance depends on your choice of subaccounts and how that particular market is doing.

If a subaccount/mutual fund is actively managed, some will do better than others in its category -- for a time. But numerous studies show that no mutual fund manager outperforms the markets in the long run.

Therefore, it's a waste of time to "chase" a hot performer.

However, if you're dissatisfied with the poor choice of subaccounts offered by your variable annuity contract, swapping to get a better choice (especially index funds and income funds) can be a good decision. So can swapping to get into a contract with significantly lower expenses, or life or death benefit options not available to you in your current contract.

However, also keep in mind that if you make the swap, you are subject to the back-end surrender charge penalty period of the new annuity.

Beware of agents who call you up to encourage you to make unnecessary annuities swaps -- they're looking for new commissions.

Some Low-Cost Variable Annuity Companies to Check Out

Here are some leads for low cost variable annuity contracts. I can't recommend specific securities for you, but this is a good list to start looking at:

1. Vanguard -- this company is the well-known leader is low-cost mutual funds, and this carries over to their variable annuities.

2. Dimensional Fund Advisors -- another well-known and highly regarded mutual fund family, though more focused on institutional investors.

3. Providian Life and Health -- The Advisor's Edge

4. Schwab

5. Jack White

6. T. Rowe Price

7. Fidelity

All of the above are reputable and should be checked out. Look for low expenses, high company credit ratings, favorable terms and investment choices that include as wide a range of income choices as possible (bond funds, TIPS funds, real estate investment trusts, utility funds, funds of financial institutions, funds of basic consumer goods such as Altria, McDonalds and Coca-Cola).

For Help, Look for a Fee-Only Financial Advisor Who's Not Prejudiced Against Variable Annuities

Financial advisors who act as brokers, will usually want to sell you only an expensive, load variable annuity that pays them a high commission.

Financial advisors who get paid based on a percentage of your overall assets, will steer you away from any variable annuities, because that will reduce the amount of your assets under their control -- and thereby reduce their fees.

But a knowledgeable financial advisor who's being paid a set hourly rate should give you the most objective advice. They can determine whether any variable annuity is right for you. And if so, help you choose a no-load, low-expense variable annuity with many choices of income-oriented subaccounts, and also a short back-end surrender charge period. They can also help you choose the best life insurance and living benefit features offered by the annuity contract.

And a local financial advisor should be familiar with your applicable state laws.

You can look for a fee-only financial advisor at:

The National Association of Personal Financial Advisors

http://www.napfa.org/

Questions to Ask a Broker/Financial Advisor Before Buying Any Variable Annuity Contract:

1. What is your commission?

2. What is the M & E & A expense?

3. What is the back-end surrender charge period? Are there any "catches?" Make sure there is a Defined End of Term.

4. Are there rolling back-end surrender charges?

5. How much can I withdraw without a back-end surrender penalty?

6. What is the annual contract fee? Will it be waived for contracts over a certain amount?

7. What is the management expense ratio of the subaccounts?

8. What subaccounts are available?

9. Do the subaccounts include:

   1. A high dividend paying stock fund?

   2. A TIPS bond fund?

   3. An intermediate, investment-grade corporate bond fund?

   4. A utility fund?

   5. A REIT fund?

   6. A financial sector fund?

   7. A basic consumer goods sector fund?

   8. A Treasury bond fund?

   9. An aggregate bond index fund?

   10. An S&P 500 stock index fund?

   11. An EAFE (international) stock index fund?

   12. An international bond fund?

10. What life insurance options are available?

11. Are you charged a fee to transfer money from one subaccount to the other? If so, how much?

12. How many times per year are you allowed to transfer funds from one subaccount to another?

13. What is the company's credit rating?

14. Does the variable annuity give you a "bonus credit?" If so, know that you'll pay for it in higher expenses in some other area of the contract.

15. Are you paying for items -- such as long term care coverage insurance -- which you may be able to find elsewhere at a cheaper price?

16. Do the subaccounts charge any front-end or back-end loads?

17. If you have heirs and want to help them pay estate taxes, ask about the availability of the Earnings Enhancement Benefit and its cost.

18. Does it have any living benefits? Which ones?

19. Does it have any catastrophic clauses? What do they cover?

Expenses that greatly exceed the examples here, bonus credits, rolling back-end surrender charges, no defined end of term, subaccount loads, lack of income-oriented subaccounts, a poor credit rating, and a long back-end surrender charges period (more than 8 years) are major RED FLAGS -- keep shopping. With a new broker/advisor.

Free Look Period

Every variable annuity contract has a "free" look period, which can vary from 3 to 20 days, depending on the company and your state's regulations. Take advantage of that. If you decide within the annuity's free look period that it isn't right for you, return it to the company or your broker.

BOTTOM LINE:

Variable annuities are too complicated to just say YES or NO.

You may have detected from reading this chapter that I am of two minds still about them. While writing about the tax-deferment they offer while you're saving for retirement, I got all excited about the benefits of tax-deferring as much savings as you could afford, without the contribution limits imposed on convention retirement accounts such as IRAs.

However, when thinking about all their expenses and the limitations of the subaccount structure (forced on them by the government), I wasn't so happy about them.

Clearly, there's no one right solution that fits everybody.

If you are determined to ignore the advice in the rest of this book, and want to invest for capital gains (even if through an index fund), then sheltering your gains inside a variable annuity for many years is probably smart for you. In the long term, they have many advantages over taxable, open-ended mutual funds.

In 2002 the PriceWaterhouseCoopers, LLP performed a study comparing mutual funds and variable annuities held for the long term -- for retirement.

The title gives away their conclusion: REPORT: ANNUITIES ARE BETTER THAN MUTUAL FUNDS FOR RETIREMENT. They updated their findings in 2004, and came to the same basic conclusion.

However, given the long term advantages of investing for income, I believe that in the long run you'll do best by achieving financial freedom by focusing on increasing your income from your investments.

The goal is to receive enough income from investments to live well on, after paying taxes, and to keep that investment income growing to beat or meet inflation.

I've made clear that actively traded, open-ended mutual funds are not a good investment vehicle for this job.

Variable annuities are not perfect (yes, I wish you could invest in the right exchange traded funds, REITs and master limited partnerships -- but you can't).

Even the best annuities are not right for everybody. If they're good for you, put a significant portion of your retirement savings into them.

Always keep some of your money outside of the annuity contract!

Variable Annuity Resources

Here's one of the best websites for keeping up with news on variable annuities:

http://www.annuityfyi.com/

Books

GUARANTEED INCOME FOR LIFE: How Variable Annuities can Cut Your Taxes, Pay You Every Year of Your Life, and Bring You Financial Peace of Mind by Michael F. Lane

INVESTING WITH VARIABLE ANNUITIES: Fifty Reasons Why Variables Annuities May Be Better Long-Term Investments Than Mutual Funds by John P. Huggard

THE HANDBOOK OF VARIABLE ANNUITIES by Jeffrey K. Dellinger

Next: Variable annuities from the most financially secure life insurance companies in the world.

Chapter Forty-Three

Swiss Annuities Explained

What if you could get all the benefits of fixed and variable annuities described in the last chapter AND --

1. You could choose from among the life insurance companies with the highest credit ratings in the world? Since 1885, no company in this group has ever failed? (Prominent American and British life insurance companies have gone out of business.)

2. You could elect to hold your investments in one of the world's strongest currencies -- that's over 100% backed by gold reserves . . . and which has strengthened against the U. S dollar by 336% in the past 35 years?

3. You would have almost ironclad protection against creditors and lawsuits?

4. It was up to you to notify the IRS and pay taxes on your taxable income proceeds (when you take them)?

All these benefits are available through investing in Swiss annuities.

No, not Swiss bank accounts.

Let's get THAT out of the way right up front. I'm NOT advising you to open up a Swiss bank account, certainly not one of the infamous "numbered" accounts so beloved of thriller novelists.

Swiss bank accounts have to be reported to the IRS on your annual 1040 or on Treasury form 90-22.1. Swiss annuities don't have to be declared. However, when you start to draw out earnings, they are taxable in the U.S. and should therefore go on your 1040. You are not required to report to the U.S. government the mere ownership of a foreign life insurance policy or annuity.

(If you live in another country, you'll have to look up your nation's laws regarding Swiss annuities. However, odds are they won't be any tougher than the U.S., which is historically fanatical about collecting income taxes.)

Plus, the Swiss government requires foreigners to pay an onerous 35% tax on bank account earnings. This is not true of Swiss annuities.

Switzerland Has Long Been Renowned for Quality and Safety

Switzerland has a long-standing reputation for quality and safety, in many ways.

As an American, I was surprised to learn the Swiss democracy predates the American Revolution. It was founded over 700 years ago in 1291. They're actually the world's oldest still-existing democracy, not the U.S. (Hey, fellow Americans, that doesn't make our achievement any less. We are still the world's second oldest, pre-existing democracy -- and the Swiss didn't have to defeat the world's then-largest empire.)

In 1515, the Swiss adopted a strict policy of neutrality outside their borders combined with a policy that they will defend their borders at all costs. Both policies are still in effect to this day.

Long before Chairman Mao talked about the Army being one with the people, Switzerland made this a reality. Every Swiss adult is a part of their Army. They are armed, trained and have a job to do if their country is attacked. Since 1515 they haven't attacked any other country, have never been conquered by another country, and have been attacked only a few times.

(Of course, this is an ethically double-edged sword. During World War II, the willingness and readiness of every Swiss citizen to defend their country deterred the Nazis from invading them, thus preventing the Nazis from committing any atrocities against Swiss residents. Yet, the Swiss also failed to help stop the atrocities the Nazis committed just beyond their borders.)

Advantages

In addition to the tax-deferral of the investment earnings on your contributions, Swiss annuities offer these advantages:

1. You can diversify into the Swiss franc, euro, and/or pounds sterling.

You can elect to take out a Swiss annuity in U.S. dollars, but if you're a U.S. resident, you should not do this, because your main income is in U.S. dollars.

Use Swiss Annuities to Diversify Your Currency Risk

That goes for everybody. Take out Swiss annuities in as many currencies as you can afford -- except the currency of the country where you live, which is normally the currency of your main source of income. (Usually you must put in at least $US 25,000 or equivalent per currency.)

If you can put in only enough for one currency, make it the Swiss franc.

Everybody should diversify into currencies outside their home country!

(You can switch currencies, but I advise against this. If you have a crystal ball that allows you to accurately determine chances in currency values, you can get easily get rich as a foreign exchange trader. If you don't have such a crystal ball, don't waste your time and money trying. Just set up annuities in currencies other than the source of your income, so you're diversified.)

2. Asset protection and financial privacy

Swiss annuities taken out in Switzerland are governed by Swiss law. Swiss law places primary importance on people taking care of their families. Therefore, if the beneficiary of your annuity is a spouse or a descendant (child, grandchild and so on), creditors cannot touch it.

Also, creditors cannot touch your annuity if your beneficiary is someone else, but you've made an irrevocable election. That is, you've made a friend, cousin or someone else your beneficiary, and that cannot be changed.

By the way, you must take out the Swiss annuity either 6 months or 1 year (I've seen both figures) prior to any lawsuit or bankruptcy proceedings, and it account for every annuity. If they had to, they could meet all their financial responsibilities by issuing checks tomorrow.

Disadvantages

1. When you choose to receive immediate annuity payments, you can choose only annual, semiannual or quarterly payments. Monthly checks are reserved for Swiss residents.

2. The minimum amount you can start a Swiss annuity with is around $US 25,000 per currency selected. The minimum subsequent deposit allowed is usually around $US 10,000.

3. It's my understanding that if you choose a Swiss fixed annuity, under U.S. law, you get no tax-deferral of the earnings on your investment, even if actual payment is deferred. That's because a foreign fixed annuity contract is considered an original issue discount debt instrument.

However, Swiss variable annuities still qualify for tax-deferral, because the life insurance aspect makes them not a debt instrument. Therefore, U.S. citizens and residents should consider accumulating assets only in Swiss variable annuities -- not fixed annuities.

Swiss variable annuities qualify for U.S. tax deferral only if they're NOT "self-directed." If they are, there is no tax deferral. This is not a big deal, because NO American variable annuities are self-directed. As I wrote in the previous chapter, the U.S. government outlawed annuity contract owners investing in individual securities. So you must allow the Swiss company to control your investments, but you can still choose the subaccounts, so long as it's at least five, same as for American variable annuity contracts.

Check with your tax advisor for more details.

4. The additional costs of these investments may reduce their total returns, so you must weigh the advantages and disadvantages carefully.

Don't Be Fooled Into Thinking You Can Buy a Swiss Annuity in the U.S. or Canada -- You Can't

Make sure your annuity is really a Swiss annuity -- that is, governed by Swiss law.

There're Swiss life insurance companies operating inside the United States that will be glad to sell you annuities -- but since they're operating within the U.S., they're governed by U.S. law.

You must take out the annuity directly from a Swiss life insurance company in Switzerland or Bermuda. You can do this by mail or by flying to one of these places if you choose. Make sure that the company signs the contract in Switzerland or Bermuda.

Also, if you already own an American annuity, you can do a 1035 tax-free swap for an equivalent Swiss annuity, as explained in the chapter on variable annuities. Let the Swiss company handle the details. Don't handle any of the money. The swap must be between the American insurance company and the Swiss insurance company.

(However, remember that if you're still in the back-end surrender charge period of the first variable annuity contract, you'll still owe a penalty for terminating the contract too early.)

If you're a good candidate for a fixed or variable annuity in the U.S. or whatever country you live in, then you should also consider putting at least a sizable fraction of your money in a Swiss annuity.

This is especially true for all U.S. residents, because we have the most litigious lawyers on the planet. Anybody who appears to have money is a potential target.

This is especially true for American doctors, nurses, lawyers, landlords and business owners -- anybody in a profession where being sued in an occupational hazard.

Right now, the value of the U.S. dollar is falling rapidly against the euro and other world currencies.

This may or may not continue. Remember, I'm not a fortune teller.

If your home currency is the euro, don't feel too complacent. I've seen credible predictions that EU politicians are going to have to crank the printing presses up to high speed to send your baby boomer population the old age assistance checks they've been promised all their lives by Socialist governments.

Japan's government is also spending huge amounts of money, thus threatening the long term value of the yen.

Therefore, while the Swiss franc may not ever become one of the world's reserve currencies, its value seems fated to rise for at least the rest of our lives.

BOTTOM LINE:

Again, variable annuities from any country are not for everybody.

But if variable annuities are a worthwhile investment for you, you should consider putting at least 25% of your annuity money into Swiss annuities.

Swiss Annuity Resources

BETTER THAN GOLD: An Investor's Guide to Swiss Annuities by William T. McCord and Donald J. Moine

This book is a little out of date, but great at giving lots of background and reassuring you that investing in Swiss annuities is a good idea.

THE CONSUMER GUIDE TO SWISS ANNUITIES by Jean-Francois Meillard

This is from the Swiss Annuity Consumer Bureau.

Next: Summing up the investment vehicles available to you.

Chapter Forty-Four

What to Invest In, and How to Invest In It

You may have noticed something while reading through the last chapters -- there's no one perfect type of investment or investment vehicle.

If there were, life would be simple. I'd say, buy what's perfect. End of book.

They all have their advantages and disadvantages.

All of them are right for some people, some of the time.

Hey, life is complicated - what can I do to change that? I wish I had one simple formula that applied to everybody in every financial situation, but I don't. And neither does anybody else.

Here's my boiled-down summary. Then I'll move on to tell you how this applies to people in different age groups.

Investment Vehicles, in Order of Desirability:

1. Exchange Traded Funds

2. Unleveraged Closed End Funds

3. Index Mutual Funds

4. Mutual Funds

5. Individual Securities

NOTE: There are important exceptions -- you should buy Treasuries as individual securities. They have no credit risk, so you don't need to diversify. The U.S. Treasury allows you to open up an account with them, online or by phone, and you can have up to $100,000 at no expense. When you want to buy more than $100,000 worth of Treasuries, just open up a second account!

I'm not even listing hedge funds. I just included a chapter on them to be complete, and so you'd understand that you're not missing anything by not having enough money for them.

Next: Getting a handle on the various types of investments

Chapter Forty-Five

Investment Types -- Big Advantages and Major Disadvantages

1. Basic consumer product, utility and financial company dividend-paying stocks

   Big Advantage -- income grows with inflation so future potential is high

   Major Disadvantage -- income is low in the present and near-term

2. Real estate investment trusts (REITs)

   Big Advantage -- fairly high current income that will keep growing

   Major Disadvantage -- limited in scope of business

3. Master Limited Partnerships

   Big Advantage -- High current income

   Major Disadvantage -- long term prospects probably good, but untested by time

4. Canadian Income Trusts

   Big Advantage -- High current income

   Major Disadvantage -- disappearing in 2011

5. Treasuries

Big Advantage -- No credit risk

Major Disadvantage -- Inflation will erode purchasing power of the interest and principal

6. Investment-Grade, Intermediate-Term Corporate Bonds

Big Advantage -- High current yield

Major Disadvantage -- Inflation will erode purchasing power of the interest

7. Investment-Grade, Intermediate-Term Municipal Bonds

Big Advantage -- No federal taxes on income. In some situations, no state or local taxes.

Major Disadvantage -- Inflation will erode purchasing power of the interest

8. Treasury Inflation Protection Securities -- TIPS

Big Advantage - Guaranteed real return despite inflation

Major Disadvantage -- Must pay taxes on "phantom" income if held outside a retirement account

9. I Bonds

Big Advantage -- Guaranteed real return despite inflation

Major Disadvantage -- limited to $30,000 per year, and you must cash them in to get the interest

10. Preferred stock

Big Advantage -- High current yields

Major Disadvantage -- high credit risk

Next: Matching investment types with the optimum investment vehicles

11. Variable Annuities

Big Advantage -- tax deferral, protection for heirs

Major Disadvantage -- high expenses

12. Swiss Variable Annuities

Big Advantage -- currency diversification, low risk

Major Disadvantage -- high expenses

Chapter Forty-Six

Matching Investment Types to the Optimum Investment Vehicle

```
***************************************************
```
PLEASE NOTE!

I am not a broker. I have no license to sell securities. The following is simply my opinion about the best way to invest in the best income investments.

This is not a solicitation for the sale of these securities.

You cannot buy any of these securities from or through me.

Except where otherwise noted, you should buy them through your own deep discount broker.

This is general advice intended to guide the reader. It is NOT personal financial advice. Only you know your personal financial circumstances. You must take my suggestions and think through how they apply to you and your family.

Consult with a qualified financial planner if you need more help.

```
******************************************************************
```

Many of these securities are new -- that's good. It means that the Exchange Traded Funds companies are responding to marketplace demand.

I. Intermediate-Term and Long-Term Treasuries

Individual securities --

http://www.treasurydirect.gov/

(No credit risk and no expenses, but low income.)

II. Government bonds (not U.S. Treasuries)

Exchange Traded Funds

1. SPDR Capital International Treasury Bond ETF: BWX

This ETF tracks the Barclays Capital Global Treasury ex-US Capped Index . The Index covers fixed-rate local currency sovereign debt of investment grade countries outside of the US, in local currencies, with a remaining period of one year or more.

Because this ETF uses local currencies, it's a great way for everyone to diversify currency risk.

III. Investment-Grade, Intermediate-Term Corporate Bonds

Exchange Traded Funds --

1. Vanguard Intermediate-Term Corporate Bond ETF (VCIT)

There is no index for these securities, so Vanguard buys a representative sample.

Individual Securities

So long as you buy only bonds from InterNotes, Direct Access Notes or Core Notes, you do not have to pay the outrageous fees that bond brokers and dealers charge anyone who's not buying at least 6 figures worth at once.

http://www.internotes.com/

http://www.directnotes.com/

http://corenotes.ml.com/

Buying individual bonds allows you to forget about fluctuations in market price. Just buy and hold until maturity.

Also, by buying individual bonds, you can control your reinvestment risk by "laddering." That's the widely accepted technique of having your bonds mature in a string of years -- 2020, 2021, 2022 etc.

Essentially, you are diversifying by maturity date. You're spreading out your reinvestment risk.

With individual bonds you are taking on the risk of default by one particular company, so you should buy as many as 30 to 50. If you don't have a large enough lump sum to spend doing that, you can do this over time by buying the bonds as you have the money.

IV. Investment-Grade, Intermediate-Term Municipal Bonds

Exchange Traded Funds

1. iShares S&P National AMT-Free Municipal Bond Fund: MUB

Tracks the S&P National AMT-Free Municipal Bond Index.

2. SPDR Barclay's Capital Municipal Bond ETF: TFI

Tracks the Barclay's Capital Municipal Managed Money Index.

Choose either one of the above. You don't need both.

3. If you live in California --

iShares S&P California AMT-Free Municipal Bond Fund: CMF

Tracks the S&P California AMT-Free Municipal Bond Index.

4. If you live in New York --

iShares S&P New York AMT-Free Municipal Bond Fund: NYF

Tracks the S&P New York AMT-Free Municipal Bond Index.

V. TIPS

Income Investing Secrets

Exchange Traded Funds

iShares Barclay's U.S. Treasury Inflation Protected Securities Bond Fund: TIP

Tracks the Barclays Capital U.S. Treasury Inflation Protected Securities (TIPS) Index (Series-L).

Because of the structure of holding TIPS within an exchange traded fund, you don't have to pay taxes on the semi-annual cost of living increase in principal -- until you sell your shares of the ETF.

Obvious conclusion: never sell any shares of TIP.

VI. I Bonds

Individual securities -- http://www.treasurydirect.gov/

You can buy up to $30,000 in one year. They're a good deal, so take advantage of it if you're still saving for retirement.

VII. Dividend-Paying U.S. Stocks - includes basic consumer brands

Exchange Traded Funds --

1. PowerShares Dividend Achievers Portfolio: PFM

This ETF tracks the performance of the Mergent Broad Dividend Achievers index. That is, all U.S. companies with a history of raising the dividends at least once a year for the past 10 years or more.

2. PowerShares High Yield Equity Dividend Achievers Portfolio: PEY

This EFT holds the 50 stocks in the Mergent Dividend Achievers 50 Index -- that's the 50 companies paying the highest dividends now. (And which have also increased their dividends every year for at least the past 10 years)

3. iShares Dow Jones Select Dividend Index Fund: DVY

This is based on the Dow Jones selection of best U.S. dividend stocks. It was the first dividend-oriented ETF, and is widely considered the best of U.S. dividend ETFs.

4. First Trust Value Line Dividend Index Fund: FVD

This ETF holds the stocks in the Value Line Dividend Index.

5. SPDR Dividend ETF: SDY

This tracks the S&P High Yield Dividend Aristocrats index.

6. WisdomTree Total Dividend Fund: DTD

The WisdomTree Dividend Index consists of all the dividend paying companies in the U.S. stock market.

7. WisdomTree High-Yielding Equity Fund: DHS

This tracks the WisdomTree High-Yielding Equity Index. This is the companies in the WisdomTree Dividend Index with the highest dividend yields.

8. WisdomTree Dividend ex-Financials Fund: DTN

The WisdomTree Dividend Top 100 Index Fund tracks the performance of the high dividend paying U.S. stocks not including financial companies.

This ETR used to simply consist of the top 100 dividend payers. Obviously, in the wake of the financial meltdown of Fall 2008 they decided to stay away from banks and other financial institutions.

A Lot of Choices Here -- What to Buy?

DVY is the best known and often touted as the "best." I like Mergent's idea of tracking the companies with a history of raising dividends. They may not continue to do so in the future, but many of them will.

We're investing in dividend-paying companies for dividend growth in the future, because current yields are lower than bonds. However, the companies that are paying the most right now will likely still be paying the most in the future, so long as they keep raising their dividends.

I also respect Dr. Jeremy Siegel, and believe the fundamental approach to weighting is worthwhile.

Therefore, my personal vote is for PEY -- the highest yielding of the Mergent index (which means that all of them also have at least a 10 year history of raising their dividends, remember). And DHS for the very highest yielding now, with the index weighted by dividend yield.

But you can't go wrong with any of them.

However, you should also diversify with equities around the world:

VIII. Dividend Paying Stocks Outside U.S. -- including basic consumer brands

1. PowerShares International Dividend Achievers Portfolio: PID

This tracks the Mergent International Dividend Achievers Index. That is, these are the stocks of companies outside the U.S. with a history of raising their dividends every year for at least five years.

2. WisdomTree DEFA Fund: DWM

This tracks the WisdomTree Dividend Index of Europe, Far East Asia and Australasia (DEFA).

3. WisdomTree DEFA Equity Income Fund: DTH

The WisdomTree DEFA Equity Index consists of the companies in the WisdomTree DEFA Index with the highest dividend yields.

4. WisdomTree Emerging Markets Equity Income Fund: DEM

This ETF tracks the performance of the WisdomTree Emerging Markets Equity Income Index. This is a way to diversify into the emerging markets of the world. However, they are still risky, so keep your portfolio allocation to this one small.

Here, my vote is for PID, since it takes any company outside the U.S. (I don't really care what continent it's on or whether it's in a developed or developing country) so long as it's raised its dividends every year for at least 5 years. DTH is a close second since it tracks the companies currently paying the highest dividends.

IX. Utilities -- inside U.S.

Exchange Traded Funds --

1. iShares Dow Jones US Utilities (IDU)

Tracks the Dow Jones U.S. Utilities Index. This includes electricity (about 75% of total), gas, water and multi-utility companies. It includes regulated utilities and unregulated merchant power generators or unregulated independent power producers.

2. Vanguard Utilities ETF VPU

This ETF tracks the MSCI (Morgan Stanley Capital International) United States Investable Market Utilities Index, an index made up of stocks of large, medium-size and small utility companies in the United States.

3. PowerShares Dynamic Utilities PUI

Tracks the Dynamic Utilities Intellidex Index -- 30 US utility stocks.

These three cover the United States. I'd have to give the nod to VPU because its expense ratio is only 0.25% and, with 88 holdings, is slightly broader based than IDU's 76 companies. And IDU's expense ratio is 0.48%.

PUI comes in third. Its expense ratio could go as high as 0.6% and it holds only 30 companies, so it's not as diversified.

X. Utilities -- outside U.S.

1. S&P Global Utilities Sector Index Fund JXI

Tracks the S&P Global Utilities Index. Expense ratio is 0.48% and it holds 76 companies in the developed world, with about 1/3 U.S. companies.

2. SPDR S&P International Utilities Sector ETF IPU

Tracks the S&P Developed Ex-U.S. BMI Utilities Sector Index, an index that tracks the utilities sector of developed global markets outside the United States.

Expense ratio is 0.5%.

Here I must advise buying IPU. If you buy a U.S. utility ETF and JXI, you're getting about 33% overlap. The idea of buying an international utility ETF is to diversify out of the United States.

However, if you can buy only one utility ETF, then JXI will cover the entire developed world including the U.S.

XI. REITs -- inside U.S.

Exchange Traded Funds --

(NOTE: Some Exchange Traded Funds track only REITs in specialized sections of the real estate markets, such as residential or commercial or retail REITs. For simplicity, I'm leaving these out. I'm including only ETFs that track a broad cross-section of the total real estate market. More specialized REITs lack diversification.)

1. Vanguard REIT ETF: VNQ

The Vanguard REIT ETF tracks the performance of the MSCI® US REIT Index.

2. The iShares FTSE NAREIT Real Estate 50 Index Fund: FTY

Tracks the performance of the FTSE NAREIT Real Estate 50 Index.

3. SPDR Dow Jones REIT ETF: RWR

Tracks the Dow Jones U.S. Select REIT Index.

4. iShares Cohen & Steers Realty Majors Index Fund: ICF

The iShares Cohen & Steers Realty Majors Index Fund tracks the performance of the Cohen & Steers Realty Majors Index.

5. iShares Dow Jones U.S. Real Estate Index Fund: IYR

This ETF tracks the performance of the Dow Jones U.S. Real Estate Index.

There's no point in buying more than one of these, as all of them will give you results that roughly correspond to the overall U.S. real estate market.

My personal vote is for VNQ, because Vanguard keeps its expense ratio so low.

However, although the U.S. is a big country, there's a lot more real estate outside it than in it, so you should also diversify internationally.

XIII. REITs Outside U.S.

1. streetTracks Dow Jones Wilshire International Real Estate ETF: RWX

2. S&P Developed ex-U.S. Property Index Fund: WPS

Tracks the S&P/ Developed ex-U.S Property Index.

3. WisdomTree International Real Estate Fund: DRW

Tracks the WisdomTree International Real Estate Index.

This is a tough call, because outside the U.S. is obviously a broad area. Real estate could be booming in Europe but plummeting in Japan.

When confronted with such a choice, my voice has to be for diversification: if you have the money, buy all 3.

XIV. Canadian Royalty Trusts

Exchange Traded Funds --

1. iShares CDN Income Trust Sector Index Fund: XTR

This one tracks the performance of the S&P/TSX Capped Income Trust Index.

XV. Master Limited Partnerships

There are currently no exchange traded funds or mutual funds for master limited partnerships.

There is a new exchange traded note (ECN) that does track the Alerian index of master limited partnerships. However, this is not an ETF. ETNs are senior, unsecured obligations of JPMorgan, so there is additional credit risk involved. In effect, ECNs are much like bonds.

1 JPMorgan Alerian MLP Index ETN: AMJ

This tracks the Alerian MLP Index (AMZ).

Since you don't own partnership units in the MLPs, the quarterly income is ordinary taxable income. This makes these ECNs suitable for tax-deferred retirement accounts, unlike direct ownership of MLP units.

Individual securities

If you have a large portfolio outside of tax-deferred retirement accounts, buy a range of the largest master limited partnerships.

Don't make them the bulk of your portfolio, but when you own them directly, you can afford to allocate a larger percentage than ECNs, because owning partnership units directly is less risky than owning them through the above ECN. However, do diversify.

Closed end funds

Tortoise Energy Infrastructure Corp. (TYG)

This closed end fund invests primarily in energy-related infrastructure (90% of holdings), with 70% of holdings being MLPs. However, it may also invest up to 25% in debt securities, bonds, of energy infrastructure companies.

Still, it's another way you can put MLPs into your tax-deferred retirement account.

XVI. Preferred Stock

Exchange Traded Funds

1. iShares S&P U.S. Preferred Stock Index Fund: PFF

This fund seeks track the performance of the S&P U.S. Preferred Stock Index.

2. PowerShares Financial Preferred Portfolio: PGF

The PowerShares Financial Preferred Portfolio (Fund) is based on the Wachovia Hybrid & Preferred Securities Financial Index.

Another tough call. There're so many preferred stocks available that no index can do anything but attempt to buy a representative sample.

So buy the one with the highest current yield and/or lowest expense ratio.

XVII. Business Development Companies (BDCs)

Exchange Traded Funds

1. PowerShares Global Listed Private Equity Portfolio ETF: PSP
This tracks the Global Listed Private Equity Index of from 40 to 60 publicly traded BDCs and other companies investing in venture capital.

13. Income Deposit Securities -- IDSes

Individual Securities -- by default

Do your due diligence. These may well prove to be great investments. But right now they're too new for me to give a blanket approval to them.

In the next few chapters I'll do my best go guide you, based on your age, on how to use the above information to your best advantage. That involves figuring out how to make the most of the advantages of the above investments and how to neutralize or minimize their disadvantages, along the lines of the 7 Principles.

Obviously, I don't know you. Everybody and their circumstances are different.

Therefore, you must apply the following information to your own particular circumstances as well as you can. If you need help, I recommend you get a fee-only financial advisor who will charge you a reasonable hourly rate to give you objective advice.

Chapter Forty-Seven

Tax-Deferred Accounts

Tax-deferred accounts are a good deal. You should first of all make maximum use of them.

Employed?

I. 401(k), 403(b) or the Federal Employee Thrift Plan

Your contributions are tax deductible, and taken right out of your paycheck.

Pay in as much as you possibly can. If your employer offers matching funds, you have no excuse for not contributing at least as much as you need to take advantage of that employer matching. That's practically free money. You've doubled your money right off. No other investment matches that.

Plans vary a lot by employer. Check out your options, then invest your money as much as possible in this order:

1. Exchange Traded Funds (ETFs) -- probably not offered

2. Index mutual funds -- Divide your money up between S&P 500 and Lehman Bond Aggregate Bond Index, or other acceptable bond index (Treasuries, TIPS, investment grade corporates), depending on what's available to you.

3. Actively traded mutual funds -- Yuck! Still, the power of a tax deduction for contributions and tax-deferral of accumulated earnings makes paying mutual fund costs worth it. As much as possible (a lot depends on what's available to you), divide your money up into stock funds focusing on dividends, investment-grade corporate bonds and TIPS or Treasuries.

4. Individual securities -- A lot of companies encourage you to buy their stock. However, remember that if you place a significant amount of your retirement funds in your employer's stock, not only are your retirement funds not

diversified, your retirement funds and your wage income are at risk together. Think: out of work Enron employees complaining how they lost their jobs and their retirement funds at the same time.

Hopefully, your employer is no Enron, but who knows for sure? You should try to make investments that will survive your company having bad times.

If they match contributions only on purchases of their stock, that's a tough call. Can you accept the matching, hold the stock for a time, then sell and transfer the money into a mutual fund?

You know your company and its prospects better than I do. Check out your options and make the best call you can. However, do whatever you can to place as much of your retirement money as possible into securities that won't go away if your employer's CEO is led off to jail.

If you're a Federal employee, divide up your money between the C (S&P 500 Index) and F (Lehman Brothers Aggregate Bond Index) funds. Those are the two that pay some income. (The money market G fund does pay dividends, but too little for long-term investing. Place your money in that fund only if you're close to retirement or quitting, and will transfer it to an IRA soon, to avoid volatility just after the cessation of your employment with the government.)

II. IRA, Roth IRA

Once you've contributed the max to a retirement fund on your job, or if you don't have that option available, open an IRA or Roth IRA.

If you're below the Roth IRA income limits, that's the one I'd choose. Although you don't get to defer taxes on your contributions, they compound tax free and you will not be forced to withdraw them by age 70 1/2.

Starting with 2010, you can convert a traditional IRA to a Roth IRA even if your income is higher than the $100,000 (individual)/$160,000 (couple) limits. You do have to pay income taxes, but you can spread it out over two years.

Self-Employed?

Open a Keogh, Simplified Employees Pension (SEP or SEP-IRA), or Solo 401(k)

Consult a financial advisor regarding the exact tax-deferred retirement accounts you should open. It may vary depending on whether you're a sole proprietorship (which you should NOT be), a general partner (ditto), or whether you use a limited liability company (LLC), C corporation or S corporation. It also varies by whether you have employees or not. And whether you want a defined benefit plan.

Chapter Forty-Eight

Income Allocation Versus Asset Allocation

Markowitz published his famous paper in 1952 that demonstrated that the best way to reduce risk (defined as market price volatility) in a portfolio is to invest in a number of different assets that went up or down more or less independently of each other.

This is known as asset allocation, and is widely used by professional fund managers.

These days, asset allocation is usually described as dividing your investments between stocks, bonds and cash.

But we don't care about the market price of the assets we own. What's important to us is income. (Right? Right!)

However, all financial securities do contain an element of what I call "real world" risk. In the real world, issuers of financial securities can and do run into cash-flow problems. They even cease to exist.

The reduction in or cessation of our income flows -- that's real world risk.

(If you didn't understand that before September 2008, you should understand now that even in financial markets, "risk" means "danger."

Therefore, we need to reduce our risk through the use of income allocation -- that's diversifying the sources of our income.

OK, that's Principle 5. I wanted to repeat this, because you can find many investing books on asset allocation and many more that discuss it. Yet you won't find any on "income allocation."

Income allocation does also mean dividing your investments between stocks, bonds and cash. Stocks can mean any kind of equities – including Canadian business trust units, master limited partnership units and so on. Bonds can mean any kind of debt, including what's effectively debt, preferred stocks.

"Cash" in this case means cash-equivalents such as money market funds and certificates of deposits.

In the rest of this book, I will not mention cash or money market funds much. Everybody should have some money stashed away in a money market fund for emergencies.

Also, if you're saving for a short-term goal such as a vacation, downpayment on a house, or a child's college tuition, you should put all those funds into a money market account.

Money market accounts are NOT for long-term, especially not retirement, investing.

The more your sources of income are diversified among income-paying investments of both equity and debt, the safer your overall income flow is.

Next, what I need to tell you about rebalancing.

Chapter Forty-Nine

Rebalancing of Income Versus Rebalancing of Assets

When you start off with a portfolio divided between stocks, bonds and cash -- as advocated by devotees of asset allocation -- you can easily divide your portfolio by market value.

Let's say that you or your financial advisor determine that the optimum asset allocation for you is:

10% cash

50% stocks

40% bonds.

However, in time, the market value of each of those investments will fluctuate.

If stocks go up 20% next year while bonds fall, in a year you could easily have a portfolio that looks more like this:

9% cash

65% stocks

26% bonds

Because these percentages are not your "optimum" asset allocation, your broker or advisor will advise you to sell some of your stock and use the money that's left over (from paying taxes on your capital gains) to buy some more bonds and add a little more to your money market fund.

By now you should understand that this violates Principle 7 -- you have to pay taxes on the capital gains, and pay additional commissions on the selling and buying of securities.

Is Rebalancing Worth It? -- Not Unless It's Done Within a Tax-Deferred Account

However, it does do one good thing -- it forces you to sell stocks when they're relatively high in price, and forces you to buy bonds when they're relatively low in price.

In time, as stocks go up and down, and bonds go up and down, you'll buy more of each when they're relatively low, and sell more of each when they're relatively high.

Rebalancing advocates don't like to admit it, but this is a form of market timing.

Asset Allocation Advocates Ignored Gold During Its Long Bear Market

Also, there is no one set, perfect or "official" way of doing this. When I first read about asset allocation many years ago, 5 asset groups were mentioned: stocks, bonds, real estate, cash and gold.

If you'd started such an asset allocation/rebalancing program back in 1980, you'd now have most of your portfolio in gold.

The price of gold has just recently passed its nominal 1980 peak. It would have taken you 27 years to see that one asset class move up. But on an inflation-adjusted basis, gold is still far behind its 1980 peak.

On an inflation-adjusted basis, gold will have to reach $2000 an ounce to exceed its 1980 peak.

Maybe it will sooner than we think.

Maybe it will then seem like a great investment. But would you have wanted to wait over 28 years?

I've noticed that it's been many years since asset allocation/rebalancing advocates have dared to mention including gold in their portfolios.

Real Estate Should Also Be Included -- REITs as Well as Your Home

They don't even include real estate, although that's gotten much easier to invest it, thanks to REITs.

I don't think anybody knows when the optimum rebalancing period is. Many rebalancers do it quarterly, but that seems to me way too short a time to capture major market moves.

Even a year may be too short. If you were rebalancing a stock portfolio during the last bull market, 1995 was too early to sell off your gains. You would have missed most of the really big tech bubble that lasted until about 2000-2001. By 1995, stocks were relatively expensive, but they were going to get a whole heck of a lot more expensive before that bull run ended.

Most of Us Have to Allocate Assets Simply Because We Can Buy Only So Many Investments At Any One Time

I advocate "rebalancing" through reinvestment/compounding of income and through adding funds to your portfolio.

Here's what I mean.

Your stock portfolio pays you dividends. You reinvest those dividends into buying new shares of stock. If stock market prices are relatively high, those dividends will be fewer new shares than if stock market prices are relatively low.

Maybe while stock market prices are relatively high, bond prices will be relatively low. You reinvest your interest from bonds into new bonds. The cheaper they are, the more you can buy.

Therefore, simply through reinvesting income back into that same income-producing security, we obtain the same positive result as rebalancing.

That is, we buy more of each security when they're relatively low in price and fewer when they're higher in price.

Without paying taxes on capital gains and commissions on the sale of securities.

We've still got to pay commissions on new securities that are bought through reinvesting income.

When you add money to your retirement savings, you can also simply buy new types of investments. Maybe when you start out, you have only enough money to buy shares in a U.S. stock dividend-paying ETR such as PEY.

When you have some more, you can buy an ex-U.S. stock dividend paying ETR, a bond ETR or a REIT ETR.

So you diversify over time, as you add money to your retirement savings.

Next: General procedures for the Secrets of Income Investing Plan

Chapter Fifty

Managing Your Investment Cash Flows

1. Take as much advantage as possible of your 401(k), 403(b) or Federal Thrift Plan on your job. That's especially true if you receive any matching funds from your employer.

For example: federal employees hired after 1984 get 100% matching from the government up to 5% of their gross pay. That is, if they contribute 2% to their Thrift Fund, the government matches it with 2%. If they contribute 3%, the government kicks in 3%. And so on, up to 5%. They can contribute up to 10%, but the government matches only the first 5%.

If you can get matching funds from your employer, take advantage. That's an immediate 100% return on your money.

You have to put your money in the choices you're given. Some plans offer more and better choices than others. Remember the order of priorities.

You probably can't buy exchange traded funds, but if you can -- do it.

Otherwise, contribute to index mutual funds.

2. Next, take out an IRA, Roth IRA (if you qualify), SEP (if you're self-employed) or other relevant tax-deferred retirement account.

Contribute the max, focusing on TIPS, corporate bonds and dividend-paying stocks.

Don't put Treasury bonds, master limited partnerships or municipal bonds into retirement accounts.

3. Open an account at a discount brokerage.

4. Open a second money market fund. Here is where you'll keep all cash waiting to be invested.

Unless you have a large lump sum to invest, you'll have to start out by saving so much a month from your paycheck. And when you do receive dividend and interest checks, they won't be high enough to immediately reinvest into each security, so you'll need to deposit them into this separate, investment-only, not for everyday expenses, money market fund.

When the balance inside the money market fund is large enough to buy the next investment on your list (see the next few chapters), then buy it.

Just keep buying investment after investment, as you have the funds to do so, from both your regular income and from dividends and interest checks on your investments.

5. If you must start small, consider using a Dividend ReInvestment Plan (DRIP).

With DRIPS, you open up an account at the company that pays the dividends. Not all companies have DRIPS, but many of the best ones do. Right now, there're over 1000 companies that run DRIPs.

You can start a DRIP account with a small amount of money, sometimes for the price of just one share of the company's common stock. The company holds the stock for you, and when it pays dividends, your share is automatically reinvested in more shares of the company's stock.

You usually don't have to pay a brokerage commission, so this can save you money when you're just getting started.

You can also add to your plan in small amounts, even having them automatically deducted from your personal checking or savings account.

Here's a good list of companies to start with:

http://www.directinvesting.com/group_membership/no_fee_co.cfm

5. If that's a hassle or if you travel a lot and don't get your mail frequently, consider opening a cash management account.

CMAs are available from brokers such as Charles Schwab, Fidelity and Merrill Lynch. Plus, I'm sure you can find many others.

They are convenient for keeping all your investment money organized. All your income from investments will be sent automatically into the CMA's money market account. Also, you can have the interest from Treasury bonds sent directly from your Treasury Department account into that money market account.

The two downsides to CMAs is that many of them have high required minimum balances. Plus, they tack on an extra layer of expenses, roughly 1%.

Before we get specific, I have to mention some personal finance type of information you probably already know but probably need to be reminded of.

Chapter Fifty-One

A Few Important Points Regarding Personal Financial Subjects

1. How you can easily and immediately earn from 10 to 30% on your money - pay off your credit cards.

Many financial advisors/writers say that you should not invest anything until after you pay off all your credit cards.

By the numbers, I agree with them.

However, we're people, not numbers.

If you and/or your spouse are shopaholics or people who see any unused line of credit on your Visa and MasterCard as both an opportunity and challenge you can't resist . . .

You should get professional counseling.

In the meantime, start investing. Forty years from now you may still be maxed out on your credit cards, but at least you'll have some retirement funds.

If you are overwhelmed by your unpaid bills, consult a competent attorney regarding filing for bankruptcy or a credit counseling agency about their services.

Right now the most visible anti-debt specialist is radio show host Dave Ramsey. Check out his radio show, web site and books. Your local church may be running a Financial Peace University.

His investing advice is conventional, but he's messianic at encouraging people to get out of debt.

Income Investing Secrets

2. Everybody should have a money market account with enough money in it to pay their bills for from 3 to 6 months, in case of financial emergencies.

Until recently, I figured prime money market accounts were safe enough. But in mid-September 2008 one prime money market account broke the buck, going to 97 cents, because of owning a lot of Lehman Brothers securities. This has caused many people to pull their cash from ordinary money market accounts and sending it into treasury money market accounts, which are guaranteed by the federal government.

3. Also, if you're saving for short-term goals such as a vacation, a child's college tuition (while they're teenagers) or a downpayment on a house -- put that money into a money market account also.

You should not be investing money you'll be needing to spend within a few years.

This book is for long-term, especially retirement, investing.

It could be adapted toward saving for a child's retirement if you start before or while they're still in grade school. Once they hit middle school, you should play it safe with that money.

Also, I believe there are some laws setting up special accounts for college savings, so search online or ask a financial advisor about them.

4. Few investment writers, or even personal finance advice writers, like to mention this -- but I will.

You can also improve your financial condition (both by paying off debt and investing) by increasing your income.

That could mean working a second job even if unskilled. (I recommend delivering pizzas).

It could mean moonlighting your skills (Be careful, though. Don't break any laws, and don't steal your employer's clients.)

It could mean furthering your education by getting a higher college degree or by taking specialized courses.

It could mean selling all your unused belongings on eBay. If you can't take a picture with a digital camera and write a description, there are people who will do it for you for a percentage of the proceeds.

It could mean working a business from home part time. You too could make extra money on eBay. Or became a part time real estate agent. Or whatever.

Next: For investors under 50.

Chapter Fifty-Two

For Investors Under 50

The traditional financial advice is to keep the percentage of your portfolio invested in bonds the same as your age.

Thus, if you're 35, they say, have 35% of your money invested in bonds.

The other 65% should be invested in stocks.

I don't know what they advise people who're over 100 years old to do. Don't laugh -- that day will come for many of us baby boomers.

I think everybody under 50 should keep most -- 90% -- of their money in equities.

Personally, I'm over 50 but under 60, and when I recently transferred my retirement fund from my job to an IRA, I put about 90% into equities and only 10% into bond.

(I followed my own advice. I selected ETRs from the lists in this book.)

You should follow the advice in the proceeding chapters, and then concentrate on investing in equities:

1. U.S. dividend-paying stocks (the ETFs track broadly diversified indexes that include basic consumer goods)

2. Outside-U.S. dividend-paying stocks (the ETFs track broadly diversified indexes that include basic consumer goods)

3. U.S. utilities

4. Outside U.S. utilities

5. U.S. REITs

6. Outside-U.S. REITs

7. Master Limited Partnerships

8. Canadian trusts

9. I Bonds

10. Investment-grade, intermediate-term corporate bonds

11. Investment-grade, intermediate-term municipal bonds

12. Treasury bonds

13. Preferred stocks

14. Business Development Corporations -- if and only when you have enough money in other investments that this can be only a small percentage of your total portfolio. And only if you are willing to take the risk. I can't recommend them, but it could well be that in time they make a lot of money. Or, maybe not. Who knows? If you like to visit casinos, you should put your gambling money into BDCs instead.

I didn't put TIPS on this list because people still saving for retirement should hold TIPS only in tax-deferred retirement accounts, and I covered those in Chapter 48.

Unless you're in very poor health, you should invest with the attitude that you won't have to live on this income for at least 50 years.

Sound incredible? Medical science keeps advancing. You're already expected to live longer than any generation before you. And medical science is going to keep advancing before Social Security allows you to retire.

In 1900, the average life expectancy in the United States was just 41 years. Now it's 77. It almost doubled in just over a century.

If you can refrain from dying any time soon, you may actually live to be 200 years or more. Especially if you practice good health habits.

Scoff if you like, but 150 years from now, as you cash quarterly dividend checks that are higher than you can even dream of right now, you may thank me (or my memory, but frankly I hope it's me) for pushing you to buy stocks with ever-growing dividends.

Next: For investors between 50 and retirement age.

Chapter Fifty-Three

For Investors Age 50 to Retirement

The traditional financial advice is to keep the percentage of your portfolio invested in bonds -- the same as your age.

Thus, if you're 35, they say, have 35% of your money invested in bonds.

The other 65% should be invested in stocks.

I actually think everybody not yet retired should still keep a lot more than that of their money in equities.

Maybe not quite 90%, but 80%.

Personally, I'm over 50 but under 60, and when I recently transferred my retirement fund from my job to an IRA, I put about 90% into equities and only 10% into bonds.

(I follow my own advice. I select ETRs from the lists in this book.)

You should follow the advice in the proceeding chapters, and then start off investing in equities, but give a higher priority to fixed income investments, by alternating what you buy:

1. U.S. dividend-paying stocks

2. I Bonds

3. Outside-U.S. dividend-paying stocks

4. Investment-grade, intermediate-term corporate bonds

5. U.S. utilities

6. U.S. REITs

7. Investment-grade, intermediate-term municipal bonds

8. Outside U.S. utilities

9. Outside U.S. REITs

10. Treasury bonds

11. Master Limited Partnerships

12. Preferred stocks

13. Canadian trusts

I didn't put TIPS on this list because until you need the income from them, they should be held only in tax-deferred retirement accounts, and I covered those a few chapters ago.

Unless you're in very poor health, you should invest with the attitude that you may live on this income for at least 30 years after you retire.

You may never totally "retire." If you're a baby boomer like me you'll want to stay active. That may include doing things that cost money, such as traveling, but also things that make money, such as consulting.

Next: For retired investors.

Chapter Fifty-Four

Income Investing Once You're Retired

Frankly, it's most difficult for me to advise you, because so much depends on each person or couple's situation.

How old are you?

Are you sick with something terminal or almost as serious?

How much money do you have now?

What form is it in? Stocks, bonds, an IRA, mutual funds?

How much of the current value of your portfolio represents capital gains?

How much money are you making now from your investments?

Are you headed for a nursing home?

If you've been investing for years in "growth" mutual funds with the object of selling off your funds as you need the money, you probably have a lot of capital gains.

I Wish I Knew a Legal Way For You to Realize Capital Gains Without Paying Taxes -- but Uncle Sam Wants You to Pay Taxes

I could name a recent book on income investing (it's not one listed in the resource section) that point blank tells you to sell all investments you own that the author believes you shouldn't. Even ordinary dividend-paying stocks.

Because he believes he can show you how to make double-digit returns.

However, I can't in good conscience tell you to do something that will give you a massive tax bill next April 15. Uncle Sam would love it if I did, but that violates Principle 7.

On the other hand -- what good is an investment that doesn't pay you any income?

(Recently I saw a Motley Fool ad that said, "If you'd invested $10,000 in X stock in 1985, you'd be sitting on $1,000,000 now." I thought to myself, who needs to sit on $1,000,000? I can buy a chair at Wal-Mart for $20 -- I want a stock that pays me to own it, not one that's only good to sit on.)

First, Figure Out Exactly What Your Capital Gains and Losses Are

You need to organize your investments and get hard figures. If necessary, have an accountant or financial advisor help you.

Learn where you have capital gains, and how much they are.

If you have income paying investments, of course hang on to them.

And do you have any capital losses?

You Can Balance Capital Losses Against Capital Gains, and That Helps

If so, you should sell securities to realize up to $3000 a year in capital losses. And you should sell securities with capital gains to match.

That way, you've offset your capital gains with equivalent losses and prevented a big tax bill.

Use the money you net from all those sales to buy income investments.

At only $3000 per year (maybe it will go up in future years, but with Democrats in charge, don't count on it.), this could take years.

The traditional financial advice is to keep the percentage of your portfolio invested in bonds -- the same as your age.

Thus, if you're 35, they say, have 35% of your money invested in bonds.

The other 65% should be invested in stocks.

I actually think everybody under the age of 85 should still keep 20% or more of their money in equities.

Everybody Needs Some Equities for Growth in Income

Heck, even if you're 100, you should still keep at least 10% of your investments in equities. If you've managed to live that long, you may well hang on another ten or fifteen years -- and inflation isn't going to stop and wait for you to pass away . . it's going to keep on whittling away at the value of our currency.

However, it makes sense to put more emphasis on fixed income investments and on equities with higher yields. Since master limited partnerships are not yet proven by time and therefore are a little more risky than consumer/utility stocks and REITs, I'm leaving them off the list despite their high yields. I'm leaving Canadian trusts off the list because 2011 will soon be here.

1. Investment-grade, intermediate-term corporate bonds

2. U.S. REITs

3. Investment-grade, intermediate-term municipal bonds

4. TIPS

5. U.S. dividend-paying stocks

6. U.S. utilities

7. Preferred stocks

8. Outside U.S. utilities

9. Outside-U.S. REITs

10. Outside-U.S. dividend-paying stocks

Unless you're in very poor health, you should invest with the attitude that you may need to live on this income for at least 20-30 more years, depending on your current age.

According to the U.S. Public Health Service a 65 year old woman today can expect to live another 19.2 years. A 65 year old man today can expect to live another 16.3.

And of course, those are just averages. Half of you will live longer.

Even if you're 90, you could still live another 20 years.

Everybody needs some of their money in investments that will grow their income over time -- again, inflation is not going to wait for you to die.

The cost of everything seniors care about, from gifts for grandchildren to health care, keeps going up.

TIPS bonds should be held only in the iShares Barclay's U.S. Treasury Inflation Protected Securities Bond Fund: TIP. That is because when they're in the ETF, you don't have to pay taxes on the increases in principal until you sell the shares of the TIP exchange traded fund -- and you should know by now, you don't ever want to do that.

If you are facing paying for care in a nursing home, see a lawyer or financial advisor specializing in that area.

Also, I don't pretend that this book is about estate planning or the best ways to leave money to your heirs. See a lawyer or financial advisor specializing in those areas.

Confused by all these options and details? In the next chapter, I reveal my proprietary, patent-pending, K.I.S.S. income investing formula.

Chapter Fifty-Five

K.I.S.S.
or -- Keep It Simple, Stooker!

This chapter is for those of you who feel overwhelmed by the last fewer chapters.

Which stock dividend ETF to select? Which REIT ETF? And on and on . . .

Until you're ready to hang it up, and hand your money over to a mutual fund manager or broker for "safe" keeping. Ha Ha Ha!

Rather than let you do that, I've come up with a simple, easy, no-brainer way of investing for income.

Anybody with a little money to spare can do this.

1. Equities

Use a deep discount broker and buy the Claymore/Zacks Multi-Asset Income Index ETF: CVY.

This tracks the Claymore/Zacks Multi-Asset Income Index.

Here's a wide range of 125 to 150 income-equities all in one fund: U.S. dividend-paying stocks, outside U.S. dividend-paying stocks, REITs, Master Limited Partnerships, closed-end funds and traditional preferred stocks.

2. Debt

If you're still saving for retirement, put TIPS bonds in your IRA or other tax-deferred accounts.

Once you've invested the maximum allowed by law in a calendar year, see the next paragraph.

If you're now retired or you've put the maximum allowed TIPS in your IRA or other tax-deferred account, invest in TIPS through buying the iShares Barclay's U.S. Treasury Inflation Protected Securities Bond Fund: TIP.

That way, you don't have to pay taxes on the principle increase in the TIPS bonds the ETF holds, until you sell the ETF shares you hold.

Don't ever sell them.

That's it -- the best of all worlds.

The younger you are, the more you should buy of the CVY fund.

The older you are, the more you should buy TIPS.

However, always hold on to some of both investments. You're never too young to protect yourself from inflation by owning a few TIPS, nor too old to want some growth in your income from equities.

Now you'll have more time to make more money at your job/career/full-time or part-time business -- or go fishing.

You can quit here or, if you choose to think about what's going to happen when all us 82 gazillion billion trillions baby boomers retire over the coming few decades (we've already started), read the next chapter.

Chapter Fifty-Six

Effects of Baby Boomer Retirements on the U.S. (and Worldwide?) Financial Markets

"But clearly, as the baby boomers age and head toward retirement . . . This will drive, we believe, a very strong demand for yield and current income producing investments that still have some modest growth associated with them - which we expect to remain unabated, in fact, increase over the next 20 years or more."

--- STEVE POWELL, Managing Director, RBC Capital Markets, Royal Bank of Canada

The first baby boomer has already filed her claim for retirement Social Security benefits. Kathleen Casey-Kirschling. She was born one minute after midnight on January 1, 1946, so she turned 62 (the U.S. minimum age to collect retirement Social Security checks) on January 1, 2008.

She's the first drop of water in a massive financial tsunami rushing to the shore of the worldwide markets.

Over the next two decades, 10,000 people a day (a total of 82 million total, per the 2000 census) will become eligible to receive Social Security retirement benefits.

What's going to happen to the stock market as the largest generation in history -- now in its most productive years -- continues to retire?

According to one figure I found, my generation (I'm a boomer) has $14 trillion invested. That's an average of only $170,000 per person. That's not a lot to live on for the rest of your life.

Yet, of course, added together it's a lot of money.

When we went to grade school we each had only one desk -- but many schools had to be built to accommodate us all.

Baby Boomer Retirements Are Likely to Depress Stock and Bond Prices in 4 Ways:

1. Right now, the vast majority of us, except Kathleen Casey-Kirschling, are still working and paying a portion of our paychecks into retirement plans of one kind or another. That is, we're buying stocks and bonds.

This doesn't make the headlines, but whether the market is dropping, rising or drifting sideways, American employees and business owners (a big chunk of them boomers) are using a portion of their incomes to buy stocks and bonds for their retirement.

As they retire, that buying pressure on the market will slow down and eventually stop altogether.

When demand for stocks and bonds drops, so will prices.

2. The conventional behavior of (advice to) retirees is to sell off accumulated assets to pay for their living expenses.

(Of course, the entire point of this book is to encourage you to avoid doing this, by accumulating assets that pay income which you can use to pay your expenses without selling assets -- but here I'm writing about what most 82 million boomers are likely to do.

I wish all 82 million boomers would buy this book, but that's not realistic.)

The fact is, conventional financial planning wisdom says that retirees using optimum asset allocation formulas for their investments can sell 4% of their assets a year to meet their expenses. So that's what many financial planners are going to advise their clients to do. Boomers who can afford to sell less, will. But many boomers, pressed for cash to pay for medicine and cruises, will sell more than 4% a year.

Income Investing Secrets

Baby boomer new retirees who have been buying stocks for capital gains and not for income will HAVE to sell off some stock just to put cash in their pockets. If they don't sell some off some of their stock, the shares are just sitting there in their brokerage accounts, not doing them any good, while they struggle to pay their bills with Social Security and pension checks.

Furthermore, this model of selling off stocks to pay for expenses may well have a self-reinforcing effect.

If stock prices do start falling (for any reason), retirees will have to sell MORE shares to raise the money they need to pay for their golf games and heart surgeries. The more stock boomers sell, the more stock boomers will have to sell, to put the money they want into their pocket. The more stock boomers have to sell to finance their lifestyle, the more stock prices will fall.

The more stock prices fall because boomers are selling stock, the more stock boomers will have to sell.

It could become a vicious, self-reinforcing bear market cycle.

And what about boomers (whether income investors or not), who try to hang on to their accumulated assets?

There's a nice wrinkle in the ERISA law of 1974. When you reach age 70 1/2, you MUST start withdrawing money from all retirement accounts (except Roth IRAs).

How many trillions of baby boomer dollars are in conventional IRAs, the federal Thrift Fund, 401(k) funds, Keogh accounts, and so on? Most of it. I'm sure that even people who now place their retirement funds in Roth IRAs have not switched the money they already had in other accounts to the Roth, because they couldn't bear the thought of paying the required taxes!

(Starting in 2010, it's now easier to convert a traditional IRA to a Roth IRA, but the taxes still have to be paid over a two-year period. It'll still be painful.)

One academic study I read about estimated that the wealthiest of baby boomers own stocks paying dividends and will simply continue to live on those dividends.

(The exact strategy I'm recommending to you with this book! Isn't it interesting that while the mainstream media exhorts you to invest for capital gains, the finance professor running this study took it for granted that the wealthy invest for dividends?)

Anyway, the same study also predicts that less than wealthy baby boomers will have to sell over $3 trillion dollars in stock.

When more people are selling more stocks, the price for stocks drops.

3. Most companies make most of their money off young consumers. People working, buying houses, marrying, starting families, buying for their children, and so on.

Some people anticipate that the retirement of baby boomers will lead to a slow-down in the overall consumer economy. Poorer baby boomers especially will not be able to buy as much as they did while still working.

Of course, there will be increased business in some sectors: golf, travel, medicine, nursing homes and, eventually, funeral parlors.

I'm not so sure of this one, myself. My generation is quite self-indulgent. When we were kids we got used to getting our Mattel toys: G.I. Joes and Barbie dolls. As teens and young adults we didn't hold back from sex, drugs and rock n roll. In the 80s successful yuppies bought the fancy cars and designer clothes. I don't think many of us are going to sit in our homes with the lights off, scrimping and saving.

However, it's also true the areas of (over)consumption will probably change. It won't be buying new and bigger houses or expensive athletic shoes for our kids, but probably buying health/athletic products for ourselves, and books, movies and music . . . since we'll have more time to enjoy those pursuits. Eating out is probably a good bet, from fast food to ethnic restaurants. Also, travel -- and not just the cruises that have traditionally appealed to the elderly, but adventure treks to the Amazon jungles and the Himalaya Mountains. Travel that's "environmental," and that allows you to see the "real" (i.e., poor) people of the world.

I believe that many baby boomers are going to spend more time volunteering to help people -- and will revive their political activities to save the world. In fact, within the next 30 years the problems and poor people of the world will be hard-pressed to not be saved.

If problems remain, it won't be because of lack of boomer effort at solving them.

Still, it's also true that retired people don't buy as many sports cars, washing machines and kegs of beer.

If corporations take in less money, their stock prices will drop.

4. None of this will happen overnight. The first years of baby boomers are the smallest, so as those born in 1946 start retiring, the above effects on the stock market will take a few years to begin. The vast majority of the boomers will still be working and buying stocks out of their paychecks.

By that time, the mass media will be talking about the baby boomers retiring.

If you're buying stocks for your retirement, even if you're still young but especially if you're close to retirement age yourself, and the media is talking about how the baby boomers are going to cause the market to crash for the next 20 years, are you going to keep on buying stocks?

If you're smart and buying stocks for income and retirement as I advise in this book, yes -- you should (especially when they are cheap!).

But most people aren't going to buy this book. They're still caught in the capital gains trap. They're still brainwashed. They're going to switch their retirement accounts over to bonds or even money funds.

The more people sell stocks and stop buying them, the more the price of stocks will drop.

The Bear Market Won't Last Forever -- Look for a New Bull Starting about 2022

Demographer Harry S. Dent made a compelling case that the U.S. stock market would keep rising through 2008, but would peak sometime in 2009 or 2010. Then enter a decline that will last until about 2022, when demographics will again force it up.

We obviously did not peak in 2009. We don't yet know what will happen in

2010 and beyond, but prospects for the mid-term future don't look good.

Not everybody agrees that the retirement of baby boomers is going to adversely affect the market.

In INCOME INVESTING TODAY Richard Lehman simply says that baby boomers are not going to retire, we're just going to keep on working.

I agree with that to a degree. According to AARP Segmentation Analysis: Baby Boomers Envision Their Retirement, 8 out of 10 boomers anticipate continuing to work, at least on a part time basis. Others plan to start their own businesses.

However, I believe that many boomers plan to flee jobs they hate, and work at jobs they enjoy. Writing grants for the neighborhood Foundation for Peace, Love and Freedom is unlikely to pay as high a salary as Plant Superintendent for a major corporation. And stores selling Tibetan beads at the mall are not as likely to offer a 401(k) plan to their clerks. Also, although there are tax-deferred retirement accounts for the self-employed, you have to have a positive net profit. Most new businesses lose money.

Besides, realistically, the vast majority of boomers are going to quit somewhere short of dropping dead. (Of course, some will drop dead while working.) Yes, we're going to live longer, and we're going to have healthier old ages than any preceding generation, but sooner or later most people will reach a point where they're physically or mentally unable to hold down a productive job, like it or not. We're not going to live and work forever.

If all boomers delay retirement past age 65, that will simply delay the problem caused by our retirement. Postpone it, not solve it.

Retirement Account Laws Will Force Boomers to Sell Assets

Even if boomers try to hang on to their accumulated stocks and bonds, once they turn 70 1/2 they'll be required by law to start withdrawing them from all their tax-deferred retirement accounts.

That's required by the ERISA law, as described on page 213.

So the problem could be delayed until lots of boomers are age 70 1/2, but that's again postponing, not solving the problem.

In THE FUTURE FOR INVESTORS Dr. Jeremy Siegel discusses the problem in depth and concludes that people from developing countries, principally China and India, are going to prop up our stock market by buying up the shares our companies sold by retired baby boomers.

Searching online, I found this quote from Dr. Siegel:

"The demographic trends of the past have just not been strong enough to offset all the other influences on the stock market. But this is the granddaddy of all demographic shifts. We have never witnessed anything like this, and I am convinced it is going to be a determinant of asset prices going forward."

He believes that stock market could decline by as much as 50%.

Dr. Siegel is a finance professor at Wharton and the author of STOCKS FOR THE LONG RUN. He's been as much the cheerleader of buying stocks "for the long run" as anybody. If he's expecting such a steep decline, that's bad news for stock owners counting on capital gains to finance their purchases of the latest electronic gadgets.

According to Dr. Siegel in an interview with BUSINESS WEEK, the stock market will decline by 40-50% unless we allow global investors to buy stock. Most of the developing world is still young, and their economies are growing quickly. They will wind up financing America's baby boomer retirements.

Will the Developing World's Nouveau-Riche Save Us?

However, I'm somewhat skeptical of this scenario.

Right now, from all I read, China is investing heavily . . . in China. That is a tremendously large country, with a tremendously large number of people to keep busy. There is still a lot of poverty in China, especially in rural areas. Plus, China has its own problems caused by an aging population. Thanks to their long time "One Family, One Child" policy, their aging population is not being fully replaced by their youth.

However, it's not impossible that someday the government of China might decide to use its vast inventory of U.S. dollars to buy up shares in American companies.

India is also a large country with a billion plus people, and a large and fast-growing economy. However, it also has hundreds of millions of people who live a lifestyle little changed from 4,000 years ago. It's going to take a huge amount of money to upgrade India's infrastructure.

Plus, India is still faced with the problem of Pakistan. Islamic jihadists are making war in India's Kashmir region. Faced with the potential threat of China to their north and Pakistan to their west, India is spending a lot of money on beefing up their military.

Of course, there're a lot of other developing countries. I've seen the rise of modern office buildings and shopping malls. The spread of cell phones and Internet cafes.

Yet . . . in and around the modern buildings, and outside the major cities, developing countries are still crowded with extremely poor people.

And people who are poor by world/historical standards, NOT the modern day American "poor." I'm not talking about people who are "poor" because they get food stamps and Section 8 housing. I'm talking about people who are poor because their only income is begging or selling food from carts. Who sleep on the sidewalk. Who have to wear the same dirty clothes every day. Who die easily and fast because they have no money with which to pay doctors.

I suspect that in many countries there'll be political pressure on the wealthy to invest in their own countries rather than to buy up securities in America/Europe/Canada/Australia/Japan.

Will Our Children Keep Buying the Securities We Sell?

One argument I read is that younger workers are saving a lot more money than us baby boomers did, because of the decline in defined pension plans. That's probably true, but it's not likely they're going to buy all the stock that 50-60 year old boomers are now buying and will eventually want to sell. Also, will they continue to buy stocks if the price seems to be on a 10-year downhill slide? They may switch to stashing their money in money market accounts instead.

Income Investing Secrets

One advisor whose books I enjoy reading, Ric Edelman, pooh-poohs the whole idea that baby boomers are going to wreck the financial markets when we retire.

He contends that stock and bond valuations are based on too many other factors.

Plus, he says that, based on his experience as a financial advisor, elderly people don't sell their investments. They do whatever they have to to hang on to their principal, because that's the only money they're ever going to have.

Plus, based again on his experience as a financial advisor, he says that the IRS rule that retirement accounts be taken out of IRAs by age 70 1/2 is not going to affect the markets because people just transfer the resources involved.

My thinking:

1. Stocks and bond market prices are based on many factors, but modern finance theory has proven that the biggest risk (80 to 90%) faced by individual stocks is market risk. Only a small percentage (10 to 20%) of a company's stock price is based on the company's individual performance instead of the market's overall performance.

Therefore, if a wave of selling hits the markets due to baby boomer retirements, that has the potential to override all other factors.

2. This entire book is based on telling you not to sell investments to live on (that is, not to take advantage of your capital gains.). Nevertheless, selling your investments to raise money to live on is exactly the advice given out by most financial experts and advisors.

But let's assume that most elderly are smart enough to want to hold on to their principal. What are they going to do about stocks that pay no dividends?

I suspect that eventually many baby boomers are going to say, "The heck with this Dell stock -- I want Coca-Cola or anything that pays me a check."

What good is a stock that doesn't pay any dividends? If it doesn't pay dividends and you don't sell it, then you're not living on it. Maybe you want to save it for your heirs, but it's useless to you. Maybe its market price is high -- but you can't spend that without selling it.

I suspect that in years to come many baby boomers will come to understand the message of this book.

The Best Financial Protection Is Investing for Income

Yes, they will want to safeguard their principal. They'll sell the shares of stocks that don't pay dividends and buy stocks that do pay dividends and bonds.

That is, they won't sell for cash, but to receive more income.

3. When they begin to reach age 70 1/2, they must begin taking money out of their IRAs and other retirement accounts. They may well transfer the money into dividend-paying stocks and bonds.

But they have to sell something -- because they must pay taxes on the withdrawals.

That's WHY the IRS insisted on that aspect of the IRA laws. Those accounts are tax-DEFERRED -- not tax-free. At age 70 1/2, the deferral begins to run out.

Plus, I have to point out that even if elderly baby boomers don't sell off their portfolios, just the slowing down of their buying new stocks and bonds through their work-related retirement plans will affect the financial markets.

My Conclusion

The aging of us 82 million baby boomers is bound to have a large, negative impact on the stock market.

Boomers continuing to work and boomers not selling off their stocks right away may delay the problem, not solve it. Eventually boomers will start selling off stocks, or at least stop buying them, and become unable to work, and this will influence the market downward.

Foreign capital may step in to buy American companies, but probably not until they're screaming bargains. I could be wrong, but I suspect that the Chinese and Indians will learn from the Japanese mistakes of the 1980s – they won't buy up American properties until they're cheap. That is, for sale at severely depressed, yard-sale prices.

Income Investing Secrets

As individuals and families, our best defense is to invest for income, as advocated in the rest of this book.

The more income you get from your investments, the less you'll be tempted to sell them when their market price is low.

If you're still accumulating retirement funds, dividend-paying stocks will go on sale, and that's good news for you. Buy up high yielding stocks in well-run businesses that meet basic human needs.

And if I and everybody else who's predicting a stock market decline because of aging boomers is wrong . . . you'll still be best off by investing for income.

Next: how to have more time to make more money . . . time to work and time to let your savings compound and therefore grow to the sky.

Chapter Fifty-Seven

How to Have More Time to Make Money in Your Present-Day Life, More Time in Which to Let Your Investments Compound so You Get Richer, and Also to Better Enjoy Life

Get, or remain, healthy.

That's the short version of this chapter.

I already told you that I don't think it's worth your time to read 100 investing books a year, hang out at online investing forums or read annual reports. I said that instead, you should do things that will make you more money in your job, career or business. Then you'll have more money to invest.

Many of you groaned, I'm sure.

It's not easy to find the time to go to school or work part time, or sell on eBay part time or any of that other stuff.

Especially if your day job tires you out so much that all you want to do is collapse in front of the TV.

But investing time in your good health will pay off in both the short and long term. You'll have more energy, you'll feel better, and you'll spend less time sick in bed.

That will give you more time and ability to make more money, so you have more money to invest.

And remember Principle 2 -- the longer you compound your investments, the more they'll grow. Remember Anne Schieber. She grew $5000 into $22 million not just because she was smart and reinvested her interest on interest, but because she lived to age 101.

So adding years to your life will add money to your investments.

Plus, you'll spend less money on doctor bills, medicine and hospitals.

Plus, you'll just plain enjoy life more when you can make love, dance and go swimming with your great-grandchildren than if you're sitting in a wheelchair in a nursing home.

Since I understand that you didn't get this income investing program for health advice, you can skip this chapter if you choose, but here it is:

1. Air

Oxygen is our most basic need. Most of us don't get enough. We'd all be a lot healthier if we took 10 deep breaths, 3 times a day.

This book focuses on the weight-loss aspect of breathing, but that's OK. You may or may not need to lose weight. We all need to breath more.

JUMPSTART YOUR METABOLISM by Pam Grout

2. Water

If I describe someone as "wrinkled, desiccated, dried out, like a prune" -- do you think they're young or old?

Of course -- old.

Intuitively, we all associate water with life and youth.

Healthy babies are plump and smooth-skinned. But if babies dehydrate (lose water through diarrhea) they die. It's one of the most common causes of death among infants in the developing world.

After we're older, we don't die of dehydration right away, but too many of us live our lives partially dehydrated. For optimum health, we need more water.

(By the way, we need to drink more water -- not milk, juice, tea, coffee, soda, energy drinks, or lemonade -- WATER!)

YOUR BODY'S MANY CRIES FOR WATER by F. Batmanghelidj, M.D.
WATER FOR HEALTH, FOR HEALING, FOR LIFE by F. Batmanghelidj, M.D.

3. Healthy food

The most bio-available nutrition comes from food itself, not tablets or pills. Yet the food in our groceries stores is depleted of natural vitamins, minerals and phytonutrients.

Fortunately, we've learned that certain foods have incredible amounts of nutrition -- spirulina, blue-green algae, chlorella, barley and many more "superfoods."

Obviously, we're not going to eat a forkful of algae. But we can add a superfood powder to juice or other foods and thereby greatly increase our intake of phytonutrients and vitamins.

We should all take at least one tablespoon a day of superfoods.

3. Healthy overall diet

For optimum health, we need the proper balance of the three main food ingredients: protein, carbohydrates and fat.

Most of us overwhelm our bodies with carbohydrates, and that probably contributes to vast increase we've seen in modern times in obesity, diabetes, heart disease, strokes, cancer and probably many other health conditions.

THE ANTI-INFLAMMATION ZONE by Dr. Barry Sears

4. Vitamins/minerals and other important nutrition

Buy and take high-quality vitamins, minerals and other supplements. You won't find "high-quality" supplements at Wal-Mart, or even GNC. Shop carefully online to find the most powerful, bio-available brands.

5. Joint health

Arthritis, joint pain and lack of mobility can really hinder our enjoyment of life as we add on the years. According to this author, it doesn't have to be this way:

THE EGOSCUE METHOD OF HEALTH THROUGH MOTION by Pete Egoscue
PAIN FREE: A REVOLUTIONARY METHOD FOR STOPPING CHRONIC PAIN by Pete Egoscue

6. Aerobic fitness

The conventional advice is to run, walk, swim or cycle for long distances. Here's the best way to build up your fitness:

PACE: Rediscover Your Native Fitness by Al Sears MD

7. General fitness

Lots of exercise gurus tell you to lift weights. Save your money and effort. Also, don't bother joining that expensive health club. You can keep yourself strong and fit just by using the weight of your own body. It's more convenient and a lot safer.

There are quite a few bodyweight exercise (remember when we just called calisthenics?) books available.

7. Advanced exercise programs

I did a lot of yoga when I was a young kid, and I'm convinced it help lay a foundation of good health that benefits me to this day, though I have to admit that it's been years since I stood on my head.

I have never practiced T'ai Ch'ai, but by all accounts it's also an excellent system of mild exercise to achieve and maintain good health, even into advanced old age.

I've also never practiced Pilates, but from everything I've read about it, it's another great system of youth-enhancing, age-defying exercises.

Next: Investing Resources

Chapter Fifty-Eight

Additional Investing Resources

For more information on income investing.

These are the best available on these subjects. Unfortunately, as of this writing, there're no books devoted to master limited partnerships or some of the other, more exotic, income investments.

Modern finance

CAPITAL IDEAS by Peter L. Bernstein
A RANDOM WALK DOWN WALL STREET by Burton Malkiel
A MATHEMATICIAN PLAYS THE STOCK MARKET by John Allen Paulos
FOOLED BY RANDOMNESS: The Hidden Role of Chance in Life and in the Markets by Nassim Nicholas Taleb

Investing for income

YES, YOU CAN BE A SUCCESSFUL INCOME INVESTOR by Ben Stein and Phil DeMuth
INCOME INVESTING TODAY by Richard Lehman

Stocks that pay dividends

THE DIVIDEND GROWTH AND INVESTMENT STRATEGY by RoxAnn Klugman
THE STANDARD & POOR'S GUIDE TO BUILDING WEALTH WITH DIVIDEND STOCKS by Joseph Tigue
BEATING THE S&P WITH DIVIDENDS: How to Build a Superior Portfolio of Dividend Yielding Stocks by Peter O'Shea and Jonathan Worrall

Bonds

THE BOND BOOK by Annette Thau

THE ONLY GUIDE TO A WINNING BOND STRATEGY YOU'LL EVER NEED by Larry E. Swedroe and Joseph H. Hempen

Real Estate Investment Trusts

INVESTING IN REITS by Ralph L. Block

Canadian trusts

CANADIAN INCOME FUNDS by Peter Beck and Simon Romano

Afterword

This book was to give you a plan to follow to provide yourself with a prosperous retirement.

My website:

http://www.IncomeInvestHome.com/

contains a lot more particular information about each type of investment, if you choose to do more research.

However, my site doesn't contain the 7 Principles. It doesn't try to evaluate which income investments belong in your portfolio. It doesn't give you the overall plan. That's what you bought this book for.

The site is like a jigsaw puzzle, although in a logical order. It gives you the individual pieces – not the big picture.

This book is intended to give you the underlying principles and the plan for you to fit the pieces into your financial life.

I wish I could make successful investing as easy as One Two Three -- but, life is complicated. People are in a wide variety of personal and financial circumstances. The financial markets are complicated.

However, I've cut through the hype about capital gains that you encounter every day, when financial writers, investing experts and your friends automatically assume that "making money in the markets" means buying and then selling for a profit.

Even the federal government. If the Federal Trade Commission (FTC) ever investigates my site or this book (Which they might, because they're online actively seeking out investment-related scams.), they'll want me to tell you that I can't guarantee your investment results.

And they mean that I can't guarantee that any particular security will go up in price in the future.

That's fine. I don't promise any such thing. I have no desire to. So long as you buy securities that pay you income -- I don't want you to care whether they ever go up in price or not, because I don't want you to ever sell them.

I also cannot guarantee you how much of an income you'll receive from your investments. Financial markets and investments continue to change. I can't predict the future.

A company may be paying $1 per share in dividends this year, but increase it to $1.10 per share next year -- or reduce it to 90 cents.

Or stop paying dividends. Or even go out of business.

Protecting yourself from these real dangers is why I advise you to focus on dividend payers that meet basic human needs and to diversify as much as you can afford to.

The "never sell" part part of my advice is what the federal government -- especially the IRS and politicians -- will hate about this book – when people follow my advice, they won't pay more capital gains taxes!

So, screen out the hype and assumptions regarding the necessity for capital gains, and put your long-term retirement money into a wide variety of income investments.

Don't sell them.

Reinvest your earnings so you compound your "gold eggs" -- and have a happy, prosperous retirement!

many thanks again,

Rick Stooker

Other books by Richard Stooker . . .

COMPUTER CAREER SECRETS

Maybe you're stuck in a dead-end job. Or you're unemployed. Or you're not fulfilled in your current position. Or you just love computers.

Demand for info tech workers does fluctuate, but there's always some need for those services, because we keep on using computers in more and new ways. And clever IT workers can use their skills to make money from self-employment.

Learn your options now.

"I read your book and am very impressed. As an experienced career changer to IT, I'm in agreement with your assessments, and also learned a few new things that may save me some grief.

"In the course of my personal efforts I have endured an unbelievable lack of real, comprehensive knowledge on the subject of what it really takes to get a start in IT, not to mention a preponderance of misinformation from the media, sellers of courses, certifications and degrees - even many "professional" counselors.

"I wish I had read your book before I started my journey into IT. It would have saved me a lot of wrong turns and self questioning. Obviously you did your homework and then some. Thanks."
    -- Ron Mitchell

"Your report is excellent. I have a lot of experience in the IT industry, but for someone who is just getting started or changing careers, your book would be a MUST! It would save one a great deal of time and money, and also alleviate much confusion regarding the whole certification/training issue. Thanks,"

    -- Len Van Sant

"I thought this book was excellent!!!

Thomas J Leary DDS

VIRGIN BLOOD

"Janie is one of the best fictional characters I've come across in a long time -- beaten but not broken, earthy yet innocent, a thoroughly modern saint. . . . at the end of the book, I almost broke into tears. And you have the stylistic sophistication to be able to blend gritty realism and outright magic and pull it off. In short, VIRGIN BLOOD is a marvelous book."

-- Dave King, Dave King Editorial Services www.davekingedits.com

If you're like most readers, you hope to find 4 things in the novels you read:

1. Heroes you love to love.
2. Villains you love to hate.
3. Nerve-ripping suspense.
4. A heart-squeezing, unforeseen conclusion.

If do like imaginative elements intermixed with nitty gritty reality . . . if you like Stephen King . . . if you like Dean R. Koontz . . . you'll enjoy VIRGIN BLOOD.

To the late-night ER staff struggling to save her life, Janie Braxton one more big city crime victim. But to the spirit of an ancient Native American chief who once reigned supreme over the middle of pre-Columbian North America, she's an incomplete sacrifice holding the key to regaining his long-lost power.

Pursued by Janie's rapist Dewie and his gang, her two small daughters trek through the mean streets of St Louis . . .

While Marilyn and Jim search for them, discovering that Dewie is possessed of a supernatural power threatening the balance of forces in the entire universe . . .

Culminating in a split-second final showdown at the St Louis Abused Women's Shelter and the hospital Intensive Care Unit.

BEAT THE FLU

Flu experts agree -- a severe pandemic is just a matter of time.

But there are many other ways to protect yourself and your family. They are cheap and widely available. Everybody can take steps to protect themselves and their families.

The nightmare is another 1918-style flu that is both highly contagious and highly lethal. It could kill tens of millions of people around the globe.

Ordinary, seasonal flu kills from 20,000 to 40,000 Americans per year, and an unknown number of people in other countries.

What the experts aren't telling you is that flu vaccines are six months behind the virus. And in a severe pandemic there won't be enough Tamiflu to treat all the sick.

Besides, swine flu has already mutated into forms resistant to both vaccines and Tamiflu.

All it would take is the right flu virus mutation or recombination set loose in a highly crowded developing world big city slum full of malnourished poor people living in close, unhygienic conditions.

And then spread to the passengers of an international airplane flight.

"I have studied alternative health for many years... and still I found many nuggets of smart advice I hadn't thought of, forgotten, or flat out didn't know before I went through your flu book. Well done!"
-- *Jim Van Wyck http://jimvanwyck.com*

"Brings the facts to us in a clear, well-written style. "The Seven Perimeter Immune Defense System will help protect us -- from much more that the flu alone.

"You provide in-depth biological explanations using easily understood everyday words. Your ability to communicate complex concepts in ordinary language is phenomenal. I am very, very impressed."
-- *Dot Pecson http://dpcopywritingservice.com/*

GAMBLING FOR WINNERS

This book is for you only if you go to casinos to make money.

If your idea of "fun" and "entertainment" includes giving away your hard-earned money, I can't help you.

If you enjoy sitting in a mindless, bright lights/dinging trance while you drop quarters down a slot, this book is not for you.

If you think casinos are built and run by stupid people, you better stay out of them.

If you think you can beat a blackjack dealer by wild-assed guessing, think again.

If you play poker just because it's now so popular . . . you don't need my book.

If you believe that you can just happen to be "lucky" enough to beat the odds, you live in a fantasy world and you'd hate this book for destroying your illusions.

But if you're hard-headed, serious, willing to work, and tired of the mainstream gambling books that simply teach you how to lose less instead win . . .

If you understand that casinos don't stay in business by giving out more money than they take in . . .

If you understand that you must work with the laws of probability, not against them . . .

You too can gamble to WIN.

Richard Stooker also writes copy for web pages and emails and autoresponders series. For your free Email Autoresponder Higher Profits Secrets, just go now to --

http://www.richardstooker.com/auto/

8804703R0

Made in the USA
Lexington, KY
03 March 2011